SAFE, LEGAL, AND UNAVAILABLE?

SAFE, LEGAL, AND UNAVAILABLE?
ABORTION POLITICS IN THE UNITED STATES

Melody Rose
Portland State University

CQ PRESS

A Division of Congressional Quarterly Inc.
Washington, D.C.

CQ Press
1255 22nd Street, NW, Suite 400
Washington, DC 20037

Phone: 202-729-1900; toll-free, 1-866-4CQ-PRESS (1-866-427-7737)

Web: www.cqpress.com

Cover design: Jessica Tasch

Cover photo: Punchstock

♾ The paper used in this publication exceeds the requirements of the American National Standard for Information Sciences—Permanence of Paper for Printed Library Materials, ANSI Z39.48-1992.

Printed and bound in the United States of America

10   09   08   07   06   1   2   3   4   5

ISBN-10: 1-933116-89-7
ISBN-13: 978-1-933116-89-1

Library of Congress Cataloging-in-Publication Data

Rose, Melody.
    Safe, legal, and unavailable? : abortion politics in the United States / Melody Rose.
       p. cm.
    Includes bibliographical references and index.
    ISBN-13: 978-1-933116-89-1 (alk. paper)
    ISBN-10: 1-933116-89-7 (alk. paper)
    1. Abortion—United States.   2. Abortion—Law and legislation—United States.
3. Abortion—Political aspects—United States.   I. Title.

    HQ767.5.U5R65 2006
    363.460973—dc22   2006022032

For Eric
Sine Qua Non

CONTENTS

TABLES, FIGURES, AND MAP

"Of course, in our culture, children are sacred, but women are sacred too. . . ."
—Chief Fire Thunder, Pine Ridge Reservation, South Dakota

Early in 2006, South Dakota became the first state in the nation to pass a ban on abortion in all circumstances except when necessary to save a woman's life. Shortly thereafter, opponents of the new law threatened to challenge its legality under the landmark 1973 ruling, *Roe v. Wade*, and began an initiative process to take the issue to the voters in November.

Of course, to observers of abortion politics, this "clash of absolutes," as Laurence Tribe, Carl M. Loeb University Professor at Harvard Law School, describes it, is familiar. There are new features to this most recent chapter in abortion politics, however; one is the recently remade Supreme Court, whose new composition emboldened pro-life legislators in South Dakota to create a challenge to *Roe v. Wade*'s central holding that the right to privacy extends to abortion.

One of the most provocative and intriguing responses to the South Dakota law came from a voice rarely heard in the abortion battle; Chief Fire Thunder of South Dakota's Pine Ridge Reservation spoke strongly in opposition to the new regulation. Her voice carried loud and strong for two reasons: first, in contemporary abortion politics women of color are rarely heard. Primarily the issue of large interest groups and political parties dominated by middle-class white Americans, abortion politics is long overdue for some fresh perspectives on the national landscape. Second, the chief's statements echoed across America because her central theme is the sacredness of women. Fire Thunder's focus on the spiritual value of healthy women in her community struck a chord in what is otherwise a dissonant conversation: abortion policy today often is argued between those advocating for women's rights and those who champion the moral property of the fetus. In privileging the moral property of women in her comments, Fire Thunder voiced a view seldom heard in today's polarized debates.

This book is the product of a rare and valuable synthesis of my teaching and research interests. In teaching courses about women and politics for more than a decade, I have instructed abortion policy to many students at all levels of their education. In doing so, I have learned a simple and unsettling truth: few know the current status of abortion policy today.

In my classes, students are as likely to ask whether abortion is illegal as they are to argue that it is available on demand. These perspectives, once unpacked in the rarefied environment of an open classroom, generally reflect deeply held ideological values, not policy knowledge. I hope that in these pages I have offered an accurate reflection of the current status of abortion. By arguing that abortion is neither illegal nor available on demand, I hope that I will provide instructors with a tool for investigating a critical public policy battle with clarity, accuracy, and room for many intriguing conversations. In my moments of greatest conceit, I hope the text will allow for a spark of enlightenment in some classroom somewhere.

Still, the book is not without argument. As the title suggests, I maintain that abortion is becoming so highly regulated that while it remains both legal and safe, it is becoming more difficult to access, especially for the women for whom Fire Thunder speaks; the poor, the young, and the geographically remote are experiencing this public policy very differently than middle-class, urban, white women.

The abortion case is framed here as a classic case of social regulatory policy. In social regulatory policy formation, debates are polarized, court centered, and intuitively appealing to the casual observer. Often the associated debate takes on entrenched, ideological positions that lack substance and reflection. In these ways, abortion debates today are classic examples of social regulatory policy. I maintain, however, that contemporary abortion politics go beyond the features "typical" of social regulatory policy—the current debate is so entrenched, so polarizing, that it looks similar to another deeply dividing issue of many years ago: slavery. All social regulatory issues are the stuff of "gut" politics: they go to the core of our personal mores. But more than any other policy in this arena, abortion (as with slavery) touches upon our deepest-held beliefs about the very value of life.

The book has obvious utility in courses on social regulatory policy, women and politics, and women and the law—courses I teach regularly. But as a policy case study, this book is useful to the introductory student of American politics and to students of public policy in general. I have written the book with this wider audience in mind; the special features are designed to facilitate discussion, critical thinking, and learning among a broad spectrum of college students.

The text procedes simply. The Introduction offers a brief background to abortion law and politics, and introduces the basic concepts of the book. Chapter 1 focuses on the nuts and bolts of who gets abortions, how many women get them, and why. Chapter 2 outlines the consitutional environment of abortion. In chapter 3, the states' many abortion policies and practices are outlined, while national policies are described in chapter 4. Chapter 5 develops a party-based argument to explain why abortion policy is trending toward restriction; in chapter 6 I point to signs of change. Each chapter concludes with discussion questions meant to stimulate conversation as well as a list of further readings.

ACKNOWLEDGMENTS

I am delighted to write this note of thanks to the many people who helped me, in one way or another, to write this book. At CQ Press, I worked with an amazing group of professionals. I am indebted to Charisse Kiino, chief acquisitions editor for the College unit, for believing in my project from the beginning. For scrupulous editing and production, my thanks to Colleen Ganey, Lorna Notsch, and Anne Stewart. And to Terri Susan Fine, University of Central Florida; Wendy Martinek, Binghamton University, SUNY; Christiane Olivo, University of Northern Colorado; Robert Spitzer, SUNY Cortland; and Nikki Van Hightower, Texas A&M University, who encouraged CQ Press to print the book and who provided valuable feedback, I am grateful.

For the many students over the years who prodded me with challenging questions and let me test theories in the Abortion Politics seminar, I am eternally grateful; the book bears their mark in numerous places. My deep thanks go especially to Tina Gentzkow, Travis Kennedy, Bonnie Lander, Sunny Petit, and Laura Terrill Patten for having the patience, over and over again, to look up an arcane piece of administrative rule-making or obscure newspaper article; the book is so much better because they worked on it. And although I could not have done this without their faithful assistance, any errors in the text are mine alone.

Some longtime students may be frustrated to find the book more balanced than my own personal position. They, of course, have known my passionate position all along. Some will be disappointed to find a book that reflects many views—not just theirs, or mine. I trust, however, that they will see the virtue of a text that encourages the kind of spirited debates and thoughtful analyses we enjoyed in our courses. I reveled in these discussions and the puzzling areas of disagreement and common ground, and through writing and teaching this material I have grown and hope they have, too. In courses that invite debate, critical thinking expands, understanding mounts, and public dialogue hopefully grows more civil and compassionate. That is my purpose in this text.

A special note of thanks goes to the physicians I interviewed in the course of writing this text. Their generosity toward me benefited the book in many ways; most notably, I was able to incorporate the physicians' perspective, which is rarely integrated into abortion politics today. More than anything, spending time in their homes, offices, and clinics afforded me a richer view of the humanity and care they offer their patients, whose situations I came to learn are often sad, if not tragic. With little pay, and risk to their own lives, these doctors continue to provide compassionate care for women at a time of great need.

The book reflects the support and challenges of my colleagues and good friends at Portland State University. Without Richard Clucas's guidance, mentoring, and faith in my abilities, I would not have had the chance to write this book. Gretchen Kafoury deserves thanks for all she does to encourage and challenge me. For reading and responding to endless e-mails that began with "You're not going to believe what I found!" my deepest thanks to Regina Lawrence. I am grateful to Patricia Schechter, who provided support in the most unlikely places: campaign trail, delivery room, birthday party. For allowing me to bend her ear on the pre-school playground through my entire sabbatical, many thanks to Jennifer Ruth. I could not ask for better colleagues.

In some ways this is a book that has been ruminating for twenty years. Many thanks to Wendy Mink and Bob Meister for the exceptional undergraduate education they provided me at the University of California, Santa Cruz. Substantively, they sparked in me an interest in women, justice, and the law. But their impact on my life is much greater than that: as a first-generation college student, I would never have had the courage to go to graduate school without their early belief in my abilities. They are a testimony to the radical potential of public education, and I thank them for changing the course of my life.

I cannot believe my good fortune in academic mentors. At Cornell University, I found phenomenal mentors in Elizabeth Sanders, Mary Katzenstein, and Ted Lowi, who prepared me well for the rigors of academic life. Elizabeth consistently challenged me to dig deeper, think harder, and write better. Mary provided the warmth and understanding that every graduate student—especially one who is also a mother—deserves to have. To Ted especially I am indebted; his joie de vie and commitment to the discipline taught me that the academic life should be lived with passion; his words of encouragement and challenge still ring in my ears, although I work three thousand miles away. I can only hope one day to give a student what he gave to me.

I also am indebted to a core of friendships that support and sustain me personally. For the "other mothers" who work the carpools, make much-needed casseroles, and celebrate my victories with me, my whole family is indebted. It does take a village to raise children; I am so fortunate to have found mine.

My children are the true inspiration for this book, as they are for all that I do. They challenge and affirm me every day, always tugging me back to earth for what really matters: a warm dinner, a walk in the crinkly leaves, or a bubble bath. Simone, Madison, Cloe, and Bella are the great works of my life, and I am much improved by their existence. The world—my world—is better because they are in it. Still, they remind me each day that the hardest and most fulfilling job in the world is being a mother; I am glad I chose that role freely and with great abandon.

The job of mothering is made infinitely easier and more rewarding when it is shared. I dedicate this book to my loyal and loving companion, Eric Butler.

SAFE, LEGAL, AND UNAVAILABLE?

Introduction

*"The fear in their faces would haunt Dr. Larch forever, the epitome of
everything he could never understand about the great ambiguity in the feelings
people had for children. There was the human body, which was so clearly
designed to* want *babies—and then there was the human mind, which was so
confused about the matter. Sometimes the mind didn't want the babies, but
sometimes the mind was so perverse that it made other people have babies they
knew they didn't want. For whom was this insisting done? Dr. Larch wondered.
For whom did some minds insist that babies, even clearly unwanted ones,* must
be brought, screaming, into the world?"

—*The Cider House Rules* by John Irving

*"We respect the individual conscience of every American on the painful issue of
abortion, but believe as a matter of law that this decision should be left to a
woman, her conscience, her doctor and her God. But abortion should not only
be—abortion should not only be safe and legal, it should be rare."*

—Presidential nominee Bill Clinton at the 1996 Democratic National Convention

When he accepted the Democratic nomination for the presidency on August
29, 1996, Bill Clinton attempted to find compromise within an increasingly polarized debate over abortion in the United States by stating that abortion
should be "safe," "legal," and "rare." His statement reflected the wishes of many
Americans, that the procedure should remain both legally and medically accessible, but hardly used. It also became a catchphrase for late twentieth-century abortion politics, reflecting a desire to create harmony between the competing pro-life
and pro-choice positions. The outcome Clinton likely sought was a general agreement that abortion is an unfortunate event, and that working together to prevent
unwanted pregnancies, the pro-life and pro-choice communities would find common purpose.[1]

What Clinton perhaps did not anticipate was that the two movements, rather
than finding common ground in making abortion rare, would instead pursue
fundamentally different strategies in achieving this goal. For when the pro-choice
side of the equation hears "rare," they are moved to prevent the circumstances that

1

cause a woman to seek abortion: inadequate reproductive health education, poverty, imperfect contraceptive technologies, and gender inequality within relationships. For pro-life organizations, however, the goal has always been to stop abortions, irrespective of the circumstances that prompt women to seek them.

Clinton's objective is being fulfilled, although perhaps not in the way he intended. Abortion rates are declining, although there is little consensus on why this is so. The argument of this book is that efforts to chip away at the practical aspects of abortion access have been successful; in fact, they have been far more successful than most Americans realize. Abortion is slowly becoming rare because, among other reasons, it is increasingly difficult for some groups of women to access.

For while abortion does remain legal, the number and types of circumstances in which a woman can gain access to the procedure have diminished greatly in recent years because of new restrictions at both the state and national levels. Through a myriad of statutory and normative changes in policy and provisions over the past thirty years, a legal and safe abortion is becoming increasingly harder to procure, particularly if the woman who seeks it is young or poor.

This book documents the complete set of barriers to abortion that a woman faces in the United States in the early twenty-first century. Implicit in the movement toward more restrictive policies is a shift in concern away from women's health and rights and toward fetal protection. Much of the debate fueling this is based not on the language of philosophy, science, or rights, which is the language that pro-choice groups favor, but is instead based on the language of religion and morality, which is the language that most pro-life activists prefer.[2] With this shift in perspective comes two related, if relatively unnoticed, trends.

First, the movement toward greater restrictions marginalizes the traditional role of medical professionals in controlling access and practice. Whereas earlier periods in abortion politics in the United States elevated the physicians' gatekeeping role (for better or worse), today that role is being taken up by politicians. And while many would argue that physician-controlled access has its limitations, replacing medical judgment with political judgment would seem to insert a new host of problems into the politics and practice of abortion. Whether the nation might break free of this physician-politician dichotomy in the future is a subject I address in chapter 6.

Second, many of the new restrictions remove the assumption of the doctor's reasonableness and professionalism, supplanting physicians' judgment with that of politicians. When American abortion policy deferred to doctors in making the abortion decision with their patients, society basically embraced the reasonableness of those actors. Allowing women to make this decision with their doctors suggests that women know best the circumstances of their lives; with proper medical assistance, they can determine the best course of action when they face unwanted pregnancy. This formula also assumes the physician's reasonableness: to give pertinent information, to select the best procedure for the immediate patient, and to provide a level of care appropriate to the situation. However, current restrictions undermine both the authority, and, therefore, the legal options, of women and their doctors.[3]

A BRIEF HISTORY OF AMERICAN ABORTION POLICY

The Early Years

The earliest American abortion policy followed English Common Law, which established a "born alive" rule, meaning that the law only applied to cases in which infants were born alive, and then were subject to homicide. Abortion practices in the earliest decades of America's founding were therefore largely overlooked by local statutes. In the early to mid-nineteenth century, states began to adopt an understanding of the fetus that reflected religious doctrine, protecting fetal life only after "ensoulment." In general, most Americans believed that the fetus was imbued with a soul at the time of "quickening," or when the pregnant woman first felt the fetus move, which is generally at about eighteen weeks gestation. This view largely reflected the provision of Pope Gregory XIV, who in 1591 had declared that only ensouled fetuses were protected from abortion. Before quickening, therefore, Western society did not view the fetus as fully human, and abortion was largely unregulated until the mid-nineteenth century as a consequence.

At the end of the seventeenth century, Pope Innocent XI issued two rulings that allowed abortion, claiming at one point that "no abortion is homocide." [4] The courts generally upheld this understanding; for instance, in 1812 the Massachusetts Supreme Court upheld abortion before quickening in *Commonwealth v. Bangs,* and in 1821 Connecticut enacted the first criminal abortion law, which made abortions post-quickening illegal. By 1841, eight of twenty-six states and one territory had banned abortions, but only after quickening.[5]

Although it is not known definitively how many abortions occurred in early America, the practice is generally believed to have been widespread, in part because medical practices in the early nineteenth century favored liberal access to it. Pregnant women were cared for by other women; midwives and mature female family members assisted women in managing their reproductive lives, making the practice of fertility control quite private and a regular aspect of general health. Not until the mid-nineteenth century, when magazines began advertising abortifacients and midwifery practices, did legislators get involved in the provision of abortion.

Even then, the objective of most abortion regulations was to make abortion safe for women and to guard the discretion of doctors to make exceptions when they felt the procedure to be medically necessary to protect the health of the mother. Mid-century abortion regulations were handled exclusively at the local level, where America's founders had argued that intimate matters of morality and health properly belonged. It was not until the late nineteenth century that abortion restrictions grew in both their severity and number.

By the late nineteenth century, several key sociological and professional developments lent themselves toward a more restrictive abortion atmosphere. First, the establishment of "regular" medical schools produced a new medical industry of doctors, most of whom tried to establish themselves as the moral and professional superiors of the common midwife. In opposing abortion, the new doctors gained moral credibility at a time when abortion practices were being questioned publicly for the first time.[6] The new American Medical Association (AMA) announced its anti-abortion policy at its founding in 1847, and immediately pursued a lobbying effort to ban abortion through state law. As the states began restricting abortion access, often due to the influence of the AMA, Pope Pius IX also issued a powerful declaration in 1869, proclaiming that all abortions would lead to excommunication. This statement from the Roman Catholic Church coincided with a wave of "vice" movements in the United States that were designed to improve the health and morality of the people, often through coercive and patronizing methods.

The practice of abortion came to be challenged by physicians as well as by those concerned about the declining fertility rate of white middle-class women relative to those of recent immigrants. Just as middle-class women were gaining access to educational and social institutions, and were therefore more eager to control the number and spacing of their children, new waves of immigrants from eastern and southern Europe were entering the country in record numbers. In the final decades of the nineteenth century, social engineers asserted that the new immigrants, many of whom were Catholic, would overrun the "native" white social groups and outnumber them with their larger families.[7] At the same time, abortion became a more public topic, as the women's magazines that proliferated at this time advertised the availability of abortion as a means of controlling fertility.[8] This public exposure facilitated and enhanced public scrutiny of the practice.

As a result of these various developments, state legislatures began to regulate abortion by the 1880s with a new fervor. In addition, Congress had passed the first federal restriction on abortion in 1873; the Comstock Act criminalized the transmission of "obscenity," including materials containing abortion-related advertisements, through the postal system. The tenor of anti-abortion lobbying escalated further by the turn of the twentieth century. As political scientist Jean Reith Schroedel argues, the lobbying effort at that time included an attempt to make it illegal for midwives—the physicians' primary competitors—to perform abortions.

Abortion practices continued despite these efforts. In the early twentieth century, abortions were provided by midwives as well as by private physicians whose practices would have been jeopardized without the service. Then, state lawmakers began to pass "midwife bans," which made it illegal for anyone but physicians to perform the procedure. Although outside the cover of the law, many providers who had performed abortions for decades continued to do so. Many flourished in the early decades of the twentieth century. Ruth Barnett of Portland, Oregon, for instance, ran a thriving business for more than forty years in the heart of downtown, where local law enforcement shielded her from scrutiny, viewing her work as a public health necessity.[9] Contrary to the images of the "back-alley" abortionist, providers like Barnett offered women a safe—albeit illegal—end to their pregnancies.

Abortion provision became more dangerous in the 1940s, when the legal community began targeting not just abortion providers, but also the women who sought their services. For the first time in the history of the United States, women themselves were put on trial for the procurement of abortion services. This heightened legal scrutiny pushed the industry further underground, and resulted in the provision of fewer safe procedures. Most of the images Americans have today of back alley abortions are from the 1940s and 1950s, when many American women lost their reproductive organs or their lives in an effort to control their fertility.[10] As historian Rickie Solinger puts it, it was the law that made abortions unsafe by forcing the procedure underground, where it could not be regulated.[11]

The Movement to Re-Legalize Abortion

The movement in the 1960s to expand the availability of safe, legal abortions was initiated, surprisingly, in the medical community. Two specific events turned the medical community, which had long been opposed to legal abortion, into an advocate for increased access.

One event was the case of Sherry Finkbine. The mother of four children and the producer of a popular children's program in Arizona, Finkbine found herself pregnant with a fifth child in 1962. She soon discovered that the drug her husband had imported from a trip abroad to alleviate her morning sickness had in fact severely impaired the fetus. Finkbine learned, as many women did at this time, that abortion was available to her only through the local hospital's therapeutic abortion review board, a committee of her hospital's obstetrician-gynecologists, who would decide her case. She made her request for an abortion, arguing that she could not provide proper care for such a compromised child with four other small children at home. Initially, the board granted her request. But when the local media was alerted of this decision, the hospital reneged, relenting to the public scrutiny. Ultimately, Finkbine flew to Sweden for her procedure; upon her return, she was greeted by the American press corps at JFK airport in New York.

The Finkbine case highlights the vagaries of accessing safe abortions during the mid-twentieth century. Women whose grandmothers had accessed abortion services with relative ease through their family midwives found the hospital review board process demeaning and impersonal. It separated a woman's gynecological request from her overall health and family history—factors that the nineteenth-century midwife would have known intimately. Women objected to decisions being made on a seemingly ad hoc basis and in an intimidating setting. Furthermore, the review boards seemed to undermine the autonomy of women and their control over their bodies, sending a message that many women interpreted as stating that their judgment alone regarding their abortion decision was simply not enough to justify it.

Some doctors objected to this system as well, even though it ostensibly gave physicians greater authority over abortion than did outright bans. Many individual doctors felt hospital review boards also undermined their authority; sometimes the review boards were comprised of physicians without obstetric-gynecological experience. Experts in the field wanted the flexibility to help their patients with their abortion decision in the privacy of the examination room and with a fuller understanding of each woman's particular situation. Still, physicians were unaccustomed to the lawmaking process, and were reluctant to enter into this heated issue.

The rubella outbreaks during the late 1950s and early 1960s in San Francisco were the second major event that tipped the scales toward greater access to abortions. Some physicians were even propelled to bring their grievances into the legislative arena. As in the Finkbine case, the rubella epidemic highlighted the rigidity of prevailing local laws. Rubella was widely understood to cause terrible deformities in fetuses of women suffering from the disease, especially during the first three months of pregnancy, and still doctors in California found themselves unable to legally provide abortions to infected women. This launched the movement to reform California's abortion law, marked by the mobilization of the California Medical Association in the mid-1960s. With the help of the National Organization for Women (NOW), formed in 1966, California physicians were successful. Governor Ronald Reagan signed the California Therapeutic Abortion Act in 1967.[12] Considered the most liberal abortion law of its time, the statute allowed physicians to perform abortions when continued pregnancy would threaten a woman's physical or mental health, creating greater authority for individual physicians to provide abortions when they believed the procedure was necessary.[13]

Many other states followed. Buoyed by support from the emergent women's movement, the abortion reform effort succeeded in many states in producing more lenient abortion laws. Still, for many advocates of legal abortion, reform was not sufficient. Thus NARAL (then the National Abortion Repeal Action League) was founded in 1969, with the goal of *repealing* all abortion laws in an effort to return abortion provision to its early nineteenth-century traditions. Abortion, advocates argued, could be provided safely and humanely without the state's intervention. In response, Alaska, Hawaii, and New York decriminalized abortion by 1970.

For some, this process of state-based legislative reform was too painstakingly slow and uneven. By 1973, state-by-state lobbying efforts had produced a patchwork quilt of abortion regulations. To many in the women's movement, abortion access was so basic to women's liberation at home and at work that it was considered the right of all women—not just those who lived in progressive states. Without it, women could not control their educational and vocational aspirations. Uneven provision across the states created an inequality among women that many felt to be fundamentally unfair. Some groups therefore began to seek resolution through the courts. Just as the civil rights movement had been successful in abolishing inconsistent segregation laws through judicial channels, many feminists sought progress there, too.

Ultimately, the U.S. Supreme Court settled some abortion debates and spawned many others when it issued its landmark ruling, *Roe v. Wade*, on January 22, 1973. Although a more detailed analysis is found in chapter 2, it is important to note here that *Roe* overturned nearly all state abortion regulations existing at the time, and expanded the fundamental right of privacy established earlier in *Griswold v. Connecticut* (1965) to include abortion. Feminists lauded the case for establishing equality across the states; of course, the case also provoked the ire of abortion opponents, who would gain momentum for their own movement as a result of the Court's decision.

THE OPPOSITION EMERGES

Current efforts to roll back the abortion policy gains of the 1970s did not emerge in a vacuum: they are the result of a social movement. *Roe v. Wade* was heralded as the ultimate expression of women's progress by the groups who had fought for reproductive liberty. For those opposed to abortion, however, *Roe* signaled not only a shocking extension of federal judicial power, but also an affront to moral principles. The verdict set into motion a powerful backlash movement that identifies abortion as a grave example of the erosion of Christian values in this country.

Although the United States has a long history of evangelism fueling its social movements (witness the abolition, prohibition, and civil rights movements, for example) the contemporary pro-life movement is unique in its rapid rise and its quick integration into national party politics.[14] The pro-life movement today is part of a larger "Christian Right" movement. The Christian Right is often misrepresented in the popular media as a hegemonic political force. On the contrary, this movement is a mélange of different conservative theological traditions: charismatics, evangelicals, fundamentalists, and Pentecostals, as well as some Roman Catholics. Occasionally, Orthodox Jews join the conservative Christians over particular legislation, broadening the scope of the movement beyond Christianity.[15] The diversity within the movement is in fact one of its strengths: it cuts across denominations that traditionally have been at odds.[16] The history of this affiliation, and its emergence in national politics, is important to understand in order to grasp the character of American politics today and the key role that abortion plays in it.

During the 1960s, religious organizations were generally politically quiescent. Philosophically, most mainline Protestant churches adhered to the "dispensational" theory, which encourages religious adherents to focus on the afterlife rather than on the present. What is more, the Scopes monkey trial of 1925 made religious activism appear irrational in an era of increasing respect for science and technology.[17] However, social and political events in the 1960s, including the women's movement, the Vietnam War, and later, Watergate, helped create a sense of betrayal and anger amongst the nation's conservative religious voters. Many Christian voters ultimately viewed these social shifts as so destructive of their worldview that they were unhappily compelled to action.[18] The first denomination to enter the political realm was the Roman Catholic Church.

In 1965, the same year that Protestant minister Jerry Falwell publicly denounced the participation of religious people in politics,[19] the Second Vatican Council issued its "Church in the Modern World," which officially empowered lay Catholics to apply their faith values toward issues of social justice. From this document grew a movement toward the "Social Gospel," which formally linked theology with social action and politicized church teachings. One of the first issues the Catholic Church focused on was abortion. Three years later, when Pope Paul VI's 1968 encyclical, "Humanae Vitae," was issued, the Roman Catholic Church created the right-to-life movement by condemning abortion except when necessary to save a woman's life.[20] Not long after, in 1972, he reversed church doctrine dating back to 1679, which had officially allowed abortion prior to quickening, by declaring that official church doctrine now recognized that fetuses have inalienable rights.[21] Thus, abortion at any stage was impermissible.[22] The Catholic Church's entrance into the abortion debate, which was at that time mainly confined to the medical community,[23] lent financial resources, popular support, infrastructure, and manpower to the fledgling movement.[24]

The Catholic Church had protested abortion policy only at the local level until the *Roe* decision prompted the National Committee of Catholic Bishops to launch a national effort.[25] Even then, the Catholic Church's activities were fairly modest until 1975, when it issued the "Pastoral Plan for Pro-Life Activities," which called upon Catholics to act upon their life-affirming values. The plan provided an open-ing through which smaller church organizations could join the national abortion debate. By the late 1970s, the movement hit its stride, and many pro-life organiza-tions were formed during that period and throughout the 1980s, including Focus on the Family (1977), Moral Majority (1979), Concerned Women for America (1979), Family Research Council (1988), Operation Rescue (1988), and Christian Coalition (1989).

Still, despite the profusion of organizations, the movement lacked the legiti-macy and focus necessary to affect political change. As the following chapters describe, the early movement's efforts were so focused on an unequivocal federal abortion ban that anything short of this was viewed as a disappointment. Because of its slow early progress, the movement decided to institutionalize itself through a variety of new strategies aimed at mainstreaming its message. First, the Chris-tian Coalition, founded in 1991 by evangelist Pat Robertson as an outgrowth of his failed 1988 presidential campaign, traded alienating religious rhetoric and mil-itary metaphors for more choice- and civil rights-based language to appeal to a wider audience.[26] Starting in 1991, the organization's director, Ralph Reed, began encouraging local affiliates to

> find effective language that motivate[s] our supporters without turning off voters sitting on the fence. . . . Such rhetoric . . . sets a standard of basic civility that allow[s] secular ears to hear our message of stronger families and traditional values.[27]

The Christian Coalition combined its rhetorical shift with lobbying and policy changes. Following the 1994 election, which ushered in a new cohort of anti-abortion lawmakers, the organization embraced a strategy of "bold incremental-ism." [28] Not wanting to rush Reed's agenda and risk a backlash, the group led the Christian Right movement in an effort to move slowly with legislative change. Part of that effort entailed focusing on issues less volatile than abortion or the other pillar of their platform, homosexuality.[29] Reed began to support candidates on such issues as taxes and crime, which enhanced the ability of Christian Right activists to appeal to libertarian members of Congress (MCs) and voters:

> Libertarians and social conservatives both want smaller government. By using fiscal policy as social policy—shifting control of education to the local level, ending tax subsidies for abortion, and transferring certain welfare functions to the civil society—social conservatives could reduce the size of government in such a way as to measur-ably advance traditional values.[30]

Reed especially targeted family tax relief as an issue that could bring secular and religious families together. Both the Christian Coalition's Contract with the American Family and their Web site are evidence of this strategy. The Contract with the American Family is an initiative that targets tax relief, crime, and education choice alongside abortion, pornography, and reform of the arts. On their Web page, the organization offers readers a voters' guide to the performance of MCs on issues of special importance to its members. Such issues include all abortion votes, but also votes on the balanced budget amendment, congressional term limits, and the line-item veto as well. This strategy allows the organization to moderate its image and win broader public appeal.

As Reed put it, "Soon we discovered that it was far easier to win a school board seat than a Senate seat, and far more likely to change the vote of a state legislator than to change the mind of the president." [31] The Christian Coalition now focuses its efforts on local school board elections, city councils, and state legislatures and emphasizes the role of lay leaders within the organization.[32] Robertson's campaign had cultivated a "new generation of leaders and activists who were poised for later victory." [33] In 1992, the Christian Coalition began to mobilize this group of activists, and through separate training seminars for candidates for state legislatures and school boards, the organization began to see its members winning elective office.[34] Beginning in the mid-1990s, the success of this strategy could be seen in both state and federal legislation.

THE CURRENT DEBATE

The current battle over abortion policy is one fought largely between the pro-choice forces, who view reproductive rights as central and fundamental to women's freedom and equality, and the pro-life forces, who believe abortion in most if not all circumstances is morally reprehensible and an affront to the very definition of human life. Chapter 1 demonstrates that many Americans find themselves somewhere in between these two extreme positions. Still, the policies in place today are the work of abortion activists, most of whom take stronger and more rigid views than the majority of the nation. Whereas early anti-abortion forces wanted to make abortion illegal, given the strength of the *Roe* ruling and the lack of political will in the nation's capital, they simply could not do it. The movement then shifted its focus to making abortion inaccessible to as many groups of women as possible. By subtly redefining citizenship of the fetus, and more recently, the very definition of pregnancy, activists have been able to make tremendous inroads without the general public's awareness.

These recent restrictions limit access by favoring fetal rights over women's rights and by excluding scientific information and expertise, repressing them, or both. In all the debates between those who advocate women's rights and those who embrace fetal rights, the language of science and medicine has largely gone missing. The images and language most often wielded by pro-life advocates are vivid and emotional, as subsequent chapters demonstrate. Recent developments in imaging techniques certainly have facilitated a reliance on powerful pictures that humanize the fetus in a way not possible two decades ago. Because fetuses now can be seen in intricate detail, opponents of abortion have striking images to use in support of abortion restrictions, despite what these restrictions might mean to women's health and freedom. The results are that abortion in the United States is less accessible than it was in 1973 and women's health and freedom are threatened, especially for the young and the poor. Pro-choice advocates counter these restrictions largely through the use of the language of rights and freedom from government intrusion.

The final implication of this analysis is that the very definition of American citizenship is shifting to include the fetus (in some cases the zygote), but at the expense of women's status as complete social citizens. The pro-life policy agenda today has consequences for women's status as free and legal individuals and for the pro-choice premise that science and physicians should be controlling forces in all matters medical.

ABORTION AS SOCIAL REGULATORY POLICY

As the previous historical overview demonstrates, for most of the country's history, the federal government remained quiet on the question of abortion, as it was on most issues of morality. Scholars agree that early American political philosophy, and the Constitution itself, give little authority to the federal government in social regulatory policy. By definition, the philosophy of limited government keeps issues of intense personal morality close to the will of the people by delegating their regulation to local and state authorities. From marriage law to gun control, social regulatory policy, more commonly referred to as "morality policy," was handled by localities until the mid-twentieth century. At that time, for a variety of reasons, the central government began taking a more active role in all policies, including social regulatory policy.[35] For the purposes of this book, social regulatory policy is synonymous with morality policy.[36]

Local control serves a number of purposes. First, it allows state and local authorities to experiment with controversial policies without affecting the entire nation. Moreover, Americans are more likely to take an interest in issues of social control, and they have more opportunity for input at the local level than they do at the national level. The Founders also believed that with such a vast and diverse nation, it was possible that smaller groupings of Americans would be able to adjust policy to reflect the particular needs of their communities. Thus, social regulatory policy would vary—sometimes dramatically—by region or state. This outcome presents an obvious problem for those who believe certain social policies are a matter of right.

The Constitution of the United States codifies a governing system of layered federalism. Article I, Section 8, delegates most national legislative authority to Congress, granting flexible powers to discern proper national policy. Still, that section is balanced by the various limits placed on federal authority by the Bill of Rights and by the Tenth Amendment, which invests police powers, or social regulatory control, in the lower levels of government. From the beginning, this structure created tension between the layers of government, confirming James Madison's suspicion that national government authorities would continually seek more power, but be checked by local authorities. Through the struggle for control of social regulatory policy, individual liberty would be protected, because no one level of government would have absolute or unlimited power.

Until 1873 the federal government usually ceded authority over abortion policy to the states. That was the year Congress passed the Comstock Act, officially entitled the Act for the Suppression of Trade in, and Circulation of, Obscene Literature and Articles for Immoral Use. In some ways, even this act becomes the exception that proves the rule: opposition to this exercise of federal authority was quick and sharp, and the act was eventually allowed to expire under the stress of critical public scrutiny. Still, similar "mini-Comstock" laws were passed in Connecticut and Massachusetts, and remained in place for many years.

Through much of the twentieth century, the federal branches of government recoiled from the abortion dilemma, which was roiling in the states. While the states struggled with how to respond to the tragedy of dangerous illegal abortions and the safe, but illegal, abortions provided by some caregivers, the federal government remained silent.[37] As a consequence, the state policies at mid-twentieth century were a mish-mash of rules, regulations, and realities that reflected local prevailing sentiments. This outcome was theoretically respectful of the Founders' intentions for social policy; generally speaking, however, the loss of many women's lives and the deterioration of their health poignantly illustrated the dangers of localism.

Abortion is unlike any other policy debate in the United States because it involves the presence of one emerging life within an existing one. Although activists on all sides of the debate seek resolution by making analogies to other policy debates, the difficulty of abortion may lie in its uniqueness, which in some ways leads to its intractability. The issue cannot be resolved by finding a parallel resolution; however, abortion politics can be better understood within a broader policy framework. Because it invokes intense moral debate and public scrutiny, abortion can comfortably be categorized as social regulatory policy.

Social regulatory policy is distinct from other types of policy, both in its content and in how Americans engage it. Other types of policy, defined by Cornell University political scientist Theodore J. Lowi as patronage, regulatory, constituent, or redistributive, have existed since the nation's founding. Social regulatory policy, first identified and named in the latter part of the twentieth century, is distinct because it involves the regulation of intimate human behaviors and decisions. Whereas most other policies place boundaries on economic behaviors, social regulatory policy is personal. Abortion, prayer in schools, gay marriage, gun control, and some civil rights legislation are several contemporary examples.[38] Legislation in these areas touches directly upon intimate individual choices, rather than business decisions or the decisions of demographic groups.[39]

Social regulatory policy—be it gun control, end-of-life decisions, or abortion—is especially distinct from other policy areas because of the politics it engenders. Thirty years ago, Lowi argued that different policy types inspire different types of political behavior and resolution.[40] Each has a particular form and object of coercion. Political scientists Raymond Tatalovich and Byron W. Daynes argued that social regulatory policy is unique both in its object of regulation (the individual) and in its politics.[41] These politics tend to be more acrimonious and more polarized than the political battles in other policy areas. Given the personal nature of social regulatory policy, this intensity is understandable. And as with any policy type, some of these issues are more contested than others.[42] Abortion remains one of the most contested policy matters in modern history.

The battles in social regulatory policy are therefore infused with language about morality, right and wrong, and religion. Moreover, such policy is often image-driven. Because of such emphases, these debates overlook the economic, scientific, and sociological aspects of the policy in question. The stakes are therefore high: an economic policy might be about winning or losing more money; a social policy debate is often about winning or losing souls.

Finally, social regulatory politics is often protracted and difficult to resolve. Because these issues touch upon Americans' most deeply held core beliefs, and because they have a "gut level" appeal, politics in this arena can be theatrical and uncompromising.[43] For example, abortion lends itself to visual imagery more easily than a debate over the regulation of fuel emissions. All parties in the abortion debate are prone to wielding passionate and sometimes shocking visual images to persuade others of their position. Thus, abortion policy remains unresolved in this nation more than thirty years after the landmark Supreme Court decision that attempted to provide resolution.

The nation is long past the Court's decision to enter the abortion fray, and it might be reasonably argued that the stakes of abortion politics and the intensity of its activists have never been higher. Court intervention has in fact failed to yield either compromise or resolution. In part, this may be because abortion has features unlike other social policies. It challenges the definition of the person, the definition of the mother, and notions of morality and the role of science. It is, to activists on either side of the debate, a "clash of absolutes."[44] Besides abortion, only the slavery debate challenged so pointedly society's definitions of personhood and citizenship, lending a particular poignancy and intransigence to both issues.

James Davison Hunter, a professor of sociology and religious studies, helps form an understanding of these dynamics. In contemporary America, he argues, individuals have a tendency to line up on important social, or gut level, issues based upon their worldviews. And often, he argues, Americans see the world either through the lens of science or through the lens of morality. The two worldviews share little language for making sense of an issue like abortion. In this book, I argue that the pro-choice forces largely fall into the scientific camp, preferring to understand abortion as a medical matter with a rightful place within medical discourse and relying on scientific definitions of the fetus and pregnancy. For them, morality certainly is not absent, but it is secondary to the questions of maternal health and physical well-being that science asks. Pro-life groups, on the other hand, understand abortion through the lens of morality, and often argue that the science of abortion should be secondary to what they identify as the larger rubric of moralism.

POLITICAL LABELS

To describe the major actors in abortion politics, it is important to use the language that the social and political groups involved use to describe themselves. Some of this language has already been used in the preceding material. Understanding that this language and these labels were created in part to define the issue and promote a particular cause, the reader should feel free to think critically about them because their accuracy, their political power, and their impact are critical to the terms of the debate. In chapter 5, the "pro-choice" and "pro-life" labels are examined as they are used, for better or worse, by political parties and officeholders.

In addition, this discussion relies whenever possible on scientific definitions and terminology rather than religious or political ones, recognizing that all language in this debate is infused with political meaning. For instance, "embryo" is used when discussing the fertilized egg before four months gestation; "fetus" is used when discussing the fertilized egg at fourth months gestation until birth. "Pregnancy" refers to the time when the fertilized egg implants in the uterine wall until birth. To some, reliance on medical terminology may appear cold or distant; however, in the fevered debate over abortion, I believe scientific language provides the most accurate and neutral language available.

RESEARCH METHODOLOGY

The sources for this book are many and varied. Because it focuses on the accrual of abortion restrictions, I rely a good deal on legislative history and judicial decisions to document policy changes. For additional barriers to abortion procedures, I have relied on the input of the social movements themselves, which these days catalogue changes in abortion practices on their Web sites. I do not rely on a single "side" to document a trend or practice, but have looked broadly to verify claims.

I also availed myself of the unusually large number of abortion providers living and practicing in my community of Portland, Oregon, a city with a strong tradition of abortion provision dating back to Ruth Barnett in the early twentieth century, as well as a more recent wave of anti-abortion activism. I spoke at length with seven providers, testing theories and asking questions about medical practices and trends. While their views cannot be characterized as representative of those of practitioners nationwide, particularly because they practice within a relatively permissive legal environment, their advice and information were invaluable to me, and their words in the following chapters give color and depth to a very human subject.

Finally, newspapers, scholarly journals, and the many books on abortion-related political movements provided a consistently credible and informative set of sources. The influence of these materials is felt throughout this text.

MATERNAL AND FETAL CITIZENSHIP

Through the cumulative effect of federal and state efforts to protect the fetus, the nation has eroded women's full inclusion in the very definition of citizenship, and has slowly developed a kind of fetal citizenship sure to undermine women's rights further. This conclusion is reached by traveling two parallel roads: first, that fetal citizenship rests on a compilation of affirmative fetal protections and abortion barriers, not on an unequivocal ban in the Constitution or from a single federal statute. For while some pro-life activists once hoped for that sort of resolution, it remains distant and unfulfilled. More tenable, however, is the acquisition of fetal rights through a variety of protections and abortion regulations which, when viewed as a collection, provide a level of fetal protection not seen until now.

Second, to realize fetal citizenship, and to appreciate the consequences to women's full citizenship, there needs to be an official definition of "citizen." Justice Harry Blackmun concluded in his 1973 *Roe v. Wade* ruling that fetuses were not citizens because the Constitution refers only to born people as citizens. This observation, however, gives only a thin glimpse of the full meaning of the term.

In its most basic form, citizenship bestows a set of rights and obligations onto individuals within a nation's borders. The basic, traditional features of political citizenship imply rights relative to the state: voting, serving on juries and in elected bodies, and inclusion in the military. Still, many scholars are quick to point out that there is a "wider setting of society's institutional and cultural traditions" that affects the definition of a citizen.[45]

British sociologist T. H. Marshall first called this extended form of belonging "social citizenship." [46] Social citizenship "in its more general meaning [is] 'citizenship' [that] refers to an individual's status as a full member of a particular political community." [47] Feminist scholars have clearly demonstrated that women have historically been denied both proper political citizenship and the more loosely defined social citizenship. The social conditions for women before suffrage notwithstanding, the application of social citizenship can be seen today in abortion policy.

As political science professor Ursula Vogel and others note, culture has a gendered notion of citizenship, and that gendered perspective often shapes the way citizenship is understood in society. Citizenship, as a relationship between the individual and government, is affected by government policies and preferences. A host of scholars have documented the ways in which public policy has created bifurcated citizenship: when policies treat people differently based upon their gender, the effect is different stacks of benefits, associations, and obligations for different people.[48] Through different sets of public policies, "citizenship was rendered gender specific through a complex interplay of decisions by policymakers, institutional factors, political imperatives, and the unintended consequences of policy design which emerged in the course of implementation." [49]

Much of the literature in this area focuses on different treatment of women in the early twentieth century. However, some of this work clearly illuminates the ways in which early adoration of motherhood created a maternal citizenship: as a mother, a woman could receive greater support and rights under the law. Policies that regard a woman's role as mother as central to her societal contribution fundamentally linked full female citizenship with motherhood, laying a backdrop of citizenship against which abortion rests uncomfortably.

Abortion relates to gendered citizenship in at least two ways. First, if female citizenship in this country is based on motherhood, women who end their pregnancies risk a social stigma that threatens their full experience as social citizens. Second, if policy barriers are erected specifically for women seeking to end their pregnancies, women are losing rights and facing an obligation to bear unwanted children. Without the ability to control their fertility in the way they choose, American women will find it difficult to embrace the other aspects of full citizenship: full-time employment, community service, civil service through jury duty and public office, and the list goes on. The connection between citizenship and abortion policy has therefore led feminist legal scholars to conclude that "[w]hen women are denied the sexual and reproductive autonomy of men, they are relegated to second-class citizenship." [50]

What, then, is the basis for fetal citizenship? As Justice Blackmun noted more than thirty years ago, all references to citizenship in the Constitution refer to a born person, implying that citizenship, and all the rights and obligations it entails, begins at birth. Pro-life activists posit, however, that the fetus is a developing, or potential, citizen, and as such is worthy of state protection on these grounds. Note that minors in this country have otherwise never enjoyed full citizenship, but rather have been considered "persons belonging to the community only through the representative agency of others." [51]

The law in the United States is founded on the notion of the individual, which poses a conceptual challenge in defining the citizenship of a pregnant woman and the citizenship of a fetus within the woman's body. Pregnancy challenges this notion, says political scientist Judith A. Baer, because during pregnancy two individuals "occupy the same space." [52] How the interests of the mature female (and pregnant) citizen are weighed against those of the potential citizen reveals a great deal about American ideas about citizenship, as well as the role of religion and science in public policy. As I argue, the United States is gradually placing greater stock in the potential citizen than in the adult woman citizen through its abortion policies.

BOOK OVERVIEW

This book follows a simple path. In chapter 1, I offer the reader an overview of abortion facts: who has abortions, where, why, and when. I also discuss public opinion in order to provide a better understanding of how the nation regards the issue. Too many of these everyday facts have been obscured by political rhetoric to the point that many people are surprised to find that their preconceived notions about abortion rates do not match the facts.

In chapter 2, I concentrate on the evolution of Supreme Court findings on abortion, which demonstrates a trend away from abortion rights, per se, given the judicial successes of the pro-life movement and the development of legal protections for the fetus. Chapter 3 presents further evidence to support the argument that the pro-life movement has rolled back access to abortion by leveraging the full array of state-enacted abortion restrictions and practical barriers enacted over the last thirty years. In this regard, the pro-life strategy of using public opinion to affect and shape local legislation has been successful. I also demonstrate that the states have not ceded their role in social regulatory policy to any branch of the federal government, but rather are involved in an ongoing battle for regulatory control. In chapter 4, the full extent of recent federal abortion restrictions is considered, as well as the changes in the pro-life organizing strategy that made these restrictions possible. When chapters 3 and 4 are combined, the picture of fetal citizenship fully emerges.

Chapter 5 explores the partisan dimension to these developments, explaining the uniting of the Republican Party and the pro-life movement. Democrats and pro-choice advocates, for their part, are increasingly defensive and unsure of their position. Recently, they seem unable even to defend all aspects of abortion access. Finally, in chapter 6 I consider the future of abortion politics, which will likely include further fetal protections, and ultimately, a political backlash from the medical, feminist, and religious communities.

Each chapter is followed by resources meant to spark debate. Both the suggested additional readings and the discussion questions are intended to extend the puzzles and theories presented in the text. Additionally, there are three appendixes at the back of this book for further reference. Appendix A provides a description of pivotal judicial rulings regarding abortion. Appendix B shows the platforms of the national political parties in regard to abortion. Appendix C points the reader to a list of the nation's most significant abortion interest groups and their respective Web sites. I hope that readers of this book will take full advantage of the opportunity to ponder, argue, and challenge each other with meaningful debate through these resources.

DISCUSSION QUESTIONS

1. How did the concept of quickening affect early American views toward abortion? Why do you think this was the case?
2. How has the opinion of professionals in the medical field evolved toward abortion? How important should their voices be in the current debate?
3. Does the history of abortion in the United States pre-*Roe* resemble your perception of this historical era? How has this account changed your views on the issue?
4. What values do early abortion policies reflect about medical practices and religious beliefs? How have those values changed or remained the same in American culture? Are these changes for better or worse?
5. Are the hallmarks of early American abortion policy consistent with today's abortion policy? Should today's abortion policy be more or less consistent with historical abortion policy? Why or why not?
6. How did abortion policy become so restrictive in the late-nineteenth century? Were these new restrictions appropriate for the times? Would they be appropriate today? Why or why not?
7. Has the strategy of the pro-life movement changed with time? If so, how? Are the changes making the movement more or less effective? What possible changes could be made in this movement in the future?
8. How is social regulatory policy unlike other forms of public policy? How well does abortion fit into the social regulatory policy category? Should abortion and slavery be in a separate policy category altogether?

9. What is the nature of American citizenship? How should it be defined? Should it be extended to the fetus, and if so, on what grounds? What would full fetal citizenship mean for women's citizenship?

SUGGESTED READING

Hunter, James Davison. *Culture Wars: The Struggle to Define America.* New York: BasicBooks, 1991.

Irving, John. *The Cider House Rules.* New York: William Morrow and Company, 1985.

Solinger, Rickie. *Pregnancy and Power: A Short History of Reproductive Politics in America.* New York: New York University Press, 2005.

Tatalovich, Raymond, and Byron W. Daynes, eds. *Moral Controversies in American Politics,* 3rd ed. Armonk, N.Y.: M. E. Sharpe, 2004.

Tribe, Laurence H. *Abortion: The Clash of Absolutes.* New York: W. W. Norton, 1990.

NOTES

1. As a Democratic senator from New York, Bill Clinton's wife Hillary Clinton would make a similar argument nearly a decade later, causing an upheaval within her own political party. More on this development is contained in chapter 5.

2. There are two very famous philosophical exegeses on abortion, written just before legalization. Although they are beyond the scope of this work, students might wish to study them. See Judith Jarvis Thomson, "A Defense of Abortion," *Philosophy and Public Affairs* 1, no. 1 (Autumn 1971): 47–66 and Michael Tooley, "Abortion and Infanticide," *Philosophy and Public Affairs* 2, no. 1 (Autumn 1972): 37–65.

3. My thanks to my friend and former student Tina Gentzkow, who pointed out the relevance of the "reasonableness doctrine" to abortion policy.

4. Connie Paige, *The Right to Lifers: Who They Are, How They Operate, Where They Get Their Money* (New York: Summit Books, 1983), 35.

5. Connecticut (1821), Ohio (1834), Indiana (1835), Missouri (1835), Arkansas (1837), Mississippi (1839), Iowa Territory (1839), Alabama (1840), and Maine (1840).

6. Kristin Luker, *The Politics of Motherhood* (Berkeley: University of California Press, 1984).

7. James C. Mohr, *Abortion in America: The Origins and Evolution of National Policy, 1800–1900* (Oxford: Oxford University Press, 1978).

8. Rosalind Pollack Petcheskey, *Abortion and Woman's Choice: The State, Sexuality, and Reproductive Freedom,* rev. ed. (Boston: Northeastern University Press, 1990).

9. Rickie Solinger, *The Abortionist: A Woman against the Law* (Berkeley: University of California Press, 1994).

10. In recent years, several authors have documented the humane practice of safe abortions during the period in American history in which abortion was illegal. See, for instance, Carole E. Joffe, *Doctors of Conscience: The Struggle to Provide Abortion before and after* Roe v. Wade (Boston: Beacon Press, 1995) and Laura Kaplan, *The Story of Jane: The Legendary Underground Feminist Abortion Service* (Chicago: University of Chicago Press, 1997).

11. Rickie Solinger, *Beggars and Choosers* (New York: Hill and Wang, 2001), 38.

12. More will be said about the interesting partisan dimensions of abortion politics in chapter 5. It is an intriguing historical point to note that Ronald Reagan wrote an anti-abortion book during his presidency. This would seem to directly contradict his earlier actions as governor. See Ronald Reagan, *Abortion and the Conscience of a Nation* (Nashville, Tenn.: T. Nelson, 1984).

13. A brief history of the California abortion law is provided on California's Planned Parenthood Web site: www.ppacca.org/site/pp.asp?c=kuJYJeO4F&b= 139490.

14. Ralph Reed is quick to point out that religious-populist stirrings historically have been felt most powerfully within the Democratic Party. See his book, *Active Faith: How Christians Are Changing the Face of American Politics* (New York: The Free Press, 1996). Allen D. Hertzke makes an interesting argument about the unique role that religious activism plays in American politics. Responding to Mancur Olson's work about political passivity, Hertzke notes that religious motivation can sometimes override the rationality of not participating in political movements. See *Representing God in Washington: The Role of Religious Lobbies in the American Polity* (Knoxville: University of Tennessee Press, 1988).

15. For an excellent argument about the variety of theological and political views within the Christian Right, see Harvey Cox, "The Warring Visions of the Religious Right," *Atlantic Monthly,* November 1995, 59–69. Also see James Davison Hunter's book *Culture Wars: The Struggle to Define America* (New York: Basic-Books, 1991) for an illustration of the myriad issues that divide religious conservatives from religious liberals today. This work focuses more narrowly on the Christian Right, which is the most politically active segment of the movement in America, emphasizing the Christian Coalition specifically, the most active, although not the largest, Christian Right organization today.

16. The ability of the Christian Right to cut across denominational lines is recent. Movement leaders have made explicit their intentions to increase the movement's force by welcoming a range of denominations. Others argue that the

movement's potential is nonetheless thwarted by denominational disagreements. See, for instance, Duane M. Oldfield, "The Christian Right in the Presidential Nominating Process," in *In Pursuit of the White House*, ed. William G. Mayer (Chatham, N.J.: Chatham House Publishers, 1996), 254–282.

17. For those unfamiliar with the Scopes trial, it was a challenge to a Tennessee statute that forbade any instructor in a public school to teach evolution.

18. Both Kristin Luker and Sara Diamond have characterized those on either side of the abortion movement as having entirely different views regarding sex, marriage, and women's roles. The fundamental nature of this disagreement is in part responsible for the protracted nature of this debate and the inability of either side to compromise. See Kristin Luker, *Abortion and the Politics of Motherhood* (Berkeley: University of California Press, 1984) and Sara Diamond, *Roads to Dominion: Right-Wing Movements and Political Power in the United States* (New York: The Guilford Press, 1995).

19. Falwell comments on his earlier disavowal of political life in his book *Strength for the Journey: An Autobiography* (New York: Simon & Schuster, 1987).

20. Paige, *The Right to Lifers*.

21. This position is not universally held by practicing Catholics. See data in later chapters, and also Mary Fainsod Katzenstein, "Discursive Politics and Feminist Activism in the Catholic Church," in *Feminist Organization: Harvest of the New Women's Movement*, ed. Myra Marx Ferree and Patricia Yancey Martin (Philadelphia: Temple University Press, 1995) and Mary C. Segers, "The Loyal Opposition: Catholics for a Free Choice," in *The Catholic Church and the Politics of Abortion—A View from the States*, ed. Timothy A. Byrnes and Mary C. Segers (Boulder: Westview Press, 1992).

22. Paige, *Right to Lifers*.

23. Luker, *Abortion and the Politics of Motherhood*.

24. The entrance of the Catholic Church into abortion politics provoked the ire of liberal mainline Protestants and Jews, who immediately organized in opposition. In 1967, the Association of Reformed Rabbis and the New York unit of the United Synagogue of America led the charge, criticizing the church openly. Not long after, American Baptists, Southern Baptists, Southern Presbyterians, United Presbyterians, and the United Church of Christ issued similar statements, calling for greater sensitivity for women. See Paige, *Right to Lifers*.

25. Byrnes, "The Politics of Abortion: The Catholic Bishops."

26. This work focuses on the role of the Christian Coalition, whose membership numbered more than 1.5 million Americans at the end of the twentieth century. Two other organizations, Concerned Women for America and Focus on the Family, also figure prominently in the movement, although their emphasis has thus far been far less focused on the political parties.

27. Reed, *Active Faith,* 120.

28. Ibid., 188. This theme is echoed in William Kristol's arguments regarding abortion strategy. See Fred Barnes, "Try Again," *New Republic,* June 13, 1994, 9–10.

29. Rob Eure, "Some Coalition Members Look beyond 'Family Values'," *The Ledger-Standard* (Norfolk, Virginia), September 11, 1992.

30. Reed, *Active Faith,* 189.

31. Ibid., 132.

32. Mark J. Rozell and Clyde Wilcox, "Second Coming: The Strategies of the New Christian Right," *Political Science Quarterly* 111 (Summer 1996): 274; *Second Coming: The New Christian Right in Virginia Politics* (Baltimore: Johns Hopkins University Press, 1996), for a book-length analysis of the movement's efforts in the state of Virginia; and, for a comparative state-by-state analysis of Christian Right efforts, *God at the Grassroots: The Christian Right in the 1994 Elections* (Lanham, Md.: Rowman and Littlefield Publishers, 1995).

33. Reed, *Active Faith,* 128.

34. In response, some progressive women's organizations have begun grassroots efforts of their own. See Cheryl Hyde, "Feminist Social Movement Organizations Survive the New Right," *Feminist Organizations: Harvest of the New Women's Movement,* ed. Myra Marx Ferree and Patricia Yancey Martin (Philadelphia: Temple University Press, 1995).

35. William M. Lunch, *The Nationalization of American Politics* (Berkeley: University of California Press, 1987).

36. See, for instance, Kenneth J. Meier, *The Politics of Sin* and Christopher Z. Mooney and Mei-Hsien Lee, "Legislating Morality in the American States: The Case of Pre-*Roe* Abortion Regulation Reform," *American Journal of Political Science* 39, no. 3: 599–627.

37. Joffe, *Doctors of Conscience.*

38. Robert J. Spitzer, *The Politics of Gun Control,* 3rd ed. (Washington, D.C.: CQ Press, 2004).

39. There is an ongoing debate between those like Lowi, who believe that social regulatory policy is a subset of traditional regulatory policy, and Raymond Tatalovich and Byron W. Daynes, who argue that those categories are distinct.

40. Theodore J. Lowi, "American Business, Public Policy, Case Studies, and Political Theory," *World Politics* 16, no. 4: 677–715 and Theodore J. Lowi, "Four Systems of Policy, Politics, and Choice," *Public Administration Review* 32, no. 4: 298–310.

41. Raymond Tatalovich and Byron W. Daynes, eds., *Moral Controversies in American Politics,* 2nd ed. (Armonk, N.Y.: M. E. Sharpe, 2004).

42. Kenneth J. Meier, *The Politics of Sin: Drugs, Alcohol and Public Policy* (Armonk, N.Y.: M. E. Sharpe, 1994), 246–247.

43. James Davison Hunter, *Culture Wars* and *Before the Shooting Begins: Searching for Democracy in America's Culture Wars* (New York: The Free Press, 1994).

44. Laurence H. Tribe, *Abortion: The Clash of Absolutes* (New York: W. W. Norton, 1990).

45. T. H. Marshall, quoted on page xi by Ursula Vogel and Michael Moran, introduction to *The Frontiers of Citizenship*, ed. Ursula Vogel and Michael Moran (New York: St. Martin's Press, 1991).

46. T. H. Marshall, "Citizenship and Social Class," in *Class, Citizenship, and Social Development* (Westport, Conn.: Greenwood Press, 1964), 65–122.

47. Ursula Vogel, "Is Citizenship Gender-Specific?" in *The Frontiers of Citizenship*, 62.

48. See, in particular, Theda Skocpol, *Protecting Soldiers and Mothers: The Political Origins of Social Policy in the United States* (Cambridge: Harvard University Press, 1992); Gwendolyn Mink, *The Wages of Motherhood: Inequality in the Welfare State, 1917–1942* (Ithaca, N.Y.: Cornell University Press, 1995); Suzanne Mettler, *Dividing Citizenships: Gender and Federalism in New Deal Public Policy* (Ithaca, N.Y.: Cornell University Press, 1998); and Linda Kerber, *No Constitutional Right to Be Ladies: Women and the Obligations of Citizenship* (New York: Hill and Wang, 1999).

49. Suzanne Mettler, *Dividing Citizenships*, xii.

50. Joan Hoff, *Law, Gender, and Injustice: A Legal History of U.S. Women* (New York: New York University Press, 1991), 315.

51. Michael Moran, "The Frontiers of Social Citizenship: The Case of Health Care Entitlements," in *The Frontiers of Citizenship*, 62.

52. Judith A. Baer, ed., *Women in American Law: The Struggle toward Equality from the New Deal to the Present* (New York: Holmes and Meier, 2002), 171.

CHAPTER 1

Abortion: Just the Facts

"The law and the amendment we debate today allows an abortionist to pull the baby almost all the way out of its mother, and as shown here on this diagram, insert his scissors into the base of this pre-born American child's brainstem and vacuum out its brains. This is abuse of pre-born American children. This is violence against pre-born American babies. This is the torture and murder of future American patriots who deserve this Nation."

—Rep. Rick Renzi (R-Arizona),
Floor Debate of the Partial-Birth Abortion Ban Act of 2003, June 4, 2003

"I understand the desire to eliminate the use of a procedure that appears inhumane. But to eliminate it without taking into consideration the rare and tragic circumstances in which its use may be necessary would be even more inhumane. . . . As a result of this Congressional indifference to women's health, I cannot, in good conscience and consistent with my responsibility to uphold the law, sign this legislation."

—President Bill Clinton, upon vetoing the Partial-Birth Abortion Ban Act of 1996,
April 11, 1996

Twenty-first century abortion politics began with a debate over what abortion opponents call "partial-birth" abortion. This is often a debate regarding late-term procedures, defined sometimes as abortion of viable fetuses, or as abortion during the third trimester of pregnancy.[1] The techniques for aborting a fetus at the end of pregnancy first received public attention in 1989, when Operation Rescue, one of the nation's largest anti-abortion organizations, sent hundreds of protesters to a Maryland clinic where late-term abortions were reportedly performed. Dr. Martin Haskell prompted further public scrutiny of the practice when he described a late-term technique at a 1992 meeting of the National Abortion Federation (NAF), a professional association of abortion providers. His scholarly paper documented the procedure he and others had been using to provide abortions for women whose pregnancies were between twenty and twenty-four weeks gestation. The paper, which coined the term "Dilation and Extraction," or D&X,

ultimately received widespread public attention when right-to-life organizations received word of the presentation.

The right-to-life organizations quickly launched an appeal to ban the procedure. These early demands produced little reaction in a Congress then controlled by a pro-choice, Democratic majority. By 1995, however, the national political landscape had changed dramatically, this time in favor of the anti-abortion movement. President Bill Clinton and congressional Democrats had lost control of Congress as a result of the 1994 election. Wounded politically by this defeat, and later by his 1998–1999 impeachment proceedings and the associated decline in public trust toward the president, the Clinton administration could not prevent movement of legislation directed at late-term abortions.[2]

By June 1995, legislation to ban partial-birth abortions was in committee in both chambers of Congress. Advocates of the legislation prefer the term "partial-birth," to the medical term "D&X" because it focuses attention on the most jarring aspect of the procedure: that the fetus is partially removed from its mother before it dies. The term, therefore, does not refer to a medical technique; in fact, the label was developed in anti-abortion congressional strategy meetings,[3] and first appeared in the media in the conservative *Washington Times*.[4] During debates about the ban, members of Congress continued to use this term and other political tools typically associated with social regulatory policy, which is to say that vitriolic debate and graphic imagery were common. Members opposed to late-term procedures wielded photos of aborted fetuses and compared the practice of late-term abortions to the Holocaust; members protective of women's rights reminded their audience of the horrors of illegal abortion, the nation's and the government's commitment to privacy rights, and the importance of guarding women's health. Still, the visual imagery used by abortion opponents was consistently more gripping, and their arguments ultimately proved more persuasive.

The absence of visual imagery in opposition to the bill reflects the political reality of legalized abortion: in the 1960s, supporters of legalization had the tragic images of women who had died as a result of illegal procedures to strengthen their cause; today's supporters are without such political ammunition. Not only did the fetal imagery focus debate around the fetus instead of the pregnant woman and the reasons she might choose a D&X procedure, the debate also stretched the limits of Democratic support for abortion by publicizing the most graphic aspects of it. Those opposed to the ban appeared at once heartlessly immune to the emotional pull of the fetal images and extreme in their placement of women's rights before fetal life.

As a result of the mobilization of pro-life interests, Congress twice passed a ban to end the partial-birth abortion procedure while Clinton was president; he vetoed it both in 1996 and again in 1997. In both instances, the House of Representatives overrode his veto but the Senate could not quite muster the support to do so. Clinton did lose support from pro-choice members in Congress between his first and second vetoes, when the *New York Times* reported that the source Clinton relied on to prove that D&X abortions are rare admitted he had misrepresented the data.[5]

The manner in which Clinton vetoed the ban underscores the politics of social regulatory policy. He was able to use the first veto for his political advantage, holding a press viewing and surrounding himself with women whose lives or health had been saved by a D&X abortion. This humanized the president's decision to veto the legislation, emphasizing his own morality. However, as public support for the ban mounted, he signed the second veto in 1997 amidst the shadows of his office in the early hours of the morning.

Public opposition to late-term abortion continued to swell near the end of the twentieth century and into the twenty-first century. Congress passed the ban a third time in 2003. This time, with President George W. Bush in office, it was expeditiously signed into law on November 5 of that year. True to form in regards to social regulatory policies, which ultimately tend to be decided by the courts, the law has been declared unconstitutional by U.S. District Courts in California, Nebraska, and New York. In the fall of 2005, Bush administration officials requested U.S. Supreme Court review of these lower court rulings. In February 2006, the Court agreed to hear the case, guaranteeing a judicial resolution to this particular abortion policy debate.

The federal Partial-Birth Abortion Ban, in its current form, makes a particular abortion practice illegal.[6] In general, the law is understood to restrict physicians from performing D&X abortions, the procedure used most often in advanced pregnancies in order to protect the health or future fertility of pregnant women. The attending physician would be punished by a fine, up to two years in prison, or both. The ban does not make exceptions for circumstances in which the procedure is necessary to save the health of the pregnant woman.[7]

The procedure calls for the partial removal of a live fetus, at which time the skull is collapsed to allow removal of the fetus intact. Physicians who perform this procedure explain that it is protective of women's health; the alternative method—dilation and evacuation (D&E)—requires dismemberment of the fetus, which presents higher risks for perforation of the uterus. Although the public has come to agree that D&X procedures are shocking, and possibly morally repugnant, the congressional debate over partial-birth abortion did not demonstrate that the circumstances that lead women to request a D&X procedure are themselves often tragic and frightening. Very few D&X abortions take place in this country, and most physicians refuse to perform them, but that said, they are used most often to preserve a woman's future fertility, to end a pregnancy that will end tragically anyway, or for emergency health reasons. Ironically, dilation and evacuation, which is both riskier for the woman and does not provide an opportunity for a family to hold and grieve their lost fetus, remains legal under the new law.

The history of the Partial-Birth Abortion Ban reveals the fevered pitch of contemporary abortion politics. What's more, it leaves the observer with the impression that late-term abortions are rampant, and that women are callous in their abortion choices. Little about the congressional partial-birth abortion debates centered on women's full rights as citizens or as patients with medical needs; rather, those proceedings consistently focused on the rights of the fetus at the expense of the mother's rights before the law and in medicine. Chapter 2 investigates the legal aspects of the partial-birth issue in greater depth. I address it here, however, because it is emblematic of where the abortion debate stands today: the pro-life movement has successfully framed the issue to the point that abortion rights advocates are forced to defend the most extreme aspects of abortion, and the health of the woman is eclipsed by concerns for the fetus. The purpose of this chapter, however, is to step away from the common debates over the intensely controversial aspects of abortion and educate the reader about its more common aspects: its incidence, rates, and trends. In this way the focus can be placed on the facts in what has otherwise become a debate edging ever closer to hyperbole.

The twenty-first century debate over partial-birth abortion distracts Americans from the long history of abortion practice in the United States and elsewhere. It is widely understood that abortions have occurred in all cultures across all periods of human history. What is more surprising to some is that there seems to be no relationship between the number of abortions performed and its legal status: women have abortions, regardless of whether they are legal or not. Space does not allow a consideration of the various cultural responses to abortion, but it is valuable to understand how the United States, specifically, has handled the issue throughout its history in order to understand certain features of the contemporary debate. More than anything, this discussion underscores the point that abortion is more highly regulated today than it has been in decades, and that oftentimes the science of abortion is trumped by its moral politics.

Many have the impression that since abortion became legal in 1973, it has been available to all women "on demand." Certainly, the debate over the partial birth bill suggests that this is the case. The remainder of this chapter is dedicated to laying out the statistical facts of abortion practice in contemporary America to dispel some of the myths surrounding its provision. These facts reveal that some 40% of all American women have abortions at some point during their reproductive lives, that they do so for a variety of reasons, and that most women who have abortions also become mothers. Still, although abortion in the United States is both legal and safe, the parameters of abortion law and local social conditions affect women's ability to use that law based upon their age, economic status, and geographical location.

IS THE UNITED STATES UNIQUE ON THE WORLD STAGE?

Incidence of Abortion in the United States

There are two main sources of data in regard to abortion incidence and trends. One is the Centers for Disease Control and Prevention (CDC), the main federal government organization that oversees public health policy in the United States. The other is the Alan Guttmacher Institute (AGI), a private organization that studies and advocates for women's health policy worldwide. Most of the following data are extracted from AGI, which has very different data collection techniques than the CDC. The CDC's data are gathered through voluntary reporting by the states directly to the CDC. Unfortunately, in recent years, between four and six states (including California, the most populous state) have chosen not to provide their abortion incidence reports. This subsequently has made the CDC data unrepresentative of a large portion of the country and possibly of specific demographic groups highly concentrated in California, such as particular recent immigrant groups. At AGI, researchers actively and regularly poll all known abortion providers from all states and regions in the country to compile their data. Wherever possible, I have used AGI data throughout this book; however, in places the CDC's data are more recent or relevant, as in some of the later figures.

Of course, a woman coming to a clinic for an abortion has a right to withhold certain demographic information if she chooses, even though every indication is that the vast majority of women participate in these intake surveys because the pertinent personal information in them is confidential; only aggregated data, free of identifying information, is reported to AGI or the CDC. However, abortion providers are required to document each abortion procedure and the gestational age of the fetus for state regulatory bodies, just as they would be for other medical procedures, guaranteeing that the data referenced here on abortion incidence is reasonably accurate.

In 2000, the most recent year for which data are available, approximately 1.31 million abortions were performed in the United States, which means that 2.1 percent of all women ages fifteen to forty-four had an abortion that year.[8] (Most studies of abortion use this age range because it encompasses the years that most women are fertile.) This number represents a gradual decline in the overall number of abortions in this country over the last decade, despite the fact that the population of women has increased over that same time period. Despite that decline, roughly 20 percent of all pregnancies in the United States will end in abortion; another 15 percent of known pregnancies end in miscarriage.[9]

Of course, raw numbers by themselves are not very informative. While political leaders and abortion activists of all stripes may use aggregate numbers to bolster their political positions, the purpose here is more scholarly. Figure 1.1 documents

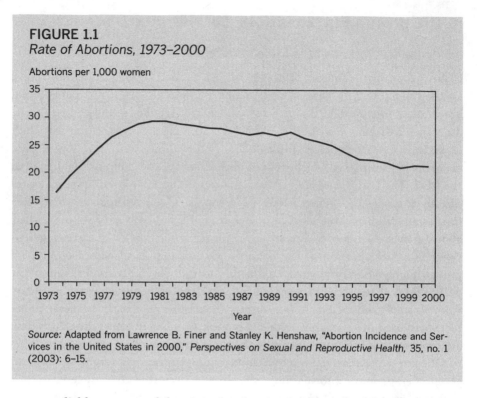

FIGURE 1.1
Rate of Abortions, 1973–2000

Abortions per 1,000 women

Source: Adapted from Lawrence B. Finer and Stanley K. Henshaw, "Abortion Incidence and Services in the United States in 2000," *Perspectives on Sexual and Reproductive Health,* 35, no. 1 (2003): 6–15.

a more reliable measure of abortion: the abortion rate. Knowing the abortion rate is more useful than knowing aggregate numbers of abortions because the rate takes population fluctuations into account. It measures the number of abortions performed per one thousand women ages fifteen to forty-four. Recently, the rate declined from twenty-four per one thousand women in 1994 to twenty-one per one thousand women in 2000. Moreover, the overall abortion rate is hovering currently where it was in the mid-1970s, indicating that abortion incidence is trending downward.

What accounts for the overall decline in abortion incidence? While there is no definitive answer to that question, researchers point to a number of likely factors. Among the most cited reasons is the more widespread and correct use of long-acting hormonal contraceptives like Norplant, which have high reliability rates and have been effective at lowering teen pregnancy rates, and emergency contraception (including "Plan B," or the morning after pill), which impedes implantation of a fertilized egg. Both are relatively new to the U.S. market, and their use coincides chronologically with the recent decline in abortion rates. If rates of unintended pregnancy decline, rates of abortion will likely fall as a consequence.

However, it is also true that declining abortion rates coincide chronologically with new and effective barriers to abortion; abortions may be declining because the obstacles to the procedure are working. Economic trends seem to play a large role in such decisions as well. With the economic boom of the 1990s, some women had more money, and therefore more means, to support an unexpected pregnancy. This could have contributed to the abortion rate decline. On the other hand, for less affluent women who face an unexpected pregnancy, abortion may prove a potential alternative to raising a child no matter the overall economic climate.

The United States Compared to the World

The abortion rate in the United States is higher than in other industrialized nations, but lower than the rate in developing nations. For every one thousand women ages fifteen to forty-four in the world, approximately thirty-five have an abortion every year. It is estimated that for every thirty-five abortions that occur worldwide, twenty will be legal procedures, and fifteen will be illegal. In general, abortion rates are somewhat lower in advanced economies than in developing ones, probably because women have better access to birth control, financial resources, and education in those societies. Many believe that the United States has a higher-than-average rate of abortion than other industrialized nations because contraception is not as widely available or supported by insurance here as it is in most of these economies. It is critical to underscore that legality is *not* related to the rate of abortion. Abortion rates are higher in developing nations as a whole, despite the fact that in Latin America and Africa the vast majority of nations declare the procedure illegal.[10] In developed nations, where women have access to legal abortion, abortion rates are consistently lower than in those nations that prohibit the practice.[11]

Why Women Have Abortions

American women report that nearly half (49 percent) of all their pregnancies are unintended, and 54 percent of those unintended pregnancies end in abortion.[12] To understand why women choose to have abortions, it is first necessary to appreciate the reasons for unintended pregnancies. Most scholars attribute the high level of unintended pregnancy in this country to three factors: many couples do not use contraception, others use it inconsistently or incorrectly, and nearly all contraceptive methods can fail even when used correctly and consistently. Clearly contraception access and use are key to understanding abortion rates in this country and elsewhere.

In a recent study of 10,683 women nationally who had had abortions between 2000 and 2001, Rachel Jones and her colleagues at AGI found that nearly half of the women respondents had not been using any form of birth control in the month of conception. Thirty-three percent of the women not using contraception reported that they had not done so because they believed they were at low risk of becoming pregnant, 32 percent said they had concerns about contraceptive methods, 27 percent said that sex was unexpected or unwanted, and 12 percent said they had financial constraints or other problems in acquiring contraception.[13] These data are sobering for those who seek to reduce abortion rates, because the main cause of unintended pregnancies seems to be preventable by effective contraception. Therefore, one key method of abortion prevention seems directly related to policy that regulates reproductive health education and contraception access.

Of course, a failure to use contraception explains the high rate of unintended pregnancies, but does not answer why women who are unexpectedly pregnant choose to abort. The public discourse sometimes portrays such a choice as flippant or callous. Yet women consistently report a desire to end their pregnancies after giving the situation and the options available careful consideration. As one doctor I interviewed noted, "It's about choice, but it's about *agonizing* choice." [14] While the reasons vary widely, curiously, they are similar across cultures, regardless of whether abortion is legal or not.[15] One recent study conducted in the United States provided an opportunity for women to list all of their reasons for choosing to have an abortion. The surveyed women cited a variety of motivations for ending their pregnancies. Seventy-three percent indicated they could not afford to raise a baby, 74 percent reported that a child would interfere with responsibilities at work or to other dependents, and another 48 percent cited the difficulty of facing single motherhood.[16]

These reasons related directly to the socioeconomic conditions of women's lives as well as to their responsibilities beyond the immediate pregnancy.[17] In recent decades, a growing gap between high-income and low-income women in the United States might be a contributing factor to these economic-based choices.[18] Moreover, the abortion decision must be seen within the context of social and economic policy: where women face meager state and federal support, they may have a greater reluctance to bear children.

When Congress reformed welfare in 1996 and reduced benefits for recipients who have an additional child while receiving welfare, it may have inadvertently created greater economic incentives for abortion among those with lower incomes. There is no evidence that up to that point, women were getting pregnant and having children just to collect additional funds and avoid doing an honest day's work. Although "welfare moms" were commonly portrayed in the popular media as sucking the system dry, this really makes little sense, given the monies provided.

Women's particular life circumstances are related to their consideration of and possible choice to have an abortion. For instance, younger women surveyed were more likely to report that they were not ready to become mothers. Nearly four in ten women indicated they were choosing to have an abortion because they had completed their families. The overriding theme of the survey was that women place their abortion decision squarely within the larger context of their lives: children, school, work, and money create pressures on unexpectedly pregnant women. These data indicate that women choose to have the procedure because of their sense of responsibility toward the other people and commitments in their lives, contrary to the perception held by some that women make this decision lightly.[19]

A far smaller number of women opt for an abortion because of their own medical conditions, such as a chronic heart condition or diabetes. Another, very small, percentage conceive as the result of rape or incest and choose to have an abortion because of the trauma of their experiences. Some decide to have an abortion because of a fetal irregularity. In these cases, many women feel they simply cannot care for a child with intense special needs, particularly if they already have other children who need their time and attention. Often, the gravest fetal irregularities are not detectable in the first trimester of pregnancy because the most accurate diagnostic tests are performed in the second trimester. The inability of science to pinpoint fetal irregularities until mid-pregnancy creates a situation in which women who may be happily pregnant discover debilitating abnormalities in their fifth month of pregnancy, or later. And when such irregularities are detected in the late stages of pregnancy, women who seek to end these pregnancies face an uncertain abortion climate: there may be no physicians in their area willing or trained to provide late-term abortions, or their state may make abortion illegal in the third trimester unless their own lives are at risk.

Whatever their situations, American women echo the voices of their global contemporaries. Women in different nations face distinct cultural, economic, religious, and legal climates for abortion, yet when they report their reasons for having them they are the reasons outlined here. This commonality is striking, and indicates a universality in women's desire to control their fertility.

Abortion and Safety

The abortion procedure, one of the most common medical procedures performed in the United States today, has grown increasingly safe. In this country, the documented number of abortion-related deaths from legal procedures in 1965 was approximately two hundred. Today, roughly 10 women die from having a legal abortion in the United States, compared to 260 who die from pregnancy and childbirth.[20] Abortion provision is generally safe in countries where the procedure is legal, and therefore regulated for hygiene and safety. Moreover, studies in the United States indicate that women are overwhelmingly pleased with the information and level of care they receive from their providers.[21]

Of course, these numbers do not account for the many women who died from illegal procedures before 1973, when abortion was illegal in the United States. And while the estimates of deaths vary significantly, the most conservative of these project that thousands of women died per year from illegal abortions.[22] This indicates that even when women face unsafe conditions and potential health risks, they demand access to abortion services and freedom to make their own reproductive decisions. This reality is not exclusively a matter of history; recent reports have documented the stories of several women in Mississippi, where abortion is difficult to procure, who have suffered from unsafe, unregulated procedures.[23]

Global statistics underscore this point. Where abortion is mostly legal, including in North America and Western Europe, morbidity and mortality rates from abortion are quite low. But women in Africa, Latin America, and the Middle East, places in which most abortions are illegal, and in Eastern Europe and Southeastern Asia, where virtually all abortions are illegal, women face very different circumstances. The most recent data available indicate very high levels of morbidity and mortality due to abortion in these regions. The Johns Hopkins School of Public Health reports that an estimated ten million to twenty million illegal abortions are performed worldwide annually, and an estimated one hundred thousand to two hundred thousand women die as a result—about one in every one hundred. These deaths account for 20 percent to 40 percent of all maternal deaths.[24]

The World Health Organization estimates that 4.2 million unsafe abortions occur annually in Africa alone, resulting in nearly 30,000 maternal deaths.[25] In Egypt, for instance, 216,000 women were hospitalized for abortion-related reasons in 1996 alone; in fact, abortion-related hospitalizations accounted for 15.3 percent of all hospitalization of women ages fifteen to forty-four. In Ethiopia, 55 percent of maternal deaths are caused by complications from illegal abortions. This is the second leading cause of death after AIDS for women of childbearing age.[26] As a general rule, global studies indicate that legalization does not increase the incidence of abortion, but it does dramatically increase the chances a woman will survive her procedure in good health.[27]

Who Has Abortions in the United States

Many Americans have misconceptions about who has abortions. Nationwide trends illuminate important facts about abortion provision, but they paint with a broad brush. It is important to document how trends vary across particular groups of women. In examining the characteristics of women obtaining abortions, it's found that, in broad terms,

> the typical woman having an abortion is between the ages of 20 and 30, has never married, has had a previous birth, lives in a metropolitan area, is economically disadvantaged, and Christian. However, women who have abortions are diverse, and unintended pregnancy leading to abortion is common in all population subgroups.[28]

The following information supports these claims.

TABLE 1.1
Age of Women Obtaining Abortions, 1994 and 2000

	Women Obtaining Abortions (%)		Abortion Rate (per 1,000 women)		
Characteristic	1994	2000	1994	2000	% Change
Age					
< 15	1.2	.07	U	U	U
15–19*	20.6	18.6	34	25	–27
15–17	8.8	6.5	24	15	–39
18–19	11.5	12.0	48	39	–18
20–24	32.8	33.0	52	47	–9
25–29	21.4	23.1	32	32	0
30–34	14.4	13.5	18	17	–5
35–39	7.5	8.1	10	9	–3
> = 40	2.3	3.1	3	4	10
Total	**100.0**	**100.0**	**24**	**21**	**–11**

Note: U = data unavailable

* Data for younger teens significantly different from that of older teens to warrant distinct category.

Source: Adapted from Rachel K. Jones, Jacqueline E. Darroch, and Stanley K. Henshaw, "Patterns in the Socioeconomic Characteristics of Women Obtaining Abortions in 2000–2001," *Perspectives on Sexual and Reproductive Health* 34, no. 5 (2002): 226–235.

Tables 1.1 and 1.2 document the percentages of women with particular characteristics who had abortions in 1994 or 2000. The rate of abortion is calculated by group; the women's likelihood of having an abortion is compared to such factors as marital status, level of education, religious affiliation, and ethnicity; and the changes in abortion rate by group for the two years are measured. These findings indicate that the overall abortion rate fell by 11 percent between 1994 and 2000, from 24 per 1,000 women to 21 per 1,000 women. Note that this decline was not uniformly experienced by women in all categories. As Table 1.1 demonstrates, the abortion rate fell most dramatically for adolescents ages fifteen to seventeen, but actually *rose* for women aged forty or older.

Abortion rates for teens have been falling, along with their rates of pregnancy and births, since the late 1980s. Many scholars attribute this decline to increased contraceptive use, greater expectations for advanced education, and changing social norms that encourage teens to discuss and negotiate birth control with their partners.[29] Interestingly, studies suggest that recent use of "abstinence-only" programs in schools is not responsible for this decline. The National Campaign to Prevent Teen Pregnancy released a review of the nation's major abstinence-only programs, concluding that "[t]here do not currently exist any abstinence-only programs with strong evidence that they either delay sex or reduce teen pregnancy." [30] What is more, studies of teen sexuality indicate that students receiving abstinence–only instruction are less likely to use birth control when they do have sex.[31]

The teen abortion decline coincides chronologically with the rise of parental notification and consent laws nationwide (see chapter 3), which may have diminished the adolescent abortion rate. Between 1991 and 1997, the number of states with laws that mandate parental consent for or notification of an abortion for a minor rose from eighteen to thirty. However, between 1997 and 2000, that number increased by only one.[32] Despite the decline in teen birth and abortion rates, the United States has some of the highest rates of teen pregnancy and abortion rates in the developed world, on par with such less-industrialized countries as Belarus, Bulgaria, Romania, and the countries of the former Soviet Union.[33]

Table 1.2 reveals that marital status does correlate with abortion rates. Whereas married women accounted for only 17 percent of abortions in 2000, they represented 48 percent of the population. Unmarried women therefore represent a disproportionate share of abortions in this country, which probably coincides with their lower household incomes and childcare resources.

Looking at other demographic categories, Table 1.2 shows that 79 percent of women who had abortions in 2000 lived in metropolitan areas, but that they accounted for 88 percent of the abortions nationwide. This statistic underscores the significant impact that local access can have on abortion rates. When women have to travel great distances to access legal abortions, as they increasingly do in this country, they are sometimes dissuaded from doing so by the logistical hurdles they face. Chapter 3 explores the issue of the diminishing number of providers in the United States, and their concentration geographically, as a barrier to abortion for women in rural communities.

Abortion rates most obviously correlate with income and education. Whereas rates for the wealthiest women in the study declined by 39 percent from 1994 to 2000, those with the lowest incomes experienced a 25 percent *increase* despite the rising cost of the procedure and the increasing number of hurdles faced by those seeking it. The class distinction evident here also may reflect the growing class divide that began during the late 1990s stock market boom. Many middle- and upper-class families reaped the benefits of this period of prosperity, whereas the real wages of low-income workers fell and, after 1996, many women on welfare lost benefits to support the birth of additional children. Education demonstrates a similar trend: the abortion rate for the least educated women increased, whereas college graduates had a 30 percent decrease in abortion incidence. The evidence seems clear: not only can affluent women afford consistent access to reliable contraception, they also are more able to embrace the expenses associated with an unintended birth.

TABLE 1.2
Characteristics of Women Obtaining Abortions, 1994 and 2000

Characteristic	Women Obtaining Abortions (%)		Abortion Rate (per 1,000 women)		
	1994	2000	1994	2000	% Change
Marital Status					
Married	18.4	17.0	9	8	−14
Previously Married	17.1	15.6	32	29	−11
Never Married	64.4	67.3	41	35	−14
Residence					
Metropolitan	88.5	88.0	27	24	−11
Non−Metropolitan/Rural	11.5	12.0	13	12	−10
Poverty Status					
<100%	25.4	26.6	36	44	25
100−199%	24.4	30.8	31	38	23
200−299%	18.9	18.0	25	21	−13
> = 300%	31.3	24.6	16	10	−39
Race/Ethnicity					
Non−Hispanic					
White	48.0	40.9	16	13	−20
Black	30.0	31.7	54	49	−8
Asian/Pacific Islander	4.4	6.4	28	31	11
Native American	1.2	0.9	U	U	U
Hispanic	16.5	20.1	37	33	−10
Education					
Not a High School Graduate	12.0	12.7	22	23	7
High School Graduate/GED	30.4	30.3	20	20	1
Some College	40.3	40.6	29	26	−12
College Graduate	17.3	16.4	19	13	−30
Religion					
Protestant	37.4	42.8	17	18	10
Catholic	31.3	27.4	25	22	−13
Other	7.6	7.6	30	31	2
Nonpracticing	23.7	22.2	46	30	−35
Total	**100.0**	**100.0**	**24**	**21**	**−11**

Note: U = data unavailable

Source: Adapted from Rachel K. Jones, Jacqueline E. Darroch, and Stanley K. Henshaw, "Patterns in the Socioeconomic Characteristics of Women Obtaining Abortions in 2000–2001," *Perspectives on Sexual and Reproductive Health* 34, no. 5 (2002): 226–235.

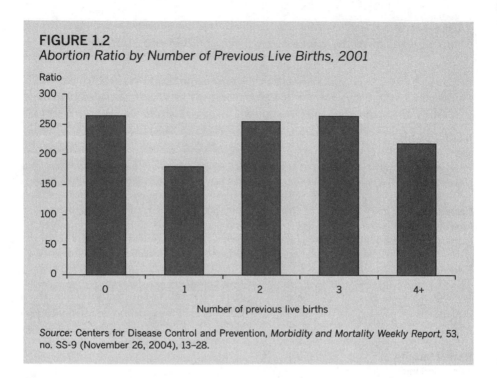

FIGURE 1.2
Abortion Ratio by Number of Previous Live Births, 2001

Source: Centers for Disease Control and Prevention, *Morbidity and Mortality Weekly Report,* 53, no. SS-9 (November 26, 2004), 13–28.

In terms of ethnicity, white women have a proportionately low number of abortions, whereas black women have the highest rate of all racial and ethnic groups. This variance is explained in part by the disproportionate number of black women in poverty, although a closer study of the table shows that black women in all income categories had higher abortion rates than white women. Abortion rates also have risen markedly for women of Asian Pacific descent.

Of all these categories, one of the most intriguing is that for religion. Protestant women account for 43 percent of abortions, a rate somewhat lower than their percentage in the population. The abortion rate for Catholic women nearly mirrors their percentage in the population: 27 percent, despite the consistent admonition against the practice from the hierarchy of their church. Interestingly, what is not shown in the table is the fact that 13 percent of women having abortions reported their religion as either "born again" or "evangelical." These categories sometimes overlap, although they may not. Those who are born again or evangelical tend to be Protestants, but are not necessarily. This incidence of abortion within these two groups indicates a disconnect between behavior and orthodoxy.

Perhaps what will be most surprising to some is the relationship between a woman's decision to have an abortion and her overall reproductive history. Some readers may have the impression that women either have children or have abortions. The data show that this is a misperception. Figure 1.2 demonstrates that although there are a good number of women having abortions who do not have children, most women who seek them have children already. Women of lesser means tend to have children earlier, and then are more likely to have an abortion after bearing children as a way to limit family size; middle- and upper-class women are more likely to have abortions early in their reproductive lives to postpone childbearing while they complete their education or lay the groundwork for a professional life outside the home. Although they may have abortions at different points in their reproductive years, many women have both children and an abortion, and 43 percent of all American women will have an abortion at some point in their lives.[34]

When Women Have Abortions

Figure 1.3 debunks yet another abortion myth: that women use abortion as a method of birth control, opting to have a series of abortions during their fertile years. While some physicians would argue that abortion is simply part of a continuum of reproductive health choices, the general public is disapproving of serial abortion use. Here it is shown that although some women do undergo multiple abortions, the most common occurrence is a woman having an abortion for the first (and only) time. The figure further indicates that about 50,000 women of the 1.3 million women obtaining abortions during that time period had had two previous abortions.

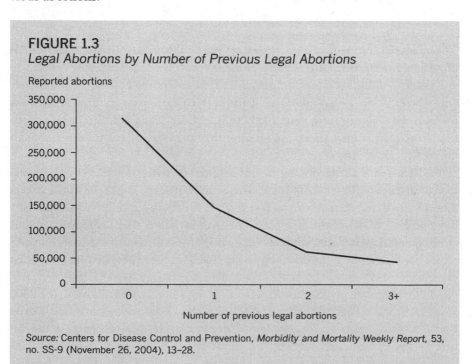

FIGURE 1.3
Legal Abortions by Number of Previous Legal Abortions

Reported abortions

Number of previous legal abortions

Source: Centers for Disease Control and Prevention, *Morbidity and Mortality Weekly Report*, 53, no. SS-9 (November 26, 2004), 13–28.

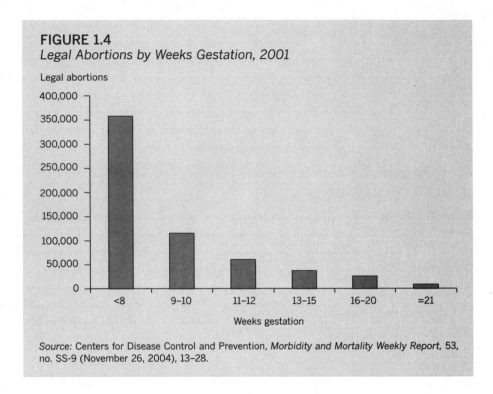

FIGURE 1.4
Legal Abortions by Weeks Gestation, 2001

Source: Centers for Disease Control and Prevention, *Morbidity and Mortality Weekly Report*, 53, no. SS-9 (November 26, 2004), 13–28.

The reasons for multiple abortions are not well known, but according to the physicians interviewed for this book, patients report that the causes are contraceptive failure and limited access to insurance that covers the cost of contraception. One small study of repeat abortion clients in Wichita, Kansas, indicates that these patients were significantly more likely to have been using contraception consistently than first-time patients, suggesting that the repeat patients experienced a failure in their contraception.[35]

As discussed at the beginning of this chapter, perhaps the greatest controversy in the current abortion debate is over late-term abortions. The high-profile debate around the Partial-Birth Abortion Ban of 2003 may have led some to believe that a large number of abortions take place later in pregnancy. As the following public opinion poll data indicate, support for legal abortion tapers off the longer a pregnancy has progressed.[36] In actuality, an increasing number of abortions are taking place earlier and earlier in pregnancy. This change in part reveals the improved techniques for detecting pregnancies earlier and more accurately. In addition, the 2000 approval by the U.S. Food and Drug Administration (FDA) of mifepristone, a drug that allows women to receive a medicinal, rather than surgical, abortion in the earliest weeks of pregnancy,[37] affords women the option of very early abortions.[38] The most recent abortion reports, shown in Figure 1.4, indicate that the vast majority of abortions occur in the first weeks of pregnancy. The D&X abortion, the target of the Partial-Birth Abortion Ban Act of 2003 and of similar legislation in a number of states, accounted for only .17 percent of all abortions in 2000.[39]

Still, some women do have mid- or late-term abortions. The most recent data available indicate that of those who end their pregnancies after sixteen weeks gestation, 71 percent report they were unaware of their pregnancy in the early months. Although this possibility may strike some as unlikely, physicians I spoke with in the course of writing this book indicated that at their practices, young and uneducated women were fairly unlikely to understand their condition, or were perhaps in denial about it. A particularly poignant example occurred as I sat in one office, interviewing a Portland physician. A woman who was seven months pregnant had just come in, seeking a pregnancy termination. The woman was schizophrenic, had been taking her medications intermittently, and had only recently realized her condition. No physician in Oregon would perform such an abortion. The physician's nurse could refer the patient to a crisis pregnancy center, or to Dr. Haskell in Wichita. When I asked the physician what the likely outcome of the pregnancy was, she replied, "She'll end up in an emergency room and the baby will become a ward of the state." While this example may not be representative of all late-term abortions, it serves to illustrate the range of possible explanations for them.

Significantly, almost half (48 percent) of those having mid- or late-term abortions report that they had difficulty making an earlier arrangement for their abortion—a point not lost on those who live in rural areas far from providers. One-third state that they were afraid to tell their parent or partner about the pregnancy; almost a quarter admitted they needed some time to make their decision. Clearly, for those who choose a second-trimester abortion, the reasons seem to be unrelated to whether they have access to late-term abortion. The most important factor seems to be lack of access to abortion during the early stages of pregnancy.[40] Ironically, barriers to abortion erected to prevent the decision to have an abortion may have the unintended effect of pushing it later into pregnancy, when it is riskier and more expensive, and when public support for the decision is significantly lower.

THE COURT OF PUBLIC OPINION

The previous section reveals how many American women have abortions, why they have them, and when they have them during their pregnancies. Public opinion in the United States in regard to abortion is fairly stable, although complex, and by no means a perfect portrayal of the country's views on this medical practice. And while several demographic variables can reasonably predict public opinion on abortion, there are still some surprises. The most surprising outcome is the significant revelation that Americans have very little support for the most common reasons women have abortions, and strong support for those very rare cases when abortion is a result of rape or incest or is needed to save the woman's life.

Public opinion polling is not an exact science. Many critics argue that polls contain inherent biases based on the wording of questions, when they are conducted, and who is polled, among other concerns. While these criticisms are warranted, public opinion polling remains the best way to document the views of a large number of people on any given subject. In an effort to avoid misrepresentations, Table 1.3 incorporates data from the General Social Survey, the largest national survey conducted in the United States, and illustrates the percentage of people who believe abortion should be available under various circumstances. This table is based upon a cumulative analysis of data from 1972–2002. Although it does not convey fluctuations from year-to-year, it does provide a large enough number of responses to analyze views based on such demographic variables as sex, race, and age.

The first intriguing point is that Americans' opinions about abortion vary dramatically depending upon why the woman is having the procedure. The first three reasons listed (life/health of the woman in jeopardy, possibility of serious fetal defect, and pregnancy is a result of rape/incest) demonstrate public support across widely different groups. When women abort for any of these three reasons, the least support is found among Americans with less than a high school education, 69 percent of whom approve of an abortion because of the possibility of serious fetal defect or because of rape or incest; still, that is a remarkably high rate of support. However, the data presented earlier in this chapter revealed that very few women actually have abortions for these reasons.

In contrast, the second set of reasons (low income/can't afford more children, not married, and abortion for any reason) produce entirely different results. In general, Americans disapprove of these reasons for ending a pregnancy, although differences can be found among demographic categories. Recalling the data reported earlier in this chapter, the reader must bear in mind that most women report aborting for precisely these economic and relational reasons, leaving the vast majority of abortions in this country on the fringes of public support.

Turning to demographics, Table 1.3 reveals some interesting agreements and disagreements across demographic groups. For instance, there is actually very little difference between women and men in any of the categories. If anything, men support abortion in greater numbers than women, although these slight differences are probably not statistically significant. This fact runs contrary to the common misperception that abortion divides women and men in the electorate.

In the category of race, whites have a consistently more favorable view toward abortion than those who identify themselves on the survey as Black or Other. Although the survey data fails to give a very nuanced picture of the relationship

TABLE 1.3

Percentage of Respondents Who Believe Abortion Should Be Available (by specific reason)

Reasons for Obtaining an Abortion	Sex	Race	Age	Education	Income	Region	Political Party
Life/Health of Woman in Jeopardy	Male: 91 Female: 89	White: 91 Black: 86 Other: 88	18–29: 93 30–49: 91 50+: 88	< HS: 81 HS: 90 College: 92 Graduate Degree: 94	< $10K: 87 10K-19,999: 87 20K-29,999: 90 30K-59,999: 91 60K-109,999: 96 110K+: 94	Atlantic: 91 N. Central: 89 S Central: 87 New England: 92 Mountain: 91 Pacific: 93	Democrat: 90 Independent: 90 Republican: 90 Other: 89
Possibility of Serious Fetal Defect	Male: 82 Female: 81	White: 83 Black: 71 Other: 80	18–29: 83 30–49: 82 50+: 79	< HS: 69 HS: 82 College: 84 Graduate Degree: 86	< $10K: 75 10K-19,999: 77 20K-29,999: 81 30K-59,999: 81 60K-109,999: 88 110K+: 81	Atlantic: 82 N.Central: 80 S Central: 75 New England: 86 Mountain: 81 Pacific: 88	Democrat: 82 Independent: 83 Republican: 80 Other: 81
Pregnancy the Result of Rape/Incest	Male: 84 Female: 82	White: 84 Black: 74 Other: 77	18–29: 85 30–49: 83 50+: 81	< HS: 69 HS: 82 College: 87 Graduate Degree: 88	< $10K: 74 10K-19,999: 78 20K-29,999: 81 30K-59,999: 82 60K-109,999: 89 110K+: 87	Atlantic: 84 N.Central: 82 S Central: 76 New England: 87 Mountain: 83 Pacific: 87	Democrat: 82 Independent: 84 Republican: 82 Other: 79

(Table continues on next page)

TABLE 1.3 (continued)
Percentage of Respondents Who Believe Abortion Should Be Available (by specific reason)

Reasons for Obtaining an Abortion	Sex	Race	Age	Education	Income	Region	Political Party
Low Income/Can't Afford More Children	Male: 50 Female: 47	White: 49 Black: 42 Other: 45	18–29: 52 30–49: 50 50+: 44	< HS: 33 HS: 44 College: 55 Graduate Degree: 66	< $10K: 37 10K–19,999: 39 20K–29,999: 45 30K–59,999: 47 60K–109,999: 70 110K+: 52	Atlantic: 50 N.Central: 44 S Central: 37 New England: 56 Mountain: 48 Pacific: 62	Democrat: 48 Independent: 51 Republican: 41 Other: 51
Not Married	Male: 47 Female: 43	White: 47 Black: 34 Other: 40	18–29: 46 30–49: 47 50+: 41	< HS: 27 HS: 40 College: 53 Graduate Degree: 64	< $10K: 34 10K–19,999: 36 20K–29,999: 29 30K–59,999: 46 60K–109,999: 62 110K+: 52	Atlantic: 46 N.Central: 41 S Central: 33 New England: 54 Mountain: 45 Pacific: 59	Democrat: 44 Independent: 46 Republican: 43 Other: 47
Any Reason	Male: 41 Female: 39	White: 41 Black: 36 Other: 37	18–29: 42 30–49: 44 50+: 36	< HS: 21 HS: 35 College: 48 Graduate Degree: 58	< $10K: 35 10K–19,999: 39 20K–29,999: 42 30K–59,999: 46 60K–109,999: 58 110K+: 53	Atlantic: 41 N.Central: 36 S Central: 29 New England: 49 Mountain: 41 Pacific: 55	Democrat: 40 Independent: 43 Republican: 36 Other: 48

Source: Adapted from James A. Davis, Tom W. Smith, and Peter V. Marsden, *General Social Surveys, 1972–2004* (Chicago: National Opinion Research Center, 2005).

of opinion on abortion to ethnicity because the Other category is very broad, the Black and White categories are interesting for at least one reason: although black Americans report less public support for abortion, the abortion rate of black women is statistically higher than that of white women.

Moving on, the table shows that older Americans generally support abortion less than younger Americans. Abortion support also is well predicted by income and education levels: the more income and education individuals have, the more likely they are to support the procedure, even though abortion rates have declined for women in these very groups. There is a slight decrease in abortion support in the highest income range; in general, however, higher income is associated with stronger support.

Predictably, there are important regional differences in abortion support scores that reflect local political leanings. As more conservative areas in general, the South Central and North Central regions support abortion less than those who live in either the Pacific or New England regions. More surprisingly, the difference in rates of abortion support between Republicans and Democrats is slight, and certainly would not appear to predict the radically different official stances the parties take on the issue (see chapter 5), suggesting that the positions the party organizations have staked out are not necessarily representative of their rank-and-file members. In four of the six sets of abortion reasons, the differences between Republicans and Democrats are imperceptible statistically. It is only in the low income/can't afford more children and any reason categories that the party differences between Americans are significant. Independents, it is interesting to note, indicate slightly more support for abortion than either of the two major parties.

The public's view of abortion is not static, of course. Much of today's shrill debate concerns people's interpretation of the public's growing acceptance of abortion as a practice. As shown in Table 1.3, the nation's views on this issue cannot be characterized by sweeping generalizations; within demographic groups lie significant differences of opinion. Just as opinion varies by demographic groups, it also varies with time, as the following figures illustrate.

Public opinion regarding abortion seems to depend on how accessible the procedure is perceived to be. Figure 1.5 is a review of public opinion on abortion. Respondents were asked whether they approved of abortion "for any reason." This form of the question tests the public's view of abortion "on demand." When asked so broadly, a modest majority of Americans do not agree with such generous access. The figure reveals an increase in support for unlimited abortion access, nearing 50 percent, during the years just following the 1992 Supreme Court ruling in *Planned Parenthood of Southeastern PA v. Casey* decision (discussed in chapter 2). Of course what exactly accounts for temporal shifts in public opinion is impossible to know, although in general, opinion is shaped by high profile, salient events like Supreme Court rulings, outbursts of violence at clinics, and Supreme Court nominations.

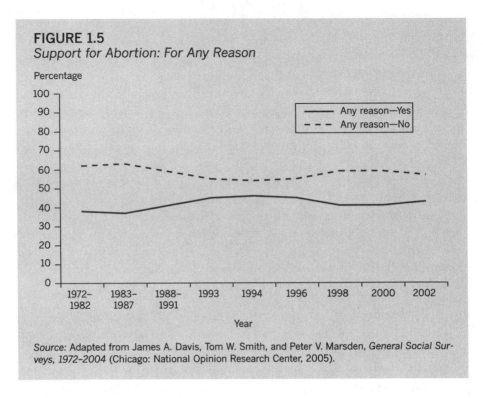

FIGURE 1.5
Support for Abortion: For Any Reason

Percentage

Legend:
——— Any reason—Yes
– – – Any reason—No

X-axis (Year): 1972–1982, 1983–1987, 1988–1991, 1993, 1994, 1996, 1998, 2000, 2002

Source: Adapted from James A. Davis, Tom W. Smith, and Peter V. Marsden, *General Social Surveys, 1972–2004* (Chicago: National Opinion Research Center, 2005).

Still, more recently, public disapproval of unlimited abortion access has grown slightly, explaining in part the rise of abortion restrictions.

However, the public shows much stronger support for abortion under limited circumstances. Figure 1.6 shows the nation's support for abortion for reasons of the woman's health, fetal deformity, or rape/incest. As the previous table indicated, Americans are most sympathetic toward abortions when the circumstances for it are beyond the woman's control. Support for women's health is the highest, reflecting the consistent support the Court has articulated for a woman's health over the life of a fetus. Still, fetal deformity and rape/incest scores hover around 80 percent, again demonstrating overwhelming public sympathy for those few women whose pregnancies will cause damage beyond their control or result from actions beyond their control.

In contrast, Figure 1.6 indicates the public seems least sympathetic and supportive of abortion when the women are perceived as having some control over their individual situations. When asked whether the respondent supports abortion when the woman cannot afford a child, has no desire to marry the father, or is not married or wants no more children, slightly less than half of Americans approve. Interestingly, these three separate questions produce nearly identical

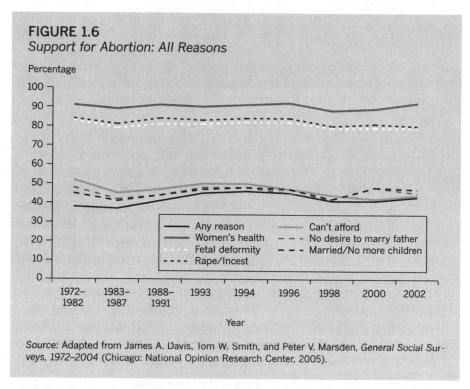

FIGURE 1.6
Support for Abortion: All Reasons

Percentage

Legend:
- Any reason
- Women's health
- Fetal deformity
- Rape/Incest
- Can't afford
- No desire to marry father
- Married/No more children

Year

Source: Adapted from James A. Davis, Tom W. Smith, and Peter V. Marsden, *General Social Surveys, 1972–2004* (Chicago: National Opinion Research Center, 2005).

responses, varying only a few percentage points at most. It may be that Americans view these reasons for abortion as less legitimate because they presume that, unlike rape or incest, these are conditions the pregnant woman can control.

One reason for this may be the belief that many of these women could choose to give their babies up for adoption upon birth. A consistent message from pro-life advocates is that there are hundreds of couples who beg to have a child to adopt, and others who spend hundreds of thousands of dollars on fertility treatments and adoption proceedings, so children born of unwanted pregnancies would have homes. While this may indeed be true, many babies and young children, especially minority children or those with physical or mental disabilities, remain in adoption and foster care systems for years.

When taken together, the statistics in Figure 1.6 reveal the relatively stable public opinion over time toward abortion; no wide swings are seen—and certainly none dramatic enough to explain the major shift in policy over the past thirty years. At the same time, these figures most graphically demonstrate the wide gap between the solid support for some circumstances and the moderate support for others. What accounts for these policy swings, if not public opinion? Later chapters address this question.

The public's disapproval of abortion when women have had full access to birth control begs the question of whether women always do, in fact, have such full access. It is true that women have more birth control options available to them today than women in previous generations, yet the current controversy over emergency contraception perhaps illustrates the limits of women's access to a full range of options.

The FDA approved emergency contraception as a prescription-only drug in 1999. Emergency contraception, or Plan B, is a higher-than-usual dose of the hormone progestin contained in birth control pills. In cases in which women are raped or traditional birth control methods fail, Plan B floods the woman's system with progestin to prevent either ovulation, or, in rare instances, implantation of the fertilized egg. When taken within seventy-two hours of intercourse, the risk of pregnancy is reduced by 75 percent. In fact, the sooner Plan B is taken, the more effective it is in preventing unwanted pregnancy. It is so effective that it has been credited by some experts as contributing to the decline of abortion in recent years. Researchers estimate that in 2000 alone, the use of Plan B prevented an estimated one hundred thousand unintended pregnancies, resulting in fifty-one thousand fewer abortions.[41]

The key to Plan B's success, however, is obtaining it and using it as soon as possible. Recently, this form of birth control has been the subject of widespread controversy. Some disapprove of Plan B because they fear it might encourage licentious behavior; others disapprove because they believe life begins when a sperm joins an egg, not when it implants in the uterus, which is the medical definition of pregnancy. As a result, pharmacists nationwide are reportedly refusing to fill Plan B prescriptions, using state "conscience," or refusal, clauses that protect them from filling prescriptions to which they are morally opposed. Other pharmacies are simply refusing to stock the drug, delaying women's access by forcing them to venue-shop for both a pharmacy that stocks the drug and a pharmacist who will fill the prescription. However, policymakers don't always allow these civilian protests to go unchecked. In Illinois, where pharmacies were reportedly denying women emergency contraception, Democratic governor Rod R. Blagojevich ordered them to fill the prescriptions.[42]

Because the effectiveness of Plan B hinges directly on how quickly it is ingested, reproductive rights and family planning advocates as well as major medical associations have urged the FDA to provide emergency contraception over the counter. In 2003, Barr Labs, Plan B's manufacturer, applied for over-the-counter (OTC) status of the drug for women sixteen years of age and older. In response, that year the FDA began its conventional review process by convening a panel of twenty-eight experts; they determined after a full review that Plan B is safe and effective, and voted twenty-three to four to recommend that it be given nonprescription status nationwide, therefore providing women with emergency contraception without the need to visit her physician or her pharmacist.

One of the dissenting members of that committee, Dr. David Hager, submitted a minority report to the FDA commissioner to express his opposition to OTC sales. Hager's action and his very presence on the committee have inspired complaints from the pro-choice and scientific communities. Although a prominent obstetrician-gynecologist, Hager is well known for his conservative Christian writings on such topics as encouraging women to pray for relief from menstrual cramps.[43] What is more, his personal integrity has recently been impugned by his divorce, prompted by his ex-wife's allegations of sexual and physical abuse. His prominent role on the committee, combined with his position in the conservative Focus on the Family anti-abortion group and the allegations of his mistreatment of his wife, has led to speculation that the FDA is being unduly influenced by an ideological interest inappropriate to a scientific body.[44]

Whatever the public controversy over Hager and his influence, the FDA has repeatedly stalled in creating OTC status for Plan B, despite the overwhelming recommendation of its outside review board to do so. Its refusal to act on its experts' recommendation ultimately led to the resignation of Dr. Susan F. Wood, Ph.D., assistant commissioner and director of the FDA's Office of Women's Health.[45] Wood, whose job description instructs her to "be a champion for women's health," stated upon her resignation that "I can no longer serve as staff when scientific and clinical evidence, fully evaluated and recommended for approval by the professional staff here, has been overruled." [46]

Citing concerns about teen access and promiscuity, groups such as the U.S. Conference of Catholic Bishops, the Family Research Council, and Concerned Women for America have opposed approval of over-the-counter use.[47] On the other side of the debate, a number of leading women politicians, including senators Hillary Clinton (D-N.Y.) and Patty Murray (D-Wash.), have voiced their distress over the sluggish FDA process. In the summer of 2005, Democrats delayed the confirmation hearings of President Bush's nominee for FDA commissioner, Lester M. Crawford, until Crawford guaranteed an FDA ruling on the Plan B recommendation by September 1 of that year. Despite this agreement, on August 26, 2005, the newly confirmed commissioner issued a press release stating that as both "a scientific and regulatory agency," the FDA would suspend judgment on Plan B and take public comment on creating OTC status for sixty days. Commissioner Crawford unexpectedly resigned from his post on September 23, 2005, stating only that at sixty-seven years old, he was ready for retirement.[48]

Two months later, in November 2005, the nonpartisan U.S. Government Accountability Office issued a report that indicated that after thorough review, it considered the process by which the FDA had delayed approval of OTC status for

Plan B highly unusual. In the other sixty-seven switch decisions made by the FDA from 1994 to 2004, the organization granted every other OTC application that received advisory committee approval.[49] The FDA's decision is now expected in the winter of 2006.

In the midst of this national debate, the states have acted on their own to solve this policy question. A number of them, including Arkansas, California, Hawaii, Maine, New Hampshire, New Mexico, and Washington, have passed laws that allow pharmacists who have collaborative practices with physicians to sell emergency contraception without prescriptions. California, New Jersey, New Mexico, New York, South Carolina, and Washington also make Plan B available in emergency rooms for victims of sexual assault. On September 15, 2005, Massachusetts was added to this list, when the state legislature overrode Governor Mitt Romney's veto of similar legislation granting wider access to Plan B without prescription. Research of Washington State indicates this legal status of Plan B is working without problems, as it does in most of Western Europe and Canada.[50]

This controversy illustrates the point that birth control is not always as easy to procure as is often thought. When one adds to this the observation that women in the aggregate have fewer financial resources than men do to raise children or to procure birth control, which can cost hundreds of dollars for the most effective methods, and that many single mothers are not well supported by either their former partners or the public safety net, it becomes harder to argue that unwanted pregnancy is a condition that women can easily control or prevent. The irony of the Plan B stalemate is that women report choosing abortion most often because of unplanned pregnancy. Birth control itself is mired in social regulatory politics and public opinion, which may in part account for the high rate of abortion in the United States relative to those of other industrialized nations. In those countries with lower abortion rates, access to contraception is often facilitated by its coverage by private or state-run insurance programs. In the United States, however, both abortion and contraception are viewed as matters of morality, which charges those who support access with defending the very existence of methods to prevent or end pregnancy.

CONCLUSION

As seen, contrary to contemporary myths and stereotypes, abortion rates in the United States are comparable to rates in other nations, and have declined in recent years. This chapter demonstrates, however, that abortion is a complex issue, showing that access and demand are strongly correlated with a woman's financial and personal resources. What is more, this chapter underscores the reality that the public's perceptions about the practices of abortion often are not supported by the facts; too often the political hyperbole of the abortion debate overshadows real trends in abortion provision, just as the fury over partial-birth abortions has obscured the rarity of all forms of late-term abortion and the reasons for it. Low-income women whose rates of abortion have risen in recent years will find little public support for their abortions, leaving them in an environment in which abortion is indeed safe and technically legal, if not socially supported. Thus, one consequence of highly regulated abortion may be the marginalization of those who seek it.

The next chapter documents the most recent trends in abortion adjudication, and indicates that the court system in the United States is no more sensitive to the particular needs of low-income women in abortion policy than is the larger culture. Recent Supreme Court rulings seem to reflect public opinion by offering little constitutional protection to the group of women who most often access the procedure. As the country adopts increasingly restrictive abortion laws, the impact will be born largely by the most vulnerable women in our society: the young and the poor.

DISCUSSION QUESTIONS

1. Why do you think women have abortions? How does the data in this chapter compare with your impressions?
2. How should data regarding why women choose to have abortions be used in policymaking?
3. In what ways (if any) do you believe that international data on abortion could be applied to the abortion debate in the United States? What does this data highlight regarding the safety of abortion in the Unites States as compared to abroad?
4. Are the restrictions on access in the United States an issue that merits government action? What kind of action could be employed?
5. Does the data regarding abortion and ethnicity refute any views that you had previously held in regard to abortion?
6. Why are Americans more comfortable with abortion when a woman has been raped than when she cannot afford to support and raise another child?
7. Why doesn't the public opinion poll data reflect the most common reasons women have abortions?

SUGGESTED READING

Cook, Elizabeth Adell, Ted G. Jelen, and Clyde Wilcox. *Between Two Absolutes: Public Opinion and the Politics of Abortion.* Boulder, Colo.: Westview Press, 1992.

Critchlow, Donald T., ed. *The Politics of Abortion and Birth Control in Historical Perspective.* University Park: Pennsylvania State University Press, 1996.

Joffe, Carole. *Doctors of Conscience: The Struggle to Provide Abortion before and after* Roe v. Wade. Boston: Beacon Press, 1995.

Kaplan, Laura. *The Story of Jane: The Legendary Underground Feminist Abortion Service.* Chicago: University of Chicago Press, 1997.

Luker, Kristin. *The Politics of Motherhood.* Berkeley: University of California Press, 1984.

Mohr, James C. *Abortion in America: The Origins and Evolution of National Policy, 1800–1900.* Oxford: Oxford University Press, 1978.

Petcheskey, Rosalind Pollack. *Abortion and Woman's Choice: The State, Sexuality, and Reproductive Freedom,* rev. ed. Boston: Northeastern University Press, 1990.

Reagan, Leslie J. *When Abortion Was a Crime: Women, Medicine, and Law in the United States, 1867–1973.* Berkeley: University of California Press, 1997.

Solinger, Rickie. *The Abortionist: A Woman against the Law.* Berkeley: University of California Press, 1994.

———, *Wake Up Little Susie: Single Pregnancy and Race before* Roe v. Wade. New York: Routledge, 1992.

NOTES

1. Fetal viability is not as straightforward as the term suggests. Because of advancing technologies, fetuses are capable of living outside the womb earlier and earlier in the gestational process. Still, techniques for determining viability such as sonograms can be interpreted differently by different physicians. Moreover, each fetus is unique, making certainty regarding viability virtually impossible.

2. For a more complete explanation of how the pro-choice Democrats in Congress lost the debate over "partial birth" abortion, see Melody Rose, "Losing Control: The Intraparty Consequences of Divided Government," *Presidential Studies Quarterly* 31, no. 4 (December 2001): 679–698.

3. Cynthia Gorney, "Gambling with Abortion: Why Both Sides Think They Have Everything to Lose," *Harper's,* November 2004, 33–46, at 38.

4. Media Matters, "Fox News Toes GOP Line, Using the Term 'Partial Birth Abortion,' " December 13, 2004, http://mediamatters.org/items/ 200412130002.

5. David Stout, "An Abortion Rights Advocate Says He Lied about Procedure," *New York Times,* February 26, 1997, A11.

6. *Partial-Birth Abortion Ban Act,* Public Law 105, 108th Congress, 2d sess. (February 2004).

7. Although these are the parameters of the law, it has not been enforced. The law was immediately enjoined, and remains so pending judicial review. It will only take effect if the Supreme Court allows its implementation.

8. Lawrence B. Finer and Stanley K. Henshaw, "Abortion Incidence and Services in the United States in 2000," *Perspectives on Sexual and Reproductive Health 35,* no. 1 (January–February 2003): 6–15.

9. Miscarriages are so common in early pregnancy that many women mistake them for a normal period, which makes estimating the total number of miscarriages a challenge. The rate used herein refers only to miscarriages of "known pregnancies," though the total number of miscarriages is thought to be much higher.

10. *Sharing Responsibility: Women, Society, and Abortion Worldwide* (New York: Alan Guttmacher Institute, 1999).

11. Ibid.

12. Stanley K. Henshaw, "Unintended Pregnancy in the United States," *Family Planning Perspectives 30,* no. 1 (January–February 1998): 24–29 and 46.

13. Rachel K. Jones et al., "Contraceptive Use among U.S Women Having Abortions in 2000-2001," *Perspectives on Sexual and Reproductive Health 34,* no. 6 (November–December 2002): 294–303.

14. Dr. Siglinda Jacobsen, personal interview with the author in her office at the Oregon Health Science Hospital.

15. Akinrinola Bankole et al., "Reasons Why Women Have Induced Abortions: Evidence from 27 Countries," *International Family Planning Perspectives 24,* no. 3 (September 1998): 117–127 and 152.

16. These numbers add up to more than 100 percent because women were allowed to choose more than one reason for their abortion decision.

17. Lawrence B. Finer et al., "Reasons U.S. Women Have Abortions: Quantitative and Qualitative Perspectives," *Perspectives on Sexual and Reproductive Health 37,* no. 3 (September 2005): 110–118.

18. For a book-length examination of the growing gap between rich and poor see *Inequality Matters: The Growing Economic Divide in America and Its Poisonous Consequences,* ed. Jim Lardner and David Smith (New York: New Press, 2005).

19. References to women's callousness in abortion decisions are easy to find in popular culture. Examples are found in Barcella L., "The A-word," *Salon.com,* September 20, 2004, http://archive.salon.com/mwt/feature/2004/09/20/t_shirts/index _np.html.

20. Rebecca Benson Gold, "Abortion and Women's Health: A Turning Point for America?" (New York: Alan Guttmacher Institute, 1990).

21. "From the Patient's Perspective: The Quality of Abortion Care," report conducted by the Picker Institute, (Menlo Park, Calif.: Kaiser Family Foundation, May 1999).

22. See, for instance, Mary Steichen Calderone, *Abortion in the United States* (New York: Paul B. Hoeber, 1958), 178–180 and J. R. Abernathy, B. G. Greenberg, and D. G. Horvitz, "Estimates of Induced Abortion in Urban North Carolina," *Demography* 7, no. 1 (February 1970): 19–29.

23. Carole Joffe, "Reproductive Regression," TomPaine.commonsense, January 26, 2003, www.tompaine.com/articles/2006/01/23/reproductive_regression. php.

24. InfoforHealth, "Population Reports," www.infoforhealth.org/pr/m12/m12 chap2_1.shtml.

25. World Health Organization, "Unsafe Abortion: Global and Regional Estimates of the Incidence of Unsafe Abortion and Associated Mortality in 2000," 4th ed., 2004, www.who.int/reproductive-health/publications/unsafe_abortion_estimates_04/index.html. Of course, unsafe abortions occur most often in countries where abortion is illegal, making the documentation of them quite difficult, and probably uneven. These numbers are based on local studies and represent the best estimates available.

26. Gavin du Venage, "U.S. Policy Blamed for Abortion Deaths in Ethiopia 'Global Gag Rule' Prevents Agencies from Discussing Pregnancy Alternatives," *San Francisco Chronicle*, December 12, 2003, www.sfgate.com/cgi-bin/article. cgi?file=/chronicle/archive/2003/12/12/MNGRE3KKJT1.DTL.

27. Alan Guttmacher Institute, *Sharing Responsibility*.

28. Rachel K. Jones et al., "Patterns in the Socioeconomic Characteristics of Women Obtaining Abortions in 2000–2001," *Perspectives on Sexual and Reproductive Health* 34, no. 5 (September–October 2002): 226–235.

29. William D. Mosher et al., demonstrate that the use of contraceptives for all women of childbearing age rose from 56 percent in 1982 to 64 percent in 1995, and then fell slightly to 62 percent in 2002. See "Use of Contraception and Use of Family Planning Services in the United States: 1982–2002," *Advance Data from Vital and Health Statistics*, no. 350 (Atlanta: Centers for Disease Control and Prevention, 2004)

30. Douglas Kirby, "Do Abstinence-Only Programs Delay the Initiation of Sex among Young People and Reduce Teen Pregnancy?" National Campaign to Prevent Teen Pregnancy, October 2002, www.teenpregnancy.org/resources/data/pdf/abstinence_eval.pdf.

31. Nicholas D. Kristoff, "Bush's Sex Scandal," *New York Times* February 16, 2005.

32. Heather Boonstra and Elizabeth Nash, "Minors and the Right to Consent to Health Care" *Guttmacher Report on Public Policy*, 3, no. 4 (August 2000), www. guttmacher.org/pubs/tgr/03/4/gr030404.html.

33. Susheela Singh and Jacqueline E. Darroch, "Adolescent Pregnancy and Child-bearing: Levels and Trends in Developed Countries, *Family Planning Perspectives* 32, no. 1 (2000): 14–23.
34. Stanley K. Henshaw, "Unintended Pregnancy in the United States," *Family Planning Perspectives* 30, no. 1 (January–February 1998): 24–29 and 46.
35. John M. Westfall and Ken J. Kallail, "Repeat Abortion and Use of Primary Care Health Services," *Family Planning Perspectives* 27, no. 4 (July–August 1995): 162–165.
36. See, for example, the ABC News/*Washington Post* poll from January 16–20, 2003, which indicates that 86 percent of Americans believe abortion should be illegal after six months gestation. Of course, this poll, like all polls, is limited in that it did not ask whether exceptions should be made to that ban. Sixty-nine percent polled argued the D&X procedure should be illegal. Reported January 22, 2003, on abcnews.com, http://abcnews.go.com/sections/us/DailyNews/abortion_poll030122.html.
37. For a book-length examination of the politics of medical abortion in the United States, see Lawrence Lader, *RU 486: The Pill that Could End the Abortion Wars and Why American Women Don't Have It* (Reading, Mass.: Addison-Wesley 1991).
38. It should be said that medical abortion is not without its detractors. Some argue that medical abortion, which prescribes to the pregnant woman a two-step process of an ingested pill and later a vaginal suppository, has negative features when compared to surgical abortion. For instance, the woman has two appointments: one to get her prescription and the other as a follow-up to verify that the products of conception are indeed gone. This two-step process, when compared to an early surgical abortion, typically produces more pain, which the woman endures without the benefit of anesthesia or medical comfort, and increases the cost of the procedure.
39. Finer and Henshaw, "Abortion Incidence."
40. Aida Torres and Jacqueline Darroch Forrest, "Why Do Women Have Abortions?" *Family Planning Perspectives* 20, no. 4 (July–August 1988): 169–176.
41. Jones et al., "Contraceptive Use among U.S. Women."
42. Monica Davey and Pam Belluck, "Pharmacies Balk on After-Sex Pill and Widen Fight in Many States," *New York Times*, April 19, 2005, www.nytimes.com/2005/04/19/national/19pill.html?ei=5070&en=cdc8410ef657.
43. W. David Hager and Linda Carruth Hager, *Stress and the Woman's Body* (Tarrytown, N.Y.: Fleming H. Revell, 1996).
44. Dr. David A. Grimes has been among the most outspoken physicians calling for approval of over-the-counter status for Plan B. In one of his most colorful statements, Dr. Grimes argues that Plan B is safer over-the-counter than fire

extinguishers. See David A. Grimes, "Emergency Contraception and Fire Extinguishers: A Prevention Paradox," *American Journal of Obstetrics and Gynecology* 187, no. 6 (December 2002): 1536–1538.

45. Dr. John Abramson, "Politics of a Pill: FDA Wrangling Mires Morning-After Availability," *Boston Herald,* September 18, 2005.

46. Marc Kaufman, "FDA Official Quits over Delay on Plan B," *Washington Post,* September 1, 2005, A08.

47. Public opinion polls routinely demonstrate that Americans are nervous about teen access to abortion, as well, and favor consent laws. See, recently, Carol Eisenberg, "Abortion Still Supported, Despite Decades of Debate on Subject, Pew Poll Shows Majority of Americans Endorse It, with Restrictions," *Newsday,* August 4, 2005, A45.

48. Maria Newman, "Embattled Commissioner of F.D.A. Resigns," *New York Times,* September 23, 2005, http://select.nytimes.com/mem/tnt.html?emc=tnt&tntget=2005/09/23/politics/23cnd-fda.html&tntemail0=y.

49. U.S. Government Accountability Office, "Food and Drug Administration Decision Process to Deny Initial Application for Over-the-Counter Marketing of Emergency Contraceptive Drug Plan B Was Unusual," GAO-06-109, (Washington, D.C.: Government Printing Office, 2005).

50. Jacqueline S. Gardner et al., "Increasing Access to Emergency Contraception through Community Pharmacies: Lessons from Washington State," *Family Planning Perspectives* 33, no. 4 (July–August 2001): 172–175.

CHAPTER 2

Abortion on Demand?

The Supreme Court and Abortion Rights

*". . . for the period of pregnancy prior to this 'compelling' point [fetal viability],
the attending physician, in consultation with his patient, is free to determine,
without regulation by the State, that, in his medical judgment, the patient's
pregnancy should be terminated. If that decision is reached, the judgment may
be effectuated by an abortion* free of interference by the State.*"
(emphasis added)*

—Justice Harry Blackmun, for the majority, *Roe v. Wade*[1]

"To promote the State's interest in potential life throughout pregnancy,
the State may take measures *to ensure that the woman's choice is informed.
Measures designed to advance this interest should be invalidated if their purpose
is to persuade the woman to choose childbirth over abortion. These measures
must not be an undue burden on the right."* (emphasis added)

—Justice Sandra Day O'Connor, for the majority,
Planned Parenthood of Southeastern P.A. v. Casey[2]

In 2004, Kansas attorney general Phil Kline subpoenaed the unedited late-term
abortion records of ninety girls and women from two women's health clinics,
maintaining that he had probable cause that they would provide evidence of felo-
nious crimes. His actions met with vitriolic responses from the nation's abortion
rights groups because those records contained each patient's name, medical history, birth control practices, psychological assessment, and sexual history. Many
claimed that his action constituted an abuse of office. Others charged him with
unethical behavior, some with political plotting, and still others with callous
indifference to women's lives. From a standpoint of abortion politics, however,
his actions were resonant with three contemporary developments in the public
understanding of abortion: first, that physicians are no longer given professional
deference in the application of abortion policy, second, that women are not considered moral agents empowered to make reproductive choices free from the
state's intervention, and third, that the state is understood as a legitimate arbiter

of abortion decisions. These trends have deep roots in a number of sources, not the least of which is recent decisions by the U.S. Supreme Court.

This chapter documents the evolution of abortion politics through Supreme Court decisions, and argues that while physicians historically have been granted professional deference in abortion decisions, today's courts are more likely to invest authority in legislatures than in doctors. As a result, public policy frequently supplants the physician's medical judgment with the politician's morality. Second, this chapter documents the rise and fall of America's faith that women can make moral decisions regarding their bodies. The chapter concludes that the current judicial framing of abortion favors lawmakers over both medical experts who provide abortions and the women who seek them. In such a context, politicians will likely extend more and more restrictions over abortion, slowly whittling away the protected, legal right of women to have the procedure.

PHYSICIANS AS AUTHORITIES

Physicians have played a public role in abortion provision and policy since the mid-nineteenth century. As University of Oregon professor of history James C. Mohr explains, "regular" doctors took up the anti-abortion cause to elevate their moral and professional status above that of midwives. Midwives were the physicians' competitors in health care provision, and in order to establish their practices in a developing medical industry, physicians routinely characterized them as amateurs and admonished their practices, namely, their practices in regard to reproductive health.[3]

In so doing, the physicians' opposition to abortion dovetailed with nativist fears of the time. Periodicals blasted the high fertility rates of recent immigrants from southern and eastern Europe and lamented the lower birth rates of "native" born, white middle-class women that were presumably caused, at least in part, by abortion and contraceptive devices, sometimes called abortifacients. Their stance on abortion also allowed physicians to ally themselves with politicians and other notable individuals of the day who could provide them with business and bolster their emerging industry through public policy.

In practice, many physicians provided abortions, but at a cost. Men became the gatekeepers of women's reproductive lives. Women were stripped of what had been woman-centered reproductive health care—private decisions between a pregnant woman and her female midwife. This relationship of relative equality and mutual understanding was replaced with one of power imbalance in which the male doctor chose whether or not to provide "relief" from pregnancy. The shift was a double loss of female agency: the male physician gained control over the female body by gaining authority over her reproductive decisions, and midwives (who were overwhelmingly women) lost their businesses because of the rise of the regular medical industry.

Midwife bans, described in the Introduction, persuaded some to seek out regular physicians over midwives. Still others were convinced to do so as a matter of class identity: those with higher education and income viewed physicians as part of the emerging knowledge class. Physicians came to be associated with better skills and higher learning, whereas midwives were viewed as old fashioned and parochial. However, because midwives often took payment in the form of bartering, poorer women continued to use their services.

High physician status within the practice and policy of abortion would remain a staple within abortion politics for more than one hundred years. Although midwifery made a return beginning in the mid-twentieth century, and women have made strides within the mainstream medical profession, men remain the dominant force in medicine, and have been, until recently, highly regarded members of the policy community. That status is demonstrated in early Supreme Court abortion rulings.

However, historical deference to male physicians never guaranteed women's access to abortion. On the contrary, as the 1920s and 1930s demonstrate, physicians have often been free to impose their own morality in their offices and in state capitals, where they often supported the repressive policies of that era. Deference to doctors in the abortion arena did at least shield abortion policy from blatant, national partisan politics, which allowed decisions to be made within the medical realm instead of a political one.

The Supreme Court's First Appearance in Abortion Policy: Challenges to the Comstock Law

The Comstock Law, so named for its chief proponent, Anthony Comstock, was an anti-obscenity law passed by Congress in 1873. The law made it a federal crime to transmit "obscene, lewd, or lascivious" information through the federal mail system. This had an impact on the transmission of birth control devices and educational materials. The law was ultimately overturned by the Supreme Court in 1936 in *United States v. One Package of Japanese Pessaries,* but by that time states had already implemented similar prohibitions, sometimes dubbed "mini-Comstock" laws.

Two early reproductive freedom cases articulate standards that until very recently regularly appeared in subsequent abortion litigation. Each case, involving birth control activist Margaret Sanger, demonstrates a general regard for and deference to doctors in determining the proper application of abortion policy. Both also put forward a standard of concern for women's health as a guiding principle in reproductive policy.

Margaret Sanger: Advocate for Women's Reproductive Rights

Margaret Sanger, although she opposed abortion, committed herself to giving women control over the timing and number of children they bore. As a nurse on the lower east side of Manhattan at the turn of the century, Sanger saw firsthand the effects of repeated, untimely pregnancies on women's bodies. Her experiences in caring for women who had little control over their fertility motivated Sanger to dedicate her life to the development and distribution of birth control. She published widely on the subject, organized conferences on world population, and in 1914 founded the National Birth Control League, which later became Planned Parenthood. In advocating for the wide distribution of birth control, Sanger sometimes found herself at odds with the law.

The first major case she was involved in was *People v. Sanger.* It was brought before the New York State Supreme Court in 1917 and was a challenge to the New York Penal Code that made dispensing contraceptive devices a misdemeanor.[4] This mini-Comstock law made only one exception: local physicians were permitted to distribute contraceptives "for the cure or prevention of disease." Sanger had been arrested and convicted under the law for opening the nation's first family planning clinic on October 16, 1916. She then took her case to the state's highest court, the New York Court of Appeals, which upheld the ruling of the lower court, but did interpret the law more broadly. Although Sanger initially had defended her actions by claiming that a woman had a right to decide what happened to her own body, the appeals court based its ruling on two other rationales. First, it determined that physicians had a right to practice medicine free from unnecessary scrutiny of local law enforcement. This aspect of the ruling reveals the deference physicians generally receive in the practice of their craft, and creates the opportunity for more personal, although potentially ad hoc, decision making by prohibiting the State of New York from second guessing the medical judgment of doctors in the application of the law.

Second, and perhaps more curious to modern sensibilities, the appeals court maintained that the medical definition of "disease" might well be understood to include pregnancy. Whereas this notion might in the modern context seem preposterous, at the time such an understanding was not so shocking. Historians point to the language of contraception and abortion from the early twentieth century to support this conclusion. Many women spoke of being "relieved" of their pregnancies, indicating that the culture of the day largely considered pregnancy a state of disease from which one could recover or be cured. What is more, the morbidity and mortality rates for pregnant women of that time would have confirmed this popular characterization. Pregnancy was indeed fraught with complications, dangers, and risk. In 1917, two years before women gained a constitutional amendment protecting their right to vote, the appeals court in the *Sanger* case acknowledged this reality and interpreted the New York statute in such a way as to allow individual physicians to use their judgment in prescribing contraceptives to prevent the disease of pregnancy. So while Sanger did serve jail time, she ultimately made inroads in her fight to allow women the means to control their fertility through protection of the physician-patient relationship and through her appeals to the public interest in women's overall health. Sanger went on to appeal her case to the U.S. Supreme Court, which in 1919 dismissed the case for lack of jurisdiction.[5]

Sanger still faced other barriers to her efforts to make contraception more widely accessible. The state statute had been reinterpreted in a way to protect physician autonomy and women's health, but the contraceptive movement still had to face federal laws that prohibited the importation and transportation of articles, "designed, adapted, or intended for preventing conception, or producing abortion."[6] To provoke further reconsideration of the Comstock Law, Sanger instructed her colleague Dr. Hannah Stone of Sanger's New York family planning clinic to purchase pessaries (a relatively common form of early birth control similar to a diaphragm) from a physician distributing them in Japan. Sanger then alerted dockworkers to expect this illicit delivery, all of which contrived to bring the issue to court in the second case pivotal to early abortion politics.

A lower court initially ruled in favor of Sanger, but the federal government then presented its case to the U.S. Court of Appeals for the Second Circuit. This court upheld the lower court's ruling in *United States v. One Package of Japanese Pessaries* (1936), stating that because the pessaries had been intended for a physician and had a legitimate, legal use, Dr. Stone could in fact import and disseminate them.[7] Here again, judicial authorities focused on the health benefits of the pessaries to women—rather than the moral claims against contraception made in the legislation—and deferred to a physician's superior medical judgment in prescribing their use. As Sanger's grandson, Alexander Sanger, has noted, these rulings did not rely on women's rights or the concept of privacy developed many years later by the landmark *Griswold v. Connecticut* (1965) ruling, but instead emphasized the primacy of the woman's health to be determined and guarded by her physician.[8] These premises would continue to frame abortion rulings for some sixty years and have only recently begun to come undone.

The birth control movement of the mid-twentieth century also solidified the validity of this model. As with abortion, many physicians publicly opposed contraception while privately providing it on an ad hoc basis. Sanger's approach to her wing of the contraceptive movement was to enlist the support of physicians in seeking legalized contraception. She emphasized the physician's unique role in providing women relief from childbearing instead of focusing exclusively on the issue from a position of women's rights. Sanger was able to align herself with the medical community and gain its cooperation in her battle for legalized contraception.

Her strategy had interesting ramifications. First, her decision to align with physicians gave her a powerful lobby with which to work, and certainly assuaged any possible fears about her legitimacy as a radical woman in a male-dominated field. A second, less obvious but no less significant, point is that her alignment with physicians left their authority over women's reproductive health unchallenged. Sanger did not call for a rebirth of the midwifery field as others did, but rather cooperated with the new male-dominated medical industry. Finally, opting to separate abortion from contraception as she did led to a bifurcated view of reproduction that had not existed previously. Many had considered abortion and contraception part of a single reproductive management continuum. In fact, many in the hierarchy of the Catholic Church and in medicine today still take this view. But by disentangling contraception from abortion, Sanger created a dichotomy that has led to the simplistic "abortion-bad, contraception-good" mentality that characterizes the reproductive rights movement today.[9]

Physicians and the Contraception and Abortion Movements

Physicians continued to assert their role in abortion practice through the middle part of the twentieth century, first by actively supporting Sanger's contraception movement, and then, beginning in the 1950s, by establishing hospital review boards as a method of abortion gatekeeping. These boards became the typical process whereby women would plead their cases for wanting or needing an abortion during the strictest abortion policy years. Of course, the boards were overwhelmingly male, as few women were doctors during this time.

Perhaps even more importantly, their composition often varied, sometimes consisting of only obstetrician-gynecologists, other times of cardiac surgeons or other specialists, and still other times representatives from all of the above. They did not necessarily include patients' primary care physicians. The ad hoc nature of these committees essentially eliminated a woman's own primary caregiver from deliberations of her request. In many instances, this obfuscated key elements of the woman's story; for while obstetrician-gynecologists might focus on the impact of a birth on the woman's physical ability to bear children in the future, primary care physicians were more likely to see the current pregnancy in the larger context of the woman's whole social, familial, and economic condition.

In addition, the case of Sherry Finkbine (discussed in the Introduction) indicates that these boards were not immune from political considerations, and typically operated under the assumption that abortions would be provided only in instances in which they were necessary for extreme medical conditions, not for social or economic reasons. This is significant, given that the data show that most women have abortions for just these reasons. The hospital review board therefore played a role in creating the present-day dichotomy between the social-economic reasons and the medical-health reasons that women might have abortions.

As University of California, Berkeley, sociologist Kristin Luker demonstrates, by the 1960s physicians further pushed for authority as the dominant political coalition in abortion politics. In contrast to one hundred years prior, physicians advocated for looser abortion restrictions that would allow them to make decisions for their patients in a variety of circumstances. Building on the authority of hospital review boards, physicians demanded a reassertion of their individual professional authority in abortion, which had been somewhat sublimated by the restrictive state policies of the 1950s. Not only did physicians desire greater flexibility to respond to situations like the German measles outbreak in San Francisco (discussed in the Introduction), but they also wanted legal protection from prosecution when they performed abortions for reasons other than the severe medical ones most likely to garner public empathy and review board clearance.[10]

In part, this reform movement helped spawn the more woman-centered repeal movement, which sought to legalize abortion entirely. The reform movement certainly evoked strong empathy for women, because it strove to accommodate women's right to have an abortion under many different circumstances. Yet the repeal movement was led by women asserting women's own claim to authority in abortion decisions. Although this wing of the abortion movement met with some success, most notably in Hawaii, it was the reform movement that gained momentum building up to the landmark abortion rulings of *Roe*.

THE U.S. SUPREME COURT ACKNOWLEDGES A RIGHT TO PRIVACY

Griswold v. Connecticut

The next landmark contraception case, *Griswold v. Connecticut*, was undertaken by the U.S. Supreme Court in 1965.[11] A summary of this case, along with those for other major judicial abortion decisions, is found in Appendix A at the back of the text. Griswold was executive director of a Connecticut Planned Parenthood clinic. She and a medical colleague were arrested and charged under a state law that forbid the counseling of married couples regarding birth control and the distribution of contraceptives to them. In its ruling, the Court did not invoke either of the *Sanger* cases, and it did not rely on the central tenets of physician autonomy and patient health developed in those cases. Rather, its ruling drew from a series of cases that had developed a nascent definition of privacy to overturn the Connecticut law.[12]

The Court ruled that the State of Connecticut had overextended its authority in making the sale of contraceptives to married couples illegal. Emphasizing the Bill of Rights, the majority argued that the U.S. Constitution provides for a right to privacy. Agreeing that various amendments create a "penumbra" of privacy, the

Court held that intimate marital decisions around family planning fit squarely within that realm. And while an explicit right to privacy exists nowhere in the Constitution, this implicit right would set the terms of the abortion debate for decades to come.[13]

Roe v. Wade

Eight years later, in *Roe v. Wade,* the Court relied on the *Griswold* verdict to extend the penumbra of privacy to the issue of abortion.[14] But the Court also returned to a greater emphasis on the *Sanger*-era physician-patient relationship and the primacy of a woman's health in defining when a state had the authority to curb the right to privacy. *Roe* codified these principles as the predominant underpinnings of the right to privacy in abortion cases that would be reiterated consistently by the Court in the years to come.[15]

In *Roe,* the Court faced a challenge by Jane Roe to a Texas law that made virtually all abortions illegal except to save the pregnant woman's life. (Because she now is an active member of the pro-life movement, the public knows Jane Roe by her real name, Norma McCorvey.) Although Roe was no longer pregnant (she did not have an abortion) by the time her case reached the high court, the Court agreed to consider the law's constitutionality. Represented by twenty-six-year-old attorney Sarah Weddington, Roe presented her case to the nine justices.

After a summer of study at the Mayo Clinic, where Justice Harry Blackmun had once served as legal counsel, the justice pondered the scientific, philosophical, and religious aspects of abortion. He concluded that while there is no definitive judgment in Western civilization regarding the moral appropriateness of the procedure, the commonness of it throughout time and across cultures had yielded some consistent social responses. The most important, for the purposes of this piece, is the discomfort Blackmun found with abortion procedures conducted after the point of viability, when a fetus might be able to live outside the mother's womb. As the Introduction to this book shows, our own society historically has adopted more restrictions on obtaining an abortion after viability than before.

Writing for the majority and looking specifically at the question of fetal personhood, Blackmun concluded that the Constitution's several references to "persons" reflect an assumption that people have been born.[16] Thus, he concluded, absent consensus from religion, philosophy, or science and without definitive inclusion of the unborn within constitutional provisions, fetal personhood has no basis in law, regardless of viability.

Still, Blackmun argued, the question of legal protections often hangs not on the question of personhood, but rather, of citizenship. And while citizenship affords an individual the Fourteenth Amendment protection of life and liberty, a fetus's status as a citizen is not clear either. The Constitution, Blackmun found, never refers to the fetus; every reference to the citizen is to a born person. He thus concluded that, given the dubious legal status of the unborn, fetuses are not due full-fledged Fourteenth Amendment protections against abortion.

Blackmun instead emphasized the right of privacy created in *Griswold*, and extended this definition to include the most intimate of all family planning decisions: the choice not to become a parent by ending a pregnancy. However, he argued that this right of privacy would not extend to all abortions. He wrote that, based upon the history of Western civilization's responses to abortion, somewhere in the middle of pregnancy a society's interest in the potential citizen increases. Thus he invoked the notion of viability as a compromise between an individual's right to privacy and a state's interest in future life. Abortion would be part of a fundamental right to privacy, and therefore any government restraint on that right would be met with strict scrutiny. In creating a standard for such scrutiny, Blackmun spelled out the rubric that would guide the Court in future cases.

He developed a trimester system to navigate this difficult terrain, arguing that in the first trimester of pregnancy a woman would be free of state constraints on her decision, and could make an abortion choice in consultation with her doctor. In the second trimester, and prior to viability, restrictions to abortion access would be permissible only when necessary as a protection of the woman's health, underscoring the *Sanger*-era doctrine of holding a woman's health above other considerations. Finally, in the third trimester when the fetus is viable, the state could invoke its interest in protecting the fetus, and could restrict abortion entirely. The state would be constrained in preventing third trimester abortions, however, when abortion was necessary to preserve a woman's life or her health.

Of course, the willingness of the majority to note and affirm a woman's individual agency in *Roe* is not to be overlooked. Women are clearly invested with a moral capacity in the ruling in that their decision to pursue an abortion is legitimized and protected. What *Roe* does is acknowledge the ability of a woman to reason through her private situation (whatever that consists of) and to act upon it, free of proscription, at least in the first and second trimesters. Although a physician can deny her an abortion during the second and third trimesters, the woman is able to consult multiple physicians to help her make the right decision. In terms of physician-woman agency, the *Roe* verdict locates choice the way the early nineteenth century did: in the confidential relationship of woman and practitioner.

What the progressive language of *Roe* obfuscates is the role of the state. On balance, what remains of state authority or responsibility within that first trimester? In other words, what does *Roe*'s "choice" mean? Examination of the ruling's language makes it plain that what *Roe* provides is the right to prefer an abortion, not the right to have one. Justice Blackmun carefully makes plain his rejection of the notion that women are to have abortions "on demand," which resonates with the public opinion data presented in chapter 1. The majority opinion states that "On the basis of elements such as these appellant and some amici argue that a woman's right is absolute and that she is entitled to terminate her pregnancy at whatever time, in whatever way, and for whatever reason she alone chooses. With this we do not agree." [17]

The right to choose an abortion in consultation with one's doctor does not necessarily mean an abortion will take place. Physicians may decline because they personally disagree with the reasons presented, because the calendar is full, or because they are going on sabbatical. A right to choice means a woman has a con-stitutionally protected ability to ask—but in the end, the answer could be "no." Ultimately, the real choice protected in *Roe* is the physician's because

> for the period of pregnancy prior to this "compelling" point, the attending physician, in consultation with his patient, is free to determine, without regulation by the State, that, in his medical judgment, the patient's pregnancy should be terminated.[18] .
>
> The decision (*Roe*) vindicates [is] the right of the physician to administer medical treatment according to his professional judgment up to the point where compelling state interests provide compelling justifications for intervention. Up to those points, the abortion decision, in all its aspects is inherently, and primarily, a medical deci-sion, and basic responsibility for it must rest with the physician.[19]

Although abortion opponents tend to focus on the progressive aspects of the *Roe* ruling, namely the decision to include abortion under the *Griswold* privacy umbrella and to extend constitutional protection to abortion, the decision does not create an environment of "abortion on demand." Feminist scholars were quick to point out this limitation. Indeed, as law professor Catharine MacKin-non poignantly remarks, *Roe* also protects the privacy of *men* by protecting the authority of male physicians to be the gatekeepers of women's decisions regard-ing abortion.[20]

Government, under *Roe*, is not to construct obstacles to the decision or forbid the decision on its face. In practice, the government's constitutional role is to let women alone, to remain neutral regarding decisions to end a pregnancy, at least through the early stages, and to allow women to consult physicians in their choice. Government is not called to provide an affirmative protection to women who choose to end their pregnancies. The responsibility of provision, of pursuing and ultimately of fulfilling the choice, is left not to the state or to the physician, but to the woman considering the abortion.

In this regard, choice equals responsibility. The woman bears the responsibility of actually securing her right at whatever cost (personal, financial, etc.) there might be for her. Presumably, this cost is different for each individual woman. *Roe* does not consider the provision of abortion to be the government's responsibility, as later cases regarding public funding and resources address.

In sum, the key elements of this decision are threefold. First, the primacy of a woman's health over the state's interest in the fetus is clear and consistent, reflecting historical protections of women's reproductive rights. Second, the Court makes clear that the state's interest in the fetus only becomes compelling at the point of viability, when a fetus, or "potential citizen," could live outside the mother's womb. Finally, the Court defers to science over morality in allowing physicians—not politicians—to determine fetal viability. By not defining viability directly, the *Roe* system invests in doctors the ability to determine the appropriateness of the abortion appeal on a case-by-case basis. Inherent in this reaffirmation of the physician's authority is the basic assumption that the physician makes sound decisions— whether scientific or moral—the deference to the doctor's choice is complete until the state's interest in the fetus emerges.

The *Roe* majority is clear to point out that "the right of personal privacy includes the abortion decision, but that this right is not unqualified, and must be considered against important state interests in regulation." [21] Compared to the prior 120 years, women's agency is improved. Presumably, a woman's reason for pursuing an abortion is irrelevant to the state (although it could be pivotal in the doctor's office). She does not have to justify her reasoning to a review board, as in the 1950s, or navigate a dangerous underground industry. Still, unlike the early 1800s, women are not in practice always able to make decisions free of physician authority and approval, which in the majority of cases is male authority and approval. Furthermore, the fulfillment of the right is left up to the woman. *Roe* is hardly the radical, abortion-on-demand ruling that it has been portrayed as in recent years. As Blackmun said himself, the construction of the verdict was a sincere attempt at compromise and national healing.

THE INTERMEDIATE YEARS: PROTECTING CHOICE, DENYING RIGHTS

By and large, and with few exceptions, the Court continued its protection of abortion as a private choice throughout the 1970s and 1980s. The cases of this era consistently contain language that indicate a respect for the medical profession and an inherent willingness to give doctors latitude in making professional judgments about the application of abortion policies and practices, especially in and around the notion of viability. The majority decisions in these cases indicate a firm unwillingness to allow the state to substitute its preferences on abortion for those of the physician. Consistent with the *Sanger* rulings of many years ago, the post-*Roe* Court emphasized women's health and physicians' autonomous decision making in its rulings regarding the right of the state to intervene on behalf of fetal interests.

The post-*Roe* Court had basically two issues to face. First, within the framework of the states' acknowledged interests in abortion regulation, that is protecting women's health and an interest in viable fetal life, which limitations on abortion access would be permissible under *Roe*? Second, did the "right" to an abortion include an affirmative state provision of abortion? The Court was quick to answer both of these questions in the late 1970s and early 1980s.

Those states whose legislatures had an enduring opposition to the practice of abortion wasted no time in testing the Court's tolerance of abortion regulations after the *Roe* decision invalidated most state abortion statutes. In three key cases the Court swiftly struck down a series of abortion access limitations, adhering consistently to its argument that a state had to demonstrate a compelling interest either in women's health or viable fetal life when constructing limits. The first case was *Planned Parenthood of Central Missouri v. Danforth* (1976).[22] The case was a challenge to a Missouri law that required parental consent to a minor's abortion; a husband's written consent to his wife's abortion; a woman's written, informed consent; a ban on second-trimester use of saline amniocentesis procedures; and a record-keeping requirement for practitioners. All but the provisions involving record-keeping and informed consent failed the Court's scrutiny. In striking down the law, the *Danforth* Court leaned heavily on *Roe*'s logic of protecting women's health and physician-patient privacy. The Court specifically remarked that the viability line drawn in the *Roe* decision is "a point purposefully left flexible for professional determination." [23] As a medical term open to interpretation and changing medical technologies, the viability determination was deliberately left to the experts: physicians.

The *Danforth* Court took pains to articulate an argument that would preclude state legislatures from substituting their own judgments regarding viability for that of physicians:

> In any event, we agree with the District Court that it is not the proper function of the legislature or the courts to place viability, which essentially is a medical concept, at a specific point in the gestation period . . . the determination of whether a particular fetus is viable is, and must be, a matter for the judgment of the responsible attending physician. The definition of viability in §2(2) merely reflects this fact. The appellees do not contend otherwise, for they insist that the determination of viability rests with the physician in the exercise of his professional judgment.[24]

The Court reaffirmed this conviction in the physician's primary role seven years later in *Akron v. Akron Center for Reproductive Health, Inc.*[25] Again the Court considered a range of state-imposed abortion restrictions, this time from the State of Ohio, including a twenty-four-hour waiting period, a hospitalization requirement for late-term abortions, parental consent for abortions for girls fifteen years of age or younger, a doctor-only counseling provision, the need to relay specific information during the counseling session, and strict instructions about disposal of abortion materials. In striking down all five of the Ohio restrictions, the Court stated plainly that "It remains primarily the responsibility of physician to ensure that appropriate information is conveyed to his patient, depending on her particular circumstances." [26] What the majority of the Court found in *Akron* was a consistent attempt by the State of Ohio to impose barriers unrelated to the *Roe* standard of compelling state interest in women's health. Although the state may ask for a woman's signed consent before an abortion procedure, under *Danforth,* the state may not create a coercive environment in which it intrudes upon the physician-patient relationship. The Court objected to "intrusion upon the discretion of the pregnant patient's physician," in the language that the state forced doctors to use with each patient, whether relevant to her case or not.[27] The Court had a similar objection to the waiting period, calling it "arbitrary and inflexible." [28]

The *Akron* Court went further, directly arguing that even though the state has an interest in both women's health and emergent fetal life, it may not impose its preference for birth over abortion in the counseling requirement:

> This does not mean, however, that a State has unreviewable authority to decide what information a woman must be given before she chooses to have an abortion. It remains primarily the responsibility of the physician to ensure that the appropriate information is conveyed to his patient, depending on her particular circumstances. *Danforth*'s recognition of the State's interest in ensuring that this information be given will not justify abortion regulations designed to influence the woman's informed choice between abortion or childbirth.[29]

The Court's refusal to allow states to insert their preferences into state law culminated in the 1986 case of *Thornburgh v. American College of Obstetricians and Gynecologists,* in which the Court was faced with many of the same issues it had considered in *Akron.*[30] This time the Court rejected a specific counseling script to be read by doctors to patients, a provision that required doctors to attempt to save fetuses in post-viability abortions, a requirement that two doctors attend post-viability abortions, and a reporting requirement that allowed the public to access abortion records. The Court remanded a fifth question regarding parental consent to the lower courts for consideration. In this case, the Court referred to the loaded required language in the counseling script as the "antithesis of informed consent," [31] and offered the strongest language to date regarding the patient-physician relationship:

> Forcing the physician or counselor to present the materials and the list to the woman makes him or her, in effect, an agent of the State in treating the woman, and places his or her imprimatur upon both the materials and the list. . . . All this is, or comes

close to being, state medicine imposed upon the woman, not the professional medical guidance she seeks, and it officially structures—as it obviously was intended to do—the dialogue between the woman and her physician.[32]

Thornburgh did not just emphasize the unique and protected relationship of the woman and her doctor. Both the majority opinion, penned by Justice Blackmun, and the concurrence written by Justice John Paul Stevens argued that the state's restrictions threatened contemporary understanding of the proper scope of government authority. First, Blackmun condemned the State of Pennsylvania's actions:

> The States are not free, under the guise of protecting maternal health or potential life, to intimidate women into continuing pregnancies. Appellants claim that the statutory provisions before us today further legitimate compelling interests of the Commonwealth. Close analysis of those provisions, however, shows that they wholly subordinate constitutional privacy interests and concerns with maternal health in an effort to deter a woman from making a decision that, with her physician, is hers to make.[33]

In concurring, Justice Stevens took an even stronger tack. Stevens directly approached the question of the state's legitimate role, claiming that in the area of privacy, that role is to be contained:

> In the final analysis, the holding in *Roe v. Wade* presumes that it is far better to permit some individuals to make incorrect decisions than to deny all individuals the right to make decisions that have a profound effect upon their destiny. Arguably a very primitive society would have been protected from evil by a rule against eating apples; a majority familiar with Adam's experience might favor such a rule. But the lawmakers who placed a special premium on the protection of individual liberty have recognized that certain values are more important than the will of a transient majority.[34]

The powerful arguments made by both justices go to the heart of the proper role and scope of government. They press the case that regulation of abortion, except for the sake of a woman's health or the potential life of a viable fetus, is outside the bounds of proper liberal democratic power. State law could not be wielded to enforce patently moral ends.

At the same time that the *Akron* and *Thornburgh* majorities were producing their arguments, the dissenting justices in those cases were laying the groundwork for a very different theory of government intervention. These arguments were successful in cases concerning abortion funding during the 1970s and 1980s, although they remained in the dissent in other cases.

In a series of cases that pertained to both federal and state funding of abortions for indigent women, the justices opposed to *Roe*'s central finding crafted a majority based in part on how *Roe* framed the abortion issue. Because the central premise of the ruling is that a woman has a constitutional protection of her abortion choice, and not a fundamental right to an abortion per se, the question of public funding was open to debate. In two landmark cases, *Maher v. Roe* (1977) and *Harris v. McRae*, (1980) the high court determined that neither the states nor the federal government would be obligated to provide abortion funding.[35]

In both rulings, the dissenting justices from *Roe* gained enough support from the others to separate a denial of funding benefits from other obstacles to abortion that the Court had recently struck down. The framing of "choice" in *Roe* essentially had created a privilege, but not an obligation by government, to ensure access to abortion services to all women. The rulings denied that an absence of state action, in this case an absence of state financial assistance, was an unconstitutional barrier to a protected right. If a woman could choose to have an abortion under *Roe*, government could choose not to fund it under *Maher* and *Harris*. The Court explains this logic in its verdict for *Harris*:

> But, regardless of whether the freedom of a woman to choose to terminate her pregnancy for health reasons lies at the core or the periphery of the due process liberty recognized in *Wade*, it simply does not follow that a woman's freedom of choice carries with it a constitutional entitlement to the financial resources to avail herself of the full range of protected choices. The reason why was explained in *Maher*: although government may not place obstacles in the path of a woman's exercise of her freedom of choice, it need not remove those not of its own creation. Indigency falls in the latter category. The financial constraints that restrict an indigent woman's ability to enjoy the full range of constitutionally protected freedom of choice are the product not of governmental restrictions on access to abortions, but rather of her indigency. Although Congress has opted to subsidize medically necessary services generally, but not certain medically necessary abortions, the fact remains that the Hyde Amendment [eliminating federal abortion funding] leaves an indigent woman with at least the same range of choice in deciding whether to obtain a medically necessary abortion as she would have had if Congress had chosen to subsidize no health care costs at all. We are thus not persuaded that the Hyde Amendment impinges on the constitutionally protected freedom of choice recognized in Wade.[36]

These rulings had at least two major implications. They created an obvious class distinction between beggars (those who cannot pay) and choosers (those who can).[37] For poor women, exercising the right to have an abortion is dependent upon an ability to pay for one.

What is more, the cases signaled the advent of a theory of negative rights that would embolden the pro-life movement. In each ruling, a majority of the Court agreed that the state or federal government could legitimately assert its preference for birth over abortion by a denial of financial assistance. The right to have an abortion could be denied through state omission, although not through active state-imposed hurdles. By denying resources and assistance, the state could constitutionally encourage some women to choose to give birth over having an abortion. These cases point to an important development in the theory of the state's role in abortion regulation: a majority of the Court agreed that the state or federal government could legitimately assert its preference for birth over abortion by codifying that view in a denial of financial assistance.

Pro-life legislators later would find other ways to deny government resources through bans on the use of government buildings and personnel in the practice of abortion. Ultimately, however, the idea that states could impose their pro-birth preferences would be extended to the imposition of outright barriers to access as well. As Alexander Sanger has noted, since the *Roe* Court never concluded that abortion in itself was a good to society, society bears no responsibility to provide it. In the liberal political framework of public versus private, once an interest is deemed private, it is essentially taken from public view and consideration. This is precisely what has happened with abortion.

As a practical matter, the funding cases affected a great many women. When Congress passed its Hyde Amendment in 1976 and the Court upheld it in 1980, the financial burden of abortion for many women shifted,[38] leading Sen. Robert Packwood (R-Ore.) to observe, "a right with no access is no right at all. . . . If we vote now to restrict Medicaid funds for poor women's abortion, we make a mockery of her right." [39] Until the Court upheld Congress's ban on federal Medicaid funding for abortion services, the federal government alone had been paying for three hundred thousand abortions per year, at an annual cost of roughly $45 million. In addition, in 1979 the Defense Department cut off funding roughly 265,000 abortions a year for military personnel. A handful of states continue to offer some abortion funding (see chapter 3), but it is fair to say that nearly all abortions in the United States today are privately funded. Ironically, because the Court required government to be neutral under *Roe*, it allowed government to deny funding to poor women seeking abortions. Still, as public policy experts know, withholding resources is not a neutral government stance any more than offering them is.

Some of the justices had argued from the beginning that the state could assert its preference for birth over abortion in ways beyond the denial of government resources. In the *Akron* and *Thornburgh* cases, which struck down state-imposed barriers to abortion, the dissenting arguments expressed the right of a state to impose barriers to abortion to reflect the state's pro-birth bias. But under *Roe v. Wade*, which declares that barriers must pass a compelling state interest test in either the woman's health or the viable fetus's interests, how could these dissenting jurists justify a state-imposed burden that existed for the sole purpose of illustrating the state's birth-preference? The only way for the justices to argue in favor of that development was to lower the hurdle over which barriers must pass. The answer was the undue burden test.

Justice Sandra Day O'Connor developed the undue burden test through her dissenting opinions in *Thornburgh* and *Akron*. A reading of the often-overlooked dissenting opinions in those two cases reveals a reiteration of the arguments that gained the majority in the funding cases and foreshadowed what would become the majority view in *Webster v. Reproductive Health Services* (1989) and later *Planned Parenthood of Southeastern P.A. v. Casey* (1992).

O'Connor's dissent in *Akron* was first and foremost an attack on the *Roe* trimester system, which she claimed is "unworkable" because the viability requirement is dependent upon shifting technology and medical knowledge. Rather than see this flexibility as a way to give professional deference to medical expertise of doctors, *Roe* opponents view it as an imposition on judges to constantly reevaluate abortion policy based upon new technologies. The *Roe* majority and others had consistently resolved that issue by relying on physicians to negotiate the flexibility of the viability line. O'Connor was not willing to place such trust in the medical establishment.

However, out of respect for the doctrine of stare decisis, the principal that precedent decisions are to be followed by the courts, O'Connor claimed that she would uphold *Roe* despite her misgivings. She argued that the Court should recognize that state interest in fetal and maternal health exists throughout pregnancy, therefore any abortion restriction that is reasonably related to those interests, and that does not impose an "undue" burden on the abortion right, should be upheld. Waiting periods and counseling requirements, she argued, satisfy the state's interest in maternal health. By lowering the hurdle over which abortion restrictions must pass, O'Connor deferred not to doctors, but to state legislatures to determine how best to satisfy the state's interests.

It is intriguing that the Court's first woman justice claimed that these impositions are necessary in order for women to be thoughtful about their abortion choice. "The waiting period is surely a small cost to impose to ensure that the woman's decision is well considered in light of its certain and irreparable consequences on fetal life, and the possible effects on her own." [40] What O'Connor did not acknowledge was the potential cost of these regulations on a woman's freedom or the paternalistic dynamic they created between the state and the woman. Waiting periods and mandatory counseling sessions imply that without the state's intervention, women are unreflective about their abortion decisions or that they cannot be trusted to arrive at the proper decision without the state's assistance.

NEUTRAL NO MORE: *WEBSTER V. REPRODUCTIVE HEALTH SERVICES*

From 1973 until 1989, the majority of the Court maintained the central holding in *Roe v. Wade*. Still, as the funding cases demonstrate, the emphasis on striking down overt state barriers to access did not extend to the denial of state support.

One case marks a clear transition between the *Roe* doctrine, which requires a *compelling* state interest in fetal life to restrict abortion, and the *Casey* doctrine, which requires a *reasonable* state interest in fetal life to restrict abortion: *Webster v. Reproductive Services.*[41]

The *Webster* case is a complicated one. Originally involving twenty different Missouri abortion provisions, the high court eventually focused on five. Appendix A at the back of this text describes how the Court resolved these five major statutory considerations; however, there is more going on in this case than an approval or rejection of the Missouri provisions.

William Rehnquist, chief justice at the time of the ruling, wrote the majority opinion in *Webster,* and changed the framing of abortion adjudication in important ways. Rehnquist's central tenet was that the state (in this case, Missouri) has no obligation to provide public facilities for abortion procedures. He argued further that a ban on public facilities would do little harm to reproductive rights:

> Nothing in the Constitution requires States to enter or remain in the business of performing abortions. Nor, as appellees suggest, do private physicians and their patients have some kind of constitutional right of access to public facilities for the performance of abortions. . . . Indeed, if the State does recoup all of its costs in performing abortions, and no state subsidy, direct or indirect, is available, it is difficult to see how any procreational choice is burdened by the State's ban on the use of its facilities or employees for performing abortions.[42]

This aspect of the *Webster* ruling conveys the Court's disinterest in the particular burdens such abortion regulations place on low-income women, and affirms the view that abortion in the modern age is a privilege rather than a right. Rehnquist's statement about the state's lack of duty in abortion procedures is only one indication of a substantive diminution in women's abortion access, however. Perhaps more compelling is the turn the Court takes in *Webster* on the meaning of viability.

The reader will recall that the *Roe* decision indicated a general discomfort with abortion post-viability. For this reason, the majority in *Roe* admitted the possibility of abortion restrictions later in pregnancy based on a state's interest in a potential citizen. The trimester system laid out in 1973 protected women's access to abortion prior to viability, and left to physicians the task of determining the gray areas of the pregnancy. The Rehnquist Court took a different tack in *Webster.* The majority argued that "There is also no reason why the State's compelling interest in protecting potential human life should not extend throughout pregnancy rather than coming into existence only at the point of viability." [43]

The majority opinion therefore created a state interest in fetal life *before* viability, extending the point at which the state may legitimately restrict a woman's abortion decision earlier into pregnancy, and undermining a central tenet of *Roe*.

This move indicates a growing wariness of the physician's role in determining fetal viability in abortion, laying the groundwork for further state protections of the fetus. The Court had set the stage for abandoning the trimester system that protected early abortions under *Roe.*

The significance of allowing a state interest in life before viability is twofold. First, under the *Webster* ruling, the state is allowed to impose mandatory viability testing on women whose pregnancies are possibly within the viability range. Earlier cases recognized the difficulty of determining viability both because individual pregnancies are unique and because advances in technology change the point of possible survival; they ultimately allowed individual doctors to determine whether a viability test would be necessary. Hence, in allowing the State of Missouri to legislate viability tests on pregnant women in the middle trimester, the medical decision of women and their physicians was replaced with the judgment of state legislators.

In practice, the newly required viability tests have implications for the cost of abortion. The additional burden of cost to the pregnant woman apparently is of less interest to the state (and the courts) than is the potentiality of human life:

> It is true that the tests in question increase the expense of abortion, and regulate the discretion of the physician in determining the viability of the fetus. Since the tests will undoubtedly show in many cases that the fetus is not viable, the tests will have been performed for what were, in fact, second-trimester abortions. But we are satisfied that the requirement of these tests permissibly furthers the State's interest in protecting potential human life, and we therefore believe §188.029 [of the Missouri statute] to be constitutional.[44]

The *Webster* case should be viewed as a pivotal move away from the *Roe* standard of protecting abortion until viability. *Roe* established a protected zone for abortion and limited the state's ability to favor birth over abortion until the fetus was viable. With *Webster,* the Court embraces a new vision of state interest in fetal life prior to viability, and a Court-protected right to withhold state resources in asserting this preference.

CASEY: SUPPLANTING DOCTOR AUTHORITY WITH STATE AUTHORITY

The premise of a doctor's authority remained the dominant position in Supreme Court rulings subsequent to *Roe.* Beginning with *Webster,* however, the Court became more flexible about allowing states to second-guess physicians and impose restrictions and specific directions (such as viability tests) on doctors' practice of abortion. Between *Webster* and *Casey,* President George H. W. Bush replaced two liberal justices (William J. Brennan and Thurgood Marshall) with two conservatives (David Souter and Clarence Thomas), changing the composition of the Court. Then in *Casey* the Court threw out its historic acceptance of physician deference in lieu of a renewed role for state legislatures when it let stand some abortion barriers found impermissible in previous cases.

One overlooked aspect of *Casey* is that it greatly undermined a doctor's authority in the abortion decision. To describe this dramatic shift, a closer look must be taken at the framework employed in the opinion by Justice O'Connor. The fundamental right of abortion was replaced by the compelling state interest standard with the far lower hurdle dubbed by O'Connor as the undue burden standard.[45] A state wishing to impose abortion restrictions must now simply demonstrate that the burden imposed on the woman's access is not "undue," which the O'Connor opinion defined as:

> A finding of an undue burden is a shorthand for the conclusion that a state regulation has the purpose or effect of placing a substantial obstacle in the path of a woman seeking an abortion of a nonviable fetus. A statute with this purpose is invalid because the means chosen by the State to further the interest in potential life must be calculated to inform the woman's free choice, not hinder it.[46]

The Court further clarified this standard later in the decision by adding that a state would not create an undue burden on the woman's abortion decision if it created restrictions designed to dissuade her from having the abortion: "under the undue burden standard, a State is permitted to enact persuasive measures which favor childbirth over abortion, even if those measures do not further a health interest." [47] In this way, the Court is saying that the state's interest in the fetus begins at conception, not at viability, as *Roe* had stated. In fact, O'Connor points out repeatedly that the *Roe* case and others since have been flawed in understating the state's interest in pre-viable life, even going so far as to argue that, "it might be said that a woman who fails to act before viability has consented to the State's intervention on behalf of the developing child." [48]

As already demonstrated, O'Connor and her likeminded colleagues had been honing the undue burden language and argument since *Akron*. The new standard eases a state's burden of justifying a restriction. More importantly for the purposes of this text, it also allows the state—rather than the physician—to define the appropriate circumstances surrounding an abortion and allows the state—not the physician—to determine what type of counseling is appropriate prior to an abortion. For the first time in recent abortion politics history, physicians are being replaced as gatekeepers by state legislatures, who are now setting the very precise terms under which abortions may take place.

In policy terms, the undue burden standard has made a whole host of restrictions available to the states that were not permissible under *Roe*'s fundamental right standard. For while *Thornburgh* and *Akron* overturned state attempts to erect waiting periods and state-mandated abortion counseling prior to an abortion, the undue burden standard allows both. Neither the physician's nor the woman's assessment of a situation can mediate against the state's judgment that such hurdles are necessary because of the state's demonstrated preference of birth over abortion.

In *Planned Parenthood of Southeastern P.A. v. Casey*, the State of Pennsylvania sought to persuade women to choose giving birth over having an abortion through five abortion regulations that subsequently came before the Court. The Court upheld a twenty-four-hour waiting period, state-mandated counseling, parental consent for minors, and a reporting requirement, while overturning only one provision under the new undue burden standard: husband notification. In upholding the waiting period and the state-mandated counseling, the Court in *Casey* overturned parts of both *Akron* and *Thornburgh*, which had found those provisions unconstitutional under the fundamental right standard of *Roe*. O'Connor argued that the first four provisions were legitimate expressions of the state's preference for birth, and as such did not rise to the level of an undue burden, despite the imposition of additional costs and stresses to the pregnant woman by the first two restrictions. Ironically, she uses the state's interest in maternal health to justify both the twenty-four-hour waiting period as well as the mandated counseling script:

> In attempting to ensure that a woman apprehend the full consequences of her decision, the State furthers the legitimate purpose of reducing the risk that a woman may elect an abortion, only to discover later, with devastating psychological consequences, that her decision was not fully informed.

This statement makes three assumptions about what regularly transpires between the physician and the patient: first, that the physician does not as a matter of course inform the patient of the risks and procedures of the abortion. Given the high costs associated with medical malpractice, and the fact that state laws require physicians to inform their patients of the risks associated with virtually any procedure, it seems reasonable that a doctor would not neglect this obligation. Given this professional and ethical context, it would seem untenable for doctors to neglect providing such information. In addition, O'Connor's statement implies that women are at risk of psychological damage without the state-mandated counseling language, despite scientific evidence to the contrary.[49] Here the Court is not relying on medical evidence but instead on highly controversial claims by abortion activists. Finally, the Court seems to be implying that without the state's counseling requirement, women would make the decision to have an abortion without information or forethought, which reinforces the stereotype that women are unreasonable in their abortion decisions.

In overturning previous cases in which the Court had rejected waiting periods and counseling requirements, it is undermining the proper role of the physician in the abortion process and assuming a paternalistic position relative to the patient. Most important, what these aspects of the ruling suggest is that the individual actors in the abortion decision (the woman and her physician) are unreasonable. Given their unreasonableness, the Court defers to the legislators the power to guide the reasonable outcome of abortion situations.

Still, it is important to note that while O'Connor's majority reduced physician control of abortion practice and cleared the way for new abortion restrictions, the Court has consistently maintained the historic interest of women's health as central to future abortion policy. What is meant by women's health, and whether doctors or politicians will be allowed to determine what is in the best interest of abortion patients, is yet to be determined. And as the most recent cases indicate, while the Court seems intent on upholding women's health as a basic premise of abortion policy, the other branches of government are pushing the envelope. The future of the health standard, created in the *Sanger* era of the early twentieth century, and maintained to some degree through *Casey*, remains at risk.[50]

STENBERG V. CARHART: A FOOTNOTE OR A SHIFT?

Much has happened in abortion politics in the wake of *Casey*. As chapters 3 and 4 demonstrate, state and federal governments have used the opportunity created by the ruling to erect new restrictions on abortion. Recently, the Court's commitment to the health provision was directly challenged; to the surprise of some on both sides of this debate, the Court ruled in favor of women's health.

Stenberg et al. v. Carhart (2000) was the first opportunity the Supreme Court has had to consider an outright ban on a particular abortion procedure, and the outcome of this case is more protective of science and physicians' authority than other recent decisions.[51] The findings in *Carhart* are important here, both because they serve as a counterexample to the general trend of the Court to protect fetuses at the expense of women's health, and because they may lend insight into how the Court will eventually approach the federal Partial-Birth Abortion Ban and other cases pending before it.

In *Carhart*, the Court ruled 5–4 that Nebraska's ban on the D&X procedure was unconstitutional because it did not provide an exception for saving a woman's health, a requirement under both *Roe* and *Casey*. The Nebraska law, like the more recent federal version, banned use of the procedure at any point in pregnancy. It did create an exception to save a woman's life. Certainly in *Roe*, and to a lesser degree in *Casey*, the Court held that when considering abortion restrictions, a woman's health must be respected above interest in the fetus. In analyzing the scientific evidence presented, Justice Stephen Breyer found in his majority opinion that while the D&X procedure may be disturbing, it remains the safest procedure available for women in the instances in which it is used:

> The State fails to demonstrate that banning D&X without a health exception may not create significant health risks for women, because the record shows that significant medical authority supports the proposition that in some circumstances, D&X would be the safest procedure.[52]

Trusting the judgment of prevailing scientific research in this area, the majority deferred to medical authorities in choosing the least risky abortion procedure to women. The case also addresses the proper role of physicians in applying abortion statutes. The Nebraska law presented the possibility that physicians might be convicted and imprisoned for performing the D&X procedure. In his ruling, Breyer argued that the possibility of jail time would dissuade many conscientious physicians from performing a D&X abortion, even when it was in the woman's best medical interest. This possibility puts women's health at risk, and therefore constitutes an undue burden on her abortion liberty, and adds some clarity to the parameters of the undue burden standard.[53]

Still, Breyer was careful not to grant physicians absolute autonomy in abortion procedures:

> By no means must a State grant physicians "unfettered discretion" in their selection of abortion methods. But where substantial medical authority supports the proposition that banning a particular abortion procedure could endanger women's health, *Casey* requires the statute to include a health exception when the procedure is "necessary, in appropriate medical judgment, for the preservation of the life or health of the mother." [54]

The decision to overturn the Nebraska ban on the D&X procedure is a counterpoint to previous rulings discussed here in that it demonstrates the Court's willingness to overturn the most extreme examples of abortion restriction and defer to scientific knowledge. The case evidence deliberately and carefully analyzed the data offered by scientists and concluded that the method outlawed in Nebraska is sometimes the most respectful of women's health.

This outcome may give an indication of the possible resolution to the federal Partial-Birth Abortion Ban, which the Court agreed to hear in late 2005 in *Gonzales v. Carhart*.[55] The Nebraska statute and the Court's judgment of it left one question unanswered that could be revisited in *Gonzales*. In banning a procedure, but not late-term abortions per se, the State of Nebraska was reflecting recent Supreme Court dicta that embraces a state's interest in fetal life throughout pregnancy. A statute that was more respectful of the precedent set forth in *Roe* would have banned the procedure post-viability, and would have made an exception to protect women's health. That the state chose neither of those routes reveals much about how the states are interpreting and applying the *Webster* and *Casey* decisions.

It is worth remembering, however, that the partial-birth abortion case, *Gonzales v. Carhart,* will be heard by a remade Supreme Court. With Chief Justice Rehnquist's death, the Court lost one of its most vociferous opponents of abortion, who had dissented in *Carhart* and voted to uphold Nebraska's law. He has been replaced by John Roberts, whose full range of abortion opinion is yet untested. More intriguing still for the outcome of these pending cases is the retirement of O'Connor, a member of the five-member *Carhart* majority. The confirmation of Samuel J. Alito as O'Connor's successor leaves this an open question. As a judge of some fifteen years, Alito voted to allow Pennsylvania's husband notification law, and wrote briefs while serving as a Reagan administration official that demonstrate a desire to undercut abortion rights. The architect of the undue burden standard, O'Connor still leaves much of that standard's interpretation to her successor. Whether economic burdens and intrusions on the privacy of the physician-patient relationship will rise to a level of undue burden will largely be defined by this currently seated Court.

The nation got very little hint at the remade Court's approach to abortion in its first ruling on the subject. *Ayotte v. Planned Parenthood of Northern New England* (2006) involved a New Hampshire parental notification requirement that does not make an exception for a minor's health. With this ruling, the Roberts Court made one final abortion decision before O'Connor's replacement by Alito.[56]

Considered the first major case to be heard by the Court since *Casey*, *Ayotte* held abortion and fetal rights in the balance. By statute, the State of New Hampshire required an abortion provider to notify a parent forty-eight hours prior to a minor's abortion. The statute was especially controversial because it provides the physician with no exception for the protection of a girl's health. The only exception to the parental involvement requirement is the rare instance in which an abortion is needed immediately to save a girl's life, but not her health. The central question before the Court was whether this New Hampshire law created an undue burden on a girl's ability to secure an abortion.[57]

To the surprise of activists on both sides of the issue, the Court simply refused to consider the merits of the New Hampshire law, choosing instead to issue a unanimous slip opinion that sent the case back to a lower court. In her last opinion on the Court, O'Connor argued on behalf of her colleagues that the lower court had erred in its decision to enjoin the New Hampshire law because the law lacked a health exception. Arguing that the lower court had overstepped its bounds, the Supreme Court sidestepped the substantive issues at stake in the law and remanded the case to the lower court for reconsideration.

CONCLUSION

The Court's long-held tradition of upholding the physician's autonomy in abortion and contraceptive cases and its respect for physicians in protecting the primacy of women's health in considering restrictions on abortion was challenged in *Webster*, and the Court pulled back considerably from its prior arguments in its *Casey* ruling. By replacing *Roe*'s holding that abortion restrictions would be held to a standard of compelling state interest with *Casey*'s rubric of undue burden, the Court today posits less commitment in maintaining women's health interests as a guidepost in its rulings. Furthermore, the long tradition of deference to the medical community in determining best practices for abortion has been outflanked by the Court's assertion that the states should be allowed to express their preferences for birth over abortion in state law. Inklings of this development were seen in *Belloti v. Baird I* (1976) and *Maher*, and were certainly foreshadowed by O'Connor's dissent in *Akron* and *Thornburgh*. Developing the undue burden standard explicitly allows a state to establish a vested interest in fetal life throughout pregnancy (not just after viability, however determined), and allows the state to use this interest to trump both the physician's historic authority in medical practice as well as the state's interest in preserving women's health. And while *Carhart* provides an intriguing footnote in the deterioration of abortion rights, whether that case is known as a curious turn in the Court's perspective or merely as a bump in the road toward diminished rights will be settled in the near future. At the very least, it is fair to say that because of *Casey*, the Court has opened up the opportunity for state-sanctioned abortion restrictions that have altered the context of abortion, especially for the young and those with little money.

One unanswered question in *Casey* is whether, when considered together, a series of restrictions together present an undue burden. Up to now, the Court has considered restrictions only individually, overlooking the cumulative effect a series of restrictions can have on particular groups of women. The next two chapters allow the reader to take this macro-level view, observing from afar the combined effect of dozens of new abortion restrictions.

DISCUSSION QUESTIONS

1. Does the historic role of midwifery in abortion have an impact on how you think abortion should be viewed today (as more female-centered)? How and why have physicians altered this traditional view?

2. Is the shift over the last one hundred years in how conception is defined in the United States (as reflected by the Comstock cases and later in *Casey*) due more to technological advancement or changes in cultural values? Explain.
3. Do you believe that the right to privacy established in *Griswold* and later extended in *Roe* is a legitimate application of the Constitution? Why or why not?
4. Do you believe the trimester system of *Roe* is reasonable? What alternative framework, if any, would be more appropriate?
5. Why do you think *Roe* has been viewed as creating "abortion on demand"? Is this characterization fair? Why or why not?
6. If abortion is a fundamental right, is the Supreme Court justified in denying funding to exercise such a right?
7. What does the concept of an "undue burden" mean to you? How should such a principle be formulated at the highest levels of constitutional jurisprudence?
8. In your view, what lies ahead in abortion adjudication? Will the new Court accept or overturn the partial-birth abortion ban passed by Congress?

SUGGESTED READING

Balkin, Jack M., ed. *What* Roe v. Wade *Should Have Said: The Nation's Top Legal Experts Rewrite America's Most Controversial Decision.* New York: New York University Press, 2005.

Faux, Marian. Roe v. Wade: *The Untold Story of the Landmark Supreme Court Decision that Made Abortion Legal.* New York: Macmillan, 1988.

Garrow, David J. *Liberty and Sexuality: The Right to Privacy and the Making of* Roe v. Wade. New York: Macmillan, 1994.

Hull, N. E. H. Hull, and Peter Charles Hoffer. Roe v. Wade: *The Abortion Rights Controversy in American History.* Lawrence: University Press of Kansas, 2001.

McCorvey, Norma, with Andy Meisler. *I am Roe: My Life,* Roe v. Wade, *and Freedom of Choice.* New York: HarperCollins, 1994.

McDonagh, Eileen L., *Breaking the Abortion Deadlock: From Choice to Consent.* New York: Oxford University Press, 1996.

Tushnet, Mark. *Constitutional Issues: Abortion.* New York: Facts on File, 1996.

Weddington, Sarah. *A Question of Choice.* New York: Penguin Books, 1993.

NOTES

1. *Roe v. Wade,* 410 u.s. 113 (1973), 164.
2. *Planned Parenthood v. Casey,* 505 u.s. 833 (1992), 838.

3. James C. Mohr, *Abortion in America: the Origins and Evolution of National Policy* (Oxford, Oxford University Press, 1978).

4. *People v. Sanger,* 179 App. Div. 939, 166 N.Y.S. 1107 (1917).

5. *Margaret H. Sanger v. People of the State of New York,* 251 U.S. 537 (1919).

6. The official title of the Comstock Act of 1873 (17 Stat. 598) is Act for the Suppression of Trade in, and Circulation of, Obscene Literature and Articles for Immoral Use.

7. *United States v. One Package of Japanese Pessaries,* 86 F.2d 737 (1936).

8. The experiences and tactics of Margaret Sanger are revived through her grandson's recent book, *Beyond Choice: Reproductive Freedom in the 21st Century* (New York: PublicAffairs, 2004).

9. Ibid.

10. Kristin Luker, *Abortion and the Politics of Motherhood* (Berkeley: University of California Press, 1984).

11. *Griswold v. Connecticut,* 381 U.S 479 (1965).

12. See especially *Meyer v. State of Nebraska,* 262 U.S. 390 (1923); *Buck v. Bell,* 274 U.S. 200 (1927); *Olmstead v. United States,* 277 U.S. 438 (1928), and *Pierce v. Society of Sisters,* 268 U.S. 510 (1925).

13. It should not be lost on the reader that the concept of privacy is controversial among judicial as well as feminist scholars. For a sampling of the criticisms scholars have of the privacy concept, see especially Catherine MacKinnon, "Privacy v. Equality: Beyond *Roe v. Wade*," in *Feminism Unmodified: Discourses on Life and Law* (Cambridge: Harvard University Press, 1987) and John Hart Ely, "The Wages of Crying Wolf: A Comment on *Roe v. Wade*," *Yale Law Journal* 82 (1973): 920, 947.

14. *Roe v. Wade,* 410 U.S. 113 (1973).

15. Jon Hart Ely objects to the extension of federal power in the *Roe* ruling in his famous piece, "The Wages of Crying Wolf: A Comment on *Roe v. Wade*," *Yale Law Journal* 82 (1973): 920–49.

16. Of course, the pro-life movement quickly adopted this refrain, and has urged the passage of a constitutional amendment that would change the definition of personhood.

17. The term "amici," Latin for "friend," refers to a brief offered to the Court for consideration. See *Roe v. Wade,* 410 U.S. 113 (1973), 154.

18. *Roe v. Wade,* 410 U.S. 113 (1973), 164.

19. It is interesting to note that all Court references to physicians until 1989 are references to the male doctor, which may account in part for the Court's comfort in resting such deference there. See *Roe v. Wade,* 410 U.S. 113 (1973), 167.

20. MacKinnon, "Privacy v. Equality."

21. *Roe v. Wade,* 410 U.S. 113 (1965), 155.

22. *Planned Parenthood of Central Missouri v. Danforth,* 428 U.S. 52 (1976).
23. Ibid., 62.
24. Ibid., 66.
25. *City of Akron v. Akron Center for Reproductive Health, Inc.* 462 U.S. 416 (1983).
26. Ibid., 444.
27. Ibid., 446.
28. Ibid.
29. Ibid., 445.
30. *Thornburgh v. American College of Obstetricians and Gynecologists,* 476 U.S. 747 (1986).
31. Ibid., 765.
32. Ibid., 764.
33. Ibid., 760.
34. Ibid., 783.
35. See *Maher v. Roe,* 432 U.S. 464 (1977) and *Harris v. McRae,* 448 U.S. 297 (1980).
36. *Harris v. McRae,* 448 U.S. 297 (1980), 317.
37. Rickie Solinger, *Beggars and Choosers: How the Politics of Choice Shapes Adoption, Abortion, and Welfare in the United States* (New York: Hill and Wang, 2001).
38. *CQ Almanac* (Washington, D.C.: Congressional Quarterly 1976), 790.
39. *CQ Almanac* (Washington, D.C.: Congressional Quarterly, 1977), 308.
40. *Akron v Akron Center for Reproductive Health, Inc.,* 462 U.S. 416 (1983), 475.
41. *Webster v. Reproductive Health Services,* 492 U.S. 490 (1989).
42. Ibid., 511.
43. Ibid., 495.
44. Ibid., 521.
45. It is a curious fact that in the debates around her replacement on the Supreme Court, Justice O'Connor has been described by actors across the ideological spectrum as the "swing vote" on the Court. While she is most often described in the media as the Court's great moderate, especially in the arena of abortion, her construction of the undue burden standard might suggest that she has been active in dismantling abortion rights.
46. *Planned Parenthood of Southeastern P.A. v. Casey,* 505 U.S. 833 (1992).
47. Ibid.
48. Ibid., 871. Interestingly, the Courts are beginning to use the concept of undue burden in other areas of privacy doctrine. See, for instance, *Washington v. Glucksberg,* 521 U.S. 702 (1997).
49. See for instance N. E. Adler, et al, "Psychological Factors in Abortion: A Review," *American Psychologist* 47, no. 10 (1992): 1194–1204.
50. A good piece of the explanation for conservative trends in abortion politics comes from changes in the religious community's commitment to legal edu-

cation. In recent years, the United States has seen the endowment of Christian law schools, including Ave Maria, Liberty, Regents, and St. Thomas, funded by evangelicals, such as Pat Robertson, and the owner of Domino's Pizza Tom Monaghan, a strict adherent to traditional Roman Catholic doctrine. Although beyond the scope of this book, that development within the Christian Right movement is significant, and would predict additional encroachments on abortion rights and access.

51. *Stenberg et al v. Carhart*, 530 U.S. 914 (2000).

52. Ibid.

53. It is likely that some legislatures, both state and federal, will amend their D&X bans to include a health exception in order to satisfy the Court's ruling in *Carhart*. Since the procedure is used specifically for a woman's health, such a law would have little practical impact on provision; still, it would send a symbolic message of restriction to those keenly watching the abortion debate.

54. *Stenberg et al v. Carhart*, 530 U.S. 914 (2000), 938.

55. Two federal appeals courts have ruled the federal Partial-Birth Abortion Ban unconstitutional; on September 26, 2005, the Bush administration appealed one of these rulings to the Supreme Court. See *Gonzales v. Carhart* No. 05-380. The Court did accept the case for review and is expected to issue its ruling in 2006 or 2007.

56. *Ayotte, Attorney General of New Hampshire v. Planned Parenthood of Northern New England et al.* No. 04-1144.

57. The Court could have considered a second, more obscure question: whether it can rule on the constitutionality of a law before it has been applied. For most of America's legal history, the Court refrained from ruling on a question unless individuals could prove they had been adversely affected. In recent years, the Court has accepted cases for review that were immediately enjoined upon enactment. That was true in *Ayotte*: there was no specific girl claiming a personal injury as a result of the law; rather, interest groups sued on behalf of those who would feel the law's effect. While an obscure topic, it is one the Court could take up in a future abortion ruling, and while obscure, this line of questioning could have the greatest reach because the Court could ultimately return to its historic position and require personal injury before plaintiffs receive standing to sue.

CHAPTER 3

Abortion Restrictions in the States

"Contained within the single cell who I once was is the totality of everything I am today."

—Dr. John Willke, National Right to Life Committee[1]

"Defending the unborn with force is considerably more than an idea whose time has come, it is a biblical duty whose time has come."

—Paul Hill, convicted of murdering Dr. John Britton and his bodyguard[2]

"I delivered babies for ten years . . there's no reason why people who have abortions shouldn't have the same compassion and treatment as those who have babies."

—Dr. Peter Bours, Portland, Oregon

With the increased latitude the Supreme Court has given to states in restricting the availability of abortion, many states have pursued new restrictions in recent years. When the Court ruled that states could advocate for birth over abortion in their policies, and that they had a vested interest in fetal life before viability, the major pro-life groups in this country, including the National Right to Life Committee, the Christian Coalition, the Catholic Conference, and Concerned Women for America, and their local affiliates got to work in state legislatures and through initiative processes across the nation.[3] Subsequently, they have had a significant impact on abortion policy at the state level. This chapter documents the state-level changes to abortion law and practice and provides an indication of some of the consequences of these policy shifts.

The states have historically governed all social policies as part of their "police powers," so it should be expected that state governments would be the logical location of abortion debates and policy. The Founders believed that issues of such personal and moral implications should be left to governments closer to the people, where they might be able to experiment with policies that reflect local culture and priorities. As a consequence, abortion law and practice were governed exclusively by the states until 1873, when Congress passed the Comstock Act. The states asserted their historic social policy role by passing statutory restrictions on abortion for most of the twentieth century, however, and have continued to regulate abortion today despite the recent interest by Congress in the subject (see chapter 4).

In some ways, the states today are locked in conflict with the national branches of government for control of abortion policy. Given the politics of social regulatory policy described in the Introduction, it is no coincidence that political actors at all levels are participating in the debate. This ongoing grappling for control between the federal and state governments will continue unabated unless the Supreme Court specifically returns control exclusively to the states in a future case or definitively establishes the parameters of all abortion policy, neither of which is a likely possibility.

As noted in the Introduction, pro-life strategies of the 1970s and 1980s included attempts to create a federal statutory or constitutional protection for fetal life; that strategy, while heartfelt for many activists, met with little success. As the public opinion poll data in chapter 1 reveal, most Americans support legal, but regulated, abortion law. After two decades of little progress and with the founding of the Christian Coalition in 1989, pro-life advocates changed course, embracing instead a strategy of incrementalism. This strategy has enjoyed much greater success at the state level, where pro-life groups began running "stealth candidates" for local offices, thereby increasing their electoral representation slowly over time.

Pro-life groups have pursued a savvy strategy of targeting those areas for which there is the least public support for abortion. As seen in chapter 1, late-term abortions, teen abortions, and abortions for socioeconomic reasons have the least public support, making regulations in these areas more palatable to moderate America, and easier for conservative activists to advocate. These statutory barriers can be viewed as a measure of the Christian Right's recent victories, but they are more than that: these barriers are the harbinger of greater restrictions on abortion, possibly in areas that will provoke greater resistance. Furthermore, while these restrictions do not create a declarative citizenship for fetuses, when viewed cumulatively, they offer state-endorsed fetal protection at the expense of the social citizenship of women.

This chapter documents both the practical barriers to abortion access and the wide variety of statutory barriers to abortion at the state level. Although the practical barriers do not have the force of law, they are equally—if not more—effective than the law in limiting the range of options women today have available to them. The growth of such practical barriers should be viewed as a heretofore unnoticed and highly effective political strategy of the pro-life movement.

The political impact of statutory barriers cannot be overlooked. When considered individually, they appear innocuous to the casual observer. When viewed cumulatively, however, the statutory obstacles to abortion create a patchwork quilt of state policies and practical circumstances that look similar to the pre-*Roe* era of abortion policy. The sum of these impediments clearly debunks the myth that abortion is available "on demand" and undermines the social citizenship of women. Still, one of the most significant consequences of these barriers is that they affect women specifically based on their region of residence, age, and economic status.

PRACTICAL BARRIERS TO ABORTION ACCESS

Some of the practical barriers to abortion are those that have the greatest impact on women's lives. It may be an obvious point, but without a sufficient number of doctors willing to provide abortions, women will not be able to have this medical need met. A little-known, but potentially decisive, barrier to access is the diminishing number of abortion providers in the United States. In addition, providers are increasingly concentrated in metropolitan areas, leaving women in outlying areas without access to skilled assistance. As a business matter, many in this field argue that it takes a population in excess of two hundred thousand to make a viable clinic business, leading independent clinics to locate in urban cores.[4] The impact of this trend on women's access has yet to be fully considered by the Court under its recently adopted undue burden standard.

Location of Providers

Table 3.1 documents the thinning number of counties in which abortion providers are located. Between 1992 and 2000 alone, women in the United States lost 11 percent of their abortion providers, leaving 87 percent of all counties without a single provider. Thirty-four percent of all women in this country live in those counties. Particular regions of the country have more providers than others. Specifically, the Midwest and the South have the greatest paucity of providers; in those areas of the country, more than 90 percent of counties do not have a single provider. Women seeking abortions in the Northeast and West fare the best; half of these women live in counties with at least one provider.

Table 3.2 breaks this data down a little further to demonstrate the precipitous decline of providers in particular states. Georgia, Kansas, Kentucky, Missouri, and Tennessee have a serious dearth of providers, losing more than half between 1992 and 2000. Kentucky, in fact, lost 77 percent. The declining number of abortion providers presents real challenges to women living in these communities, although women in some small communities might prefer the anonymity of traveling to an urban center for an abortion over seeking one in their local area.[5]

TABLE 3.1
Number of Abortion Providers by Region, 1992, 1996, and 2000

| | Number of Providers | | | | | Counties, 2000 | | |
| | | | | | | | Without a Provider | |
Region	1992	1996	2000	% Change 1996–2000	Total	% Counties	% of Women
Northeast	620	562	536	−5	217	50	16
Midwest	260	212	188	−11	1,055	94	49
South	620	505	442	−12	1,425	91	45
West	880	763	653	−14	444	78	15
U.S. Total	**2,380**	**2,042**	**1,819**	**−11**	**3,141**	**87**	**34**

Source: Lawrence B. Finer and Stanley K. Henshaw, "Abortion Incidence and Services in the United States in 2000," *Perspectives on Sexual and Reproductive Health* 35, no. 1 (2003): 6–15.

Still, the absence of a provider leads to a number of logistical, economic, and health-related dilemmas that cannot be overlooked. The lack of a local provider can cause women to delay their abortions, which increases both the cost and risk of the procedure to their own health. Many women delay their abortions because of the cost of the procedure. Such a delay leads to a spiraling set of circumstances in which proximity, gestational development, and even greater cost conspire to make the abortion both more expensive and complicated with each passing week. Many of these difficulties could be mitigated by the presence of a local provider.

Interestingly, delaying an abortion later into the pregnancy also decreases the public's support for a woman's right to have the procedure, leaving her in a moral bind that might have been avoided had both a provider and money been available earlier. One in four women surveyed reported that they traveled fifty miles or more to their abortion provider, and 8 percent had to travel in excess of one hundred miles.[6] For many of these women, the nearest provider may be in a neighboring state, and as a result, some women cross state lines to obtain legal and safe abortions.[7]

Competition and Profit Margins

Another complicating factor in the provider decline is that decreasing abortion rates have created greater competition between existing providers in urban centers. While there may be too few providers in the countryside, there may be too many in the cities. Some of the country's independent providers who have been in business for decades are finding that they cannot compete with Planned Parenthood. This organization is a formidable competitor in part because it is subsidized by its foundation, and can therefore afford to offer abortions at a lower cost than

TABLE 3.2
Number of Abortion Providers by State, 1992 and 2000

State	Number of Providers		% Change 1992–2000	Without a Provider	
	1992	2000		% Counties	% Women
Alabama	20	14	−30	93	59
Alaska	13	7	−46	85	39
Arizona	28	21	−25	80	18
Arkansas	8	7	−12	97	79
California	554	400	−28	41	4
Colorado	59	40	−32	78	26
Connecticut	43	50	16	25	9
Delaware	8	9	13	33	17
District of Columbia	15	15	0	0	0
Florida	133	108	−19	70	19
Georgia	55	26	−53	94	56
Hawaii	52	51	−2	0	0
Idaho	9	7	−22	93	67
Illinois	47	37	−21	90	30
Indiana	19	15	−21	93	62
Iowa	11	8	−27	95	64
Kansas	15	7	−53	96	54
Kentucky	9	3	−77	98	75
Louisiana	17	13	−23	92	61
Maine	17	15	−12	63	45
Maryland	51	42	−18	67	24
Massachusetts	64	47	−27	21	7
Michigan	70	50	−29	83	31
Minnesota	14	11	−21	95	58
Mississippi	8	4	−50	98	86
Missouri	12	6	−50	97	71
Montana	12	9	−33	91	43
Nebraska	9	5	−44	97	46
Nevada	17	13	−24	82	10
New Hampshire	16	14	−12	50	26
New Jersey	88	86	−2	10	3
New Mexico	20	11	−45	88	48
New York	289	234	−19	42	8
North Carolina	86	55	−36	78	44
North Dakota	1	2	100	98	77
Ohio	45	35	−22	91	50
Oklahoma	11	6	−45	96	56

(Table continues on next page)

TABLE 3.2 *(continued)*
Number of Abortion Providers by State, 1992 and 2000

State	Number of Providers		% Change 1992–2000	Without a Provider	
	1992	2000		% Counties	% Women
Oregon	40	34	−15	78	26
Pennsylvania	81	73	−10	75	39
Rhode Island	6	6	0	80	39
South Carolina	18	10	−44	87	66
South Dakota	1	2	100	98	78
Tennessee	33	16	−51	94	56
Texas	79	65	−18	93	32
Utah	6	4	−33	93	51
Vermont	16	11	−31	43	23
Virginia	64	46	−28	84	47
Washington	65	53	−18	74	17
West Virginia	5	3	−40	96	83
Wisconsin	16	10	−37	93	62
Wyoming	5	3	−40	91	88
U.S. Total	**2,380**	**1,819**	**−24**	**87**	**34**

Source: Lawrence B. Finer and Stanley K. Henshaw, "Abortion Incidence and Services in the United States in 2000," *Perspectives on Sexual and Reproductive Health* 35, no. 1 (2003): 6–15.

independent clinics can. What is more, Planned Parenthood has been offering the abortion procedure at more of its clinics, and as the nation's largest provider, probably has better name recognition than smaller, private clinics.

For example, Peter Bours, a physician in Oregon, reports that new Planned Parenthood franchises in his area are making one of his offices financially untenable; whereas he once provided one hundred or more abortions per month in his Portland office, he now performs around twenty. Referring to Planned Parenthood as the "Walmart of abortion clinics," Bours contends that the larger providers offer inferior services, and that as a result women are being poorly served by the expansion of the organization in abortion provision. Although very competitive in terms of price, Bours maintains that their level of care is lower, and that patients often see clinicians with less training than physicians at smaller facilities might have.[8]

Interestingly, the low cost of the abortion procedure discourages many physicians from offering it in their private practices. The price has not kept pace with the rising costs of other medical procedures and services, creating even greater economic disincentives for young doctors to enter this field. A $300 abortion in 1972 dollars should have cost $2,251 in 2000, yet recent studies reveal the median price for a surgical abortion at ten weeks gestation in 2001 was $370, barely above the price of thirty years prior. When coupled with the rising rates of medical malpractice insurance and security systems, it is clear that some providers will be financially strained if they offer abortion services. While discount providers like Planned Parenthood may be holding down costs in order to make abortions affordable to more women, in the end these "good intentions" may be contributing to the overall decline of abortion access.

Of all abortions performed, only 26 percent are billed to a private or public insurance program.[9] That means that 74 percent of the procedures are paid for out of pocket. Relatively reasonable rates for the abortion procedure would seem to be an obvious benefit for the women procuring them, but that might not be so if the clinics are unable to keep their doors open. And regardless of whether or not the costs of abortion services have kept apace with other medical services, that price tag is still prohibitive to a number of low-income women.

All of this said, a few states actually do have more abortion providers today than they did in 1992. Upon closer inspection, however, it can be seen that these percentage increases are somewhat misleading: both North and South Dakota increased their number of providers during this time span by 100 percent, but did so by going from one to two abortion providers—not exactly a big enough increase to offset the losses in neighboring states. In addition, South Dakota has the most restrictive state laws in regard to access to public funding, so it would be inaccurate to argue that the state is a frontrunner in helping to increase women's access to abortion services.

The Graying of a Generation

Another factor contributing to provider decline is the plain fact that the providers who remember the days before legal abortion are aging. This "graying" of the first-generation abortion providers of the post-*Roe* era is no small contributor to the looming provider shortage. Fifty-seven percent of abortion providers were fifty years old or older in 1997.[10] They continue to provide abortions because they remember the specter of the septic wards before *Roe v. Wade*. These were the days when hospitals were so burdened by botched illegal and self-executed procedures that they created special wards for the sick and dying women who appeared in their emergency rooms. Still, these doctors are retiring and dying, and younger physicians are not filling their ranks.

In a private interview, Dr. Elizabeth Newhall expressed her frustration with her obstetrician-gynecologist colleagues who do not perform abortions, naming their ambivalence as the number one barrier to abortion provision today. "I am not respectful of my own profession . . . why are there not more of my colleagues who care about this passionately?" By way of explanation, this abortion provider argued that too many ob-gyns would prefer to let clinics handle abortions because it is a procedure that offers little professional or monetary reward.[11] Dr. Siglinda Jacobsen of the Oregon Health Science University agrees. "If I'm going to be an ob-gyn, these are my patients. I need to do these for my patients and not just say, 'oh well, that's fine but go see somebody else,' because that's dumping them when they're in need." [12] By mainstreaming abortion care back into larger practices, Newhall argues that abortion patients and providers would not be targets of violence, and the level and availability of overall care would improve.

Anti-Abortion Extremism and Violence

The wave of anti-abortion extremism in the 1980s and 1990s also helps explain the declining number of providers. The rise of a small wing of extremists in the past decades has fundamentally changed the environment in which doctors choose their specialties. Although violent protesters are by far the minority of the pro-life movement, this vocal group embraces violence as a means to reduce what it sees as the violence of abortion.

Whereas most of the movement's leaders prefer legislative and judicial strategies over violent action, the more militant individuals within the group grew frustrated with the lack of impact these strategies had in the 1970s and 1980s. When Joseph Scheidler of the Pro-Life Action League in Chicago published his *Closed: 99 Ways to Stop Abortion* in 1985, instructing activists to take a more active approach to preventing abortion, the movement's extremists responded.[13] One individual in particular took notice: Randall Terry founded Operation Rescue in 1987 in order to physically block women from accessing abortion clinics, thereby "rescuing" fetuses from abortion while simultaneously shaming women for choosing to have the procedure.[14]

Seven abortion providers have been murdered in the United States as a result of these radical leaders and their influence over like-minded extremists. And there have been many more attempted murders, bombings, and letters containing anthrax. A sixteen-year-old abortion patient in Palm Desert, California, was shot in her spinal cord in April 2004, leaving her a quadriplegic. Convicted clinic terrorist Clayton Waagner describes himself in this way, "It's been clearly demonstrated that I am the anti-abortion extremist, a terrorist to the abortion industry. There's no question there that I terrorized these people any way I could." [15]

If the perpetrators of these crimes are intent upon creating an atmosphere of fear so as to dissuade individuals from working in this field, it seems to be working. According to Dr. Warren Hern of San Francisco, "I walk out of my office and the first thing I do is look at the parking garage that the hospital built two doors away and see if there is a sniper on the roof. I basically expect to be shot any day." [16] Doctors in residency programs have received their share of threats as well. Extremist organization Life Dynamics distributed a "joke book" pamphlet to thirty-three thousand medical students, recommending that providers should be shot, killed by dogs, and buried in concrete. Another pamphlet entitled "RU Crazy? One Little Pill Could Destroy Your Medical Practice," warns doctors who provide pharmaceutical abortions that it will end their careers.[17]

The leaders of such mainstream pro-life organizations as National Right to Life and Concerned Women for America distance themselves from these extreme acts of violence. Other groups and individuals, however, embrace the use of violence, as has been noted. Some, like Paul Hill of Advocates for Life Ministries in Portland, Oregon, have written extensively about "justifiable homicide," using biblical passages as support for killing a physician and his bodyguard outside a Pensacola, Florida, clinic.[18]

One of the most widely recognized and well known of these violent abortion tactics involves the Nuremberg Files Web site, which lists a "Deadly Dozen" hit-list style poster with the personal information of abortion providers across the country. The site has included such information as providers' license plate numbers, their work schedules, and the names and birth dates of family members, such as that of Dr. Newhall. Newhall and her children were featured on the "Deadly Dozen" poster in the 1990s. Her clinic was shot at, and although she writes that "My name on their pathetic hit list scares me much less than the prospect of living in a world where women do not have control of their reproductive destinies," [19] the experience impacted her personally and professionally, "The fact is, I did put in bulletproof glass. I did wear a bulletproof vest. I did borrow friends' cars. I did wear disguises in and out of clinic." [20] The Web site's accompanying legend lists working providers in black font and wounded providers in gray; the names of murdered providers are struck through with black lines. In 2003, the Supreme Court let stand a Ninth Circuit Court ruling that the site did not constitute protected speech, as it indicated a real threat to the doctors involved.[21]

Still, the work of Nuremberg Files' creator Neal Horsley has not been deterred entirely. Most recently, Horsley launched a Webcast feed of abortion clinic entrances nationwide, asking supporters to photograph women coming and going from them. Despite court orders prohibiting these sites, Horsley's work continues to reappear on the Web; he has relaunched his sites repeatedly, using different Web service providers each time until expelled. Neither the Nuremberg Files site nor the Webcast are currently running, although his Christian Gallery News Service continues to post disturbing violent images aimed at abortion access supporters when it can find a host for its site.[22]

The violence and threats of violence faced by abortion providers and clinic workers continue to be a feature of contemporary abortion politics. Figure 3.1 documents the number of clinic violence episodes per year in this country.[23] While

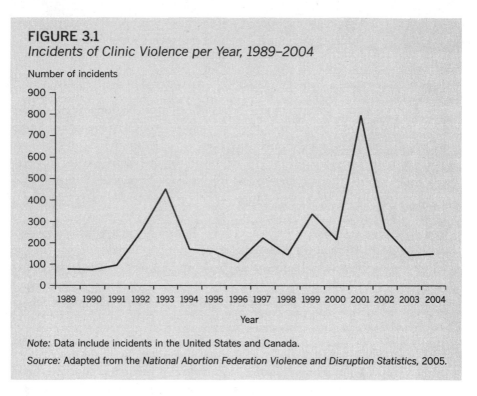

FIGURE 3.1
Incidents of Clinic Violence per Year, 1989–2004

Note: Data include incidents in the United States and Canada.

Source: Adapted from the *National Abortion Federation Violence and Disruption Statistics, 2005.*

the figure clearly demonstrates that the violence has ebbed and flowed sporadically, and seems in decline recently, the specter of that possibility still lingers with many providers.[24] The graph begins in 1989, the year the Court ruled in *Webster* and the pro-life movement was reinvigorated. In 1992–1993, there was a spike in violence just after the Court handed down its ruling in *Casey*. The largest number of violent incidents occurred in 2001, just after the Court ruled that the Nebraska partial-birth abortion ban was unconstitutional and the debate in Congress over similar legislation began heating up. Given all of this, the incidence of clinic violence appears to be event driven.

A number of factors might explain the sharp decline in clinic violence in 2002. One is presumably related to President Clinton's unprecedented use of the FBI to investigate clinic violence cases. In addition, the mainstream pro-life organizations distanced themselves from the radical, violent activists, possibly diminishing the boldness of the extremists. Finally, some have suggested that the drop in violence is directly related to the movement's legislative successes.

Both local law enforcement and the federal government responded to the spreading clinic violence of the 1980s. Many clinics successfully sought injunctions and restraining orders against the most disruptive protesters, and Congress

FIGURE 3.2
Incidence of Clinic Blockades per Year, 1989–2004

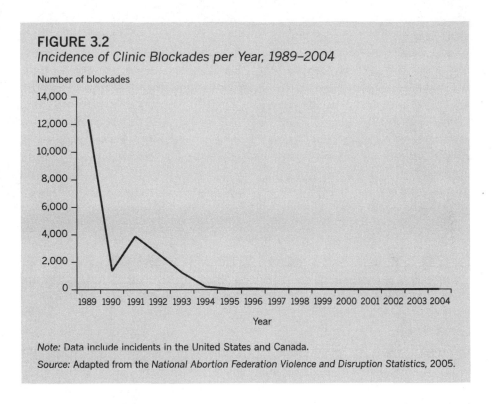

Number of blockades

Note: Data include incidents in the United States and Canada.

Source: Adapted from the *National Abortion Federation Violence and Disruption Statistics,* 2005.

passed legislation that made it illegal to block the entrance to a clinic during the course of a demonstration. The object of this legislation is to allow women greater dignity and safety while they pass through disruptive crowds en route to their appointments. Indeed, a brief period of unified Democratic government allowed that party to advance the 1994 Freedom of Access to Clinic Entrances law (FACE), which is directly responsible for the declining number of violent outbursts and blockades at clinics, actions which became federal crimes with the passage of the legislation.

Figure 3.2 illustrates the promise that protective legislation holds for women's clinics. Clinic blockades were common prior to the FACE Act, but with it, they have nearly disappeared. Only the most committed protesters are willing to go to jail and face federal charges. Federal action can and does impact the safety of clinics.

Clinic blockades were seriously curtailed by FACE, but other types of clinic disruptions remain commonplace. Figure 3.3 documents the nonviolent harassment that clinic staff and providers face on a nearly daily basis. Included are such actions as hate mail and harassing phone calls, e-mail or Internet harassment, hoax devices or suspicious packages, bomb threats, and picketing. The data indi-

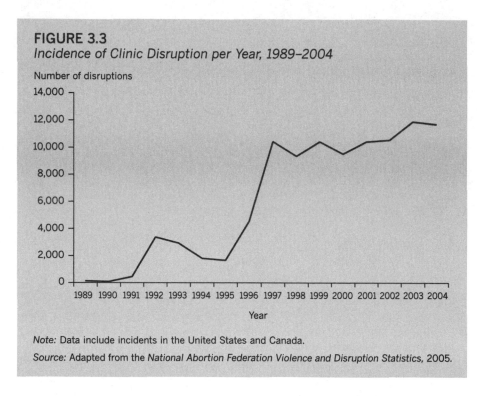

FIGURE 3.3
Incidence of Clinic Disruption per Year, 1989–2004

Number of disruptions

Note: Data include incidents in the United States and Canada.

Source: Adapted from the *National Abortion Federation Violence and Disruption Statistics*, 2005.

cate that while FACE contributed to a declining number of blockades, a rising number of other clinic disruptions resulted. This ultimately indicates the limited effectiveness of that legislation.

Pro-Choice Advocates Respond

In addition to pursuing legislative and law enforcement channels, pro-access groups such as NARAL Pro-Choice America (formerly National Abortion Repeal Action League) and NOW (National Organization for Women) attempted to use another tool against protesters: the Racketeer Influenced and Corrupt Organizations Act (RICO), a federal extortion statute. Their argument was that the tactics of abortion protesters are similar to extortion because they are designed to inhibit the business of abortion. For their part, pro-life protesters countered that RICO does not apply to their activities, as protesters were never trying to profit financially from their actions. The Supreme Court settled this question in 2003, ruling that abortion protesters did not violate the RICO law.[25] The Court had ruled in a similar fashion a decade earlier, when the majority concluded that a 1871 civil rights statute being used in Virginia to enjoin protesters from their activities did not apply to abortion protests.[26]

Pro-rights activists have met with more success in utilizing state law to create "buffer zones" around clinics and the individuals entering them. Similar to FACE, such statutes require protesters to remain a designated distance from the clinic, permitting women to walk in and out without harassment or threat of violence. These policies also force protesters to increase their numbers to have the same impact at a given location. Some have argued that this restriction inhibits the expression of free speech; the Court, however, has disagreed, ruling in three different cases that reasonably sized buffer zones permit free political dissent while simultaneously protecting women's right to enter a clinic safely.[27]

Most recently, advocates of clinic access have taken up their cause through a rather unusual venue: bankruptcy laws. In 2002, Democratic senator Charles Schumer of New York introduced a provision into a bankruptcy bill that would have denied bankruptcy protection to those using violence against clinics. The amendment passed the Senate in that year, but fell in the House. The amendment failed again in 2005.[28]

A Lack of Education

Another significant factor that discourages young doctors from practicing abortion, and one that has gained particular attention in recent years, is the lack of abortion training in medical schools in the United States. After years of classroom and lab work, medical students begin to specialize their education through intern and residency programs. Two specialty tracts would seem to lend themselves to training in abortion procedures: obstetrics and gynecology and family practice. Recent surveys of residency program directors, however, indicate that a decreasing percentage of those programs require their students to complete training in abortion procedures. In a 1995 survey of chief residents in family practice training programs, 74 percent reported that they had had no training whatsoever in first-trimester, vacuum aspiration abortions, the most common procedure practiced. Eighty-five percent indicated they had no clinical (or hands-on) experience in the procedure; only 3 percent had completed ten or more such cases.[29]

In fact, the low number of family medicine residents receiving abortion training may simply reflect the current realities of abortion provision. In contrast to earlier eras, the vast majority of abortions today are performed not in private physicians' offices or hospitals, but instead in free-standing clinics.[30] Family medicine practitioners are more likely to be affiliated with offices that do not normally provide abortion services. Knowing this is likely to be the case, the residents themselves might not seek out the training. Add to this the fact that there has been a huge decrease in the overall number of students entering into family medicine. Rural communities and low-income urban areas are having an especially difficult time getting family doctors to move to their areas and stay. So, between the reduced number of students entering the specialty and the reduced number of this total learning abortion procedures, abortion access for many women is nonexistent.

Still, training family practitioners to perform abortion has many advantages. A primary care provider is in a position to fully understand the complexity of a patient's situation: her family status, her economic condition, and her overall health picture. All of the major variables that go into a woman's abortion decision are known to the family doctor. What is more, some abortions are performed as emergencies: women face a host of health risks during pregnancy that can become life threatening. And, as one physician I interviewed pointed out, physicians who wish not to perform abortions may still need to counsel their patients about it.[31]

The fact that a large number of these physicians no longer provide abortion services means that a woman's abortion procedure is isolated from her larger health and wellness, even though the technical skills required are useful to other routine aspects of gynecological care.[32] For circumstances in which an abortion is necessary to save the life or health of the mother, a woman may find no one available at her local hospital who has practiced the procedure regularly enough to be proficient, which may in the future present a legal liability to hospitals.

In contemporary medicine it is more common today that an obstetrician-gynecologist would be expected to perform an abortion. However, there has been a decline in the number of ob-gyn residencies requiring abortion training as well. A 1991–1992 study of residency programs in obstetrics and gynecology found that 70 percent offered abortion training, but only 12 percent offered it routinely.[33] In response to that finding, the Accreditation Council for Graduate Medical Education (ACGME) adopted a requirement in 1996 that all ob-gyn residency programs offer standard abortion training. When abortion opponents in the majority party in Congress threatened legislation that would remove federal support for medical schools complying with the new ACGME abortion training requirement, the ACGME reworded its requirement so that it *encouraged* the adoption of regular clinical training in abortion.

If physicians in the two specialty areas most likely to face abortion requests (and possibly emergencies) are not trained in abortion provision, women seeking safe abortions may soon face a dubious public health environment. When in 1996 the recently founded Medical Students for Choice began advocating for more consistent abortion training, many medical schools responded of their own accord. A 1998 study of residency programs demonstrates that 81 percent of programs at that time offered first-trimester abortion instruction and 46 percent offered it routinely.[34] This does mark a substantial increase in the number of programs offering abortion training; but merely offering that training is not necessarily sufficient, when the larger context of medical school is taken into consideration.

For those students who face optional abortion training in their residency programs, the incentives to decline are powerful. Residents work grueling hours. One report indicates that the average resident works eighty hours per week, including two nights on call.[35] The process of having to procure one's own abortion training, often at a location, such as Planned Parenthood, that may be far from the place of one's residency, presents a burden to residents already facing enormous work pressures. In addition, most residents get very little compensation and often are faced with paying off student loans totaling hundreds of thousands of dollars—they literally may not be able to afford the expense of commuting to and from training. Some also have their own moral and religious objections to the procedure.[36] Finally, many residents who do receive abortion training may not be educated as to *why* the procedure is a necessary part of their future practice. As the pre-*Roe* era practitioners retire, and their stories of septic wards retire with them, fewer young doctors have a sense for why the procedure is needed.[37]

Pharmacists as Roadblocks to Abortion

A new barrier to abortion access is emerging in the twenty-first century: the local pharmacist. With the rise of both emergency contraception and medical abortion, the neighborhood pharmacy has become a new political frontier in the abortion battle. Much attention has been paid recently to cases of pharmacists refusing to fill prescriptions for Plan B, or the "morning after" pill, the emergency contraception pill that prevents implantation of a fertilized egg. In refusing to fill these legal prescriptions, pharmacists reveal an interesting trend toward seeing the beginning of pregnancy at earlier and earlier phases of development. Pregnancy, according to standard medical definitions, begins with the implantation of a fertilized egg in a woman's uterus. However, the pharmacists who refuse contraception are pushing this definition back to fertilization. From a medical standpoint, Plan B is contraception, or prevention of pregnancy, not an abortion. Still, the difficulty some women face in receiving this form of contraception indicates the increasing role pharmacies and their employees have in the abortion debate. Ironically, denying a woman access to emergency contraception may result in an abortion.

The practical barriers to abortion described here are so ingrained in medical provision and popular culture that they tend to go unnoticed. Whereas statutory barriers are often covered by the media, most of the practical barriers providers face in abortion provision are insidious. It is these barriers that are largely responsible for the declining number of abortion providers in this country, and that ultimately may prove more effective in cutting back the number of abortions in the United States than any of the following statutory restrictions. Interestingly, these practical hurdles to provision are seldom the subject of judicial review, so while they cumulatively may create an undue burden on women's reasonable access to legal and safe abortion (or in this case, contraception), they are hurdles difficult to address through traditional methods of governance and advocacy.

STATUTORY BARRIERS TO ABORTION ACCESS

By far the most common barriers to abortion are those erected in state legislatures by way of *Webster v. Reproductive Health Services* (1989) and *Casey Planned Parenthood of Southeastern P.A. v. Casey* (1992). Table 3.3 contains a list of the variety of abortion restrictions imposed by the states. As the table indicates, some of these restrictions are quite common and their meaning self-apparent. In other cases, including those found in Appendix A, the barrier and its implication require some explanation.

Illegal and Unenforceable Barriers

The first barrier listed is in truth a *potential* barrier. Statutory state bans on abortion—either throughout pregnancy or during some significant portion of pregnancy—are entirely unenforceable because they are presently unconstitutional. In some cases these laws were on the books before *Roe v. Wade,* and state legislatures have allowed them to languish there, ineffective. Other bans, however, were recently adopted. Called "trigger laws," some states have adopted presently unconstitutional abortion bans in order to have them in place if *Roe v. Wade* should ever be overturned. If that were to happen, these currently latent statutes would become enforceable without further legislative action. Through his two Supreme Court appointments, President George W. Bush may have significantly changed the balance of views on the Court, and the future of *Roe* may hang in the balance. In fact, the act of placing restrictive laws on the books now, while abortion is legal, is very savvy political strategy: if *Roe* should fall, the climate for lawmaking will be highly charged, and pro-choice activists inevitably would be highly motivated. Debating these legislations today, while the possibility of restriction seems relatively remote and while rights advocates are less mobilized, creates a more favorable political environment for passage should circumstances change.

With an intention of testing the new Court's commitment to *Roe v. Wade,* in 2006 South Dakota became the first state in the nation to pass an outright legislative ban on abortion. Supporters of the law cite Justice Samuel Alito's elevation to the bench as a motivation for their actions; they are hoping that the law, which will most certainly be challenged in court, will be cause for the Supreme Court to overturn *Roe v. Wade.* The South Dakota law would make all abortions except those needed to save women's lives illegal, irrespective of gestational development or a woman's health. Provision of an abortion in non-life threatening cases would result in physician fines and a prison sentence. In response to the ban, Cecilia Fire Thunder, chief of the Oglala Sioux Nation located on the state's Pine Ridge Indian Reservation, pledged to offer abortions within the borders of the reservation if the

TABLE 3.3
Abortion Restrictions by State

State	Abortion Ban	Husband Consent or Notification	Mandatory Counseling	Waiting Period	Minor Consent or Notification	TRAP Laws	Hospitals-Only	Physicians-Only	Gag Rules	Refusal Clause	Medicaid Ban	Insurance Ban
Alabama	X-3		X	X	X-1	X		X	X	X	X	
Alaska	X-3		X		X-1, 3	X	X	X		X		
Arizona	X-3				X-1	X		X	X	X	X	
Arkansas	X-3		X	X	X-1	X	X	X		X		
California					X-1, 3			X		X		X
Colorado	X-3	X-3			X-2			X		X	X	X
Connecticut						X		X		X		
Delaware	X-3		X-3	X	X-2	X	X	X		X	X	
District of Columbia												
Florida	X-3		X-3		X-2, 3	X		X		X	X	
Georgia					X-2	X	X	X		X	X	
Hawaii						X	X	X		X		
Idaho	X-3		X	X	X-1, 3	X		X		X	X	X
Illinois	X-3	X-3			X-2, 3	X		X	X	X		X
Indiana	X-3		X	X	X-1	X	X	X	X	X	X	
Iowa	X-3				X-2	X		X		X	X	
Kansas			X		X-2					X	X	
Kentucky	X-3	X-3	X-4	X	X-1	X		X	X	X	X	X
Louisiana	X-3	X-3	X	X	X-1	X		X	X	X	X	
Maine			X		X-1			X		X		
Maryland					X-2			X	X	X		
Massachusetts	X-3		X	X-3	X-1	X	X	X	X	X	X	X
Michigan	X-3		X	X	X-1	X		X	X	X	X	
Minnesota			X	X	X-2	X		X	X	X		
Mississippi	X-3		X-3	X-3	X-1	X	X	X	X	X	X	X
Missouri	X-3		X-3	X-3	X-1		X	X		X	X	X
Montana			X-3	X-3	X-2, 3			X		X		
Nebraska	X-3		X	X	X-2			X	X	X	X	X

(Table continues on next page)

TABLE 3.3 (continued)
Abortion Restrictions by State

State	Abortion Ban	Husband Consent or Notification	Mandatory Counseling	Waiting Period	Minor Consent or Notification	TRAP Laws	Hospitals-Only	Physicians-Only	Gag Rules	Refusal Clause	Medicaid Ban	Insurance Ban
Nevada					X-2, 3	X	X	X		X	X	
New Hampshire					X-2, 3						X	
New Jersey	X-3				X-2, 3	X	X	X		X		
New Mexico	X-3				X-1, 3			X		X		
New York						X	X	X		X		
North Carolina					X-1	X	X	X		X	X	
North Dakota	X-3	X-3	X	X	X-1	X	X	X	X-3	X	X	X
Ohio	X-3		X	X	X-2	X	X	X	X	X	X	X-3
Oklahoma	X-3				X-1, 3	X	X	X		X	X	X
Oregon										X		
Pennsylvania	X-3	X-3	X	X	X-1	X	X	X	X	X	X	X
Rhode Island	X-3	X-3	X		X-1	X	X	X		X	X	X-3
South Carolina	X-3	X-3	X	X	X-1	X	X	X	X	X	X	X
South Dakota	X-3		X	X	X-2	X	X	X		X	X	
Tennessee	X-3		X-3	X-3	X-1	X	X	X		X	X	
Texas			X	X	X-2	X		X		X	X	
Utah	X-3	X-3	X	X	X-2	X	X	X		X	X	
Vermont	X-3									X		
Virginia	X-3		X	X	X-1	X	X	X	X	X	X	X
Washington								X		X		
West Virginia	X-3		X	X	X-2					X	X	
Wisconsin	X-3		X	X	X-1	X	X	X	X	X	X	X
Wyoming					X-1			X		X		

Note:
1. State requires parental consent of either one or two parents.
2. State requires parental notice of either one or two parents.
3. State's law in this area is unconstitutional and unenforceable.
4. Kentucky's counseling law is unconstitutional only in the requirement that the state-mandated information and materials be delivered in person.

Source: Who Decides? The Status of Women's Reproductive Rights in the United States, 15th ed. (Washington, D.C.: NARAL Pro-Choice America, 2006).

law is permitted to take effect on July 1, 2006. As a sovereign nation, the tribe can legally create alternative abortion policy.

As of May 2006, ten other states—Alabama, Georgia, Indiana, Kentucky, Louisiana, Mississippi, Missouri, Ohio, South Carolina, and Tennessee—were considering legislation similar to that passed in South Dakota. A plurality of the states also has some kind of husband consent or notification law on their books, all of which are unenforceable. And while at this point no woman seeking an abortion must notify or obtain consent from her husband to secure her procedure, many women live in states with legislators who think they should. Allowing defunct laws to stay on the books allows the possibility that they will be revived, and allows states that lean pro-life to expedite their anti-abortion policies should *Roe* fall.

Legal Barriers

Other abortion hurdles have had a much more immediate impact. The most common and significant of all the abortion barriers in Table 3.3 are state-imposed counseling, mandatory delay, and parental notification/consent laws. As the table indicates, a majority of states now have all three of these provisions on their books, and more states are adopting them each year. Because the Court has approved these restrictive policies, pro-life advocates have been highly successful in pursuing them through their state legislatures.

The counseling laws vary from state to state, but in general they are provisions that require a physician to read a counseling "script" to any patient seeking an abortion. The laws ostensibly seek to ensure that all abortion patients be well informed of their procedure and its risks. There are two difficulties with these provisions: first, they are redundant, because doctors in the vast majority of states already are required to secure an informed consent form from patients undergoing any medical procedure. In this litigious age, it would be uncommonly bad judgment for a physician to perform any procedure without advising her patient.

But the second difficulty with these scripts is that they demand the relating of specific content to a patient. Written by legislators, whom *Casey* declared have a protected right to persuade women that birth is favorable to abortion, the scripts tend to be biased toward this outcome and in some cases offer medical information that is not actually pertinent to the patient. Being both redundant and possibly misleading, the counseling scripts imposed by state legislatures suggest that women facing abortion decisions are incapable of asking questions about their procedures and that their doctors are incapable of answering them in an accurate, relevant, informative, and unbiased manner.

Two examples illustrate the potentially coercive aspects of counseling requirements. An Arkansas counseling guideline mandates that doctors tell patients about their right to an ultrasound to view the image of the fetus before the abortion, and women must sign a form indicating that they were made aware of this and chose not to undergo the procedure.[38] In Texas, which passed the Woman's Right to Know Act in 2003, the law requires the Texas Department of Health to provide abortion patients with a twenty-three-page booklet that contains some medically questionable materials, such as language that describes the embryo or fetus as an "unborn child."[39] Perhaps most dubious are the discussions of the possible side effects of abortion, which include references to how women can become depressed and even suicidal following an abortion, and the potential of abortion to be linked with breast cancer. Both of these claims have been roundly criticized by the scientific community.[40] While it is safe to assume that some women may become depressed following an abortion, others may feel very differently; the pamphlet, however, does not offer that perspective. Moreover, the pamphlet speaks at length about the euphoria of giving birth, with little emphasis on the possibility of post-partum depression, a well-documented medical occurence. A balanced pamphlet would describe the full range of feelings and risks women experience through both abortion and birth, leaving a woman well informed and able to make her own decision.

Biased counseling packets like those in Arkansas and Texas seem to call into question the very reasonableness of the patient and her ability to weigh her options. They also imply that the attending physician is incapable of appropriately preparing a patient for an abortion, as Dr. Mark Nichols of Oregon Health Sciences University attests:

> Frankly, [the counseling script is] insulting, that for this one particular surgery we are scrutinized by our legislators and told how we're supposed to communicate with patients, and with every other surgical arena we're allowed to use our clinical judgment and training, and come up with information that is consenting and informing the patient properly.[41]

Mandatory delays on the abortion procedure serve a similar end. The data are very clear on abortion: it is a safe procedure, but it grows both more expensive and more risky as the gestational age of the fetus advances. Mandatory delays, imposed by legislators who want to ensure that women have thought about their circumstances, presume they have not already done so on their own. Moreover, waiting twenty-four or thirty-six hours for an abortion, after being examined and counseled by a physician, imposes greater costs, especially on women in rural areas, who require either a second trip to the clinic or an overnight stay in a hotel. Given the increasingly sparse number of providers nationwide, and particularly in the center of the country, these delays present real challenges to women already under financial constraints. Subjecting them to a wait also may increase both the cost of the procedure itself as well as the recovery time from it. The fact that abortion rates have increased for low-income women despite the paucity of providers and their uneven distribution across the country and the costs of the procedure—all while statutory barriers like mandatory waiting periods have flourished—speaks to the urgency these women must feel.

Of all the common barriers to abortion access, parental involvement laws have some of the highest public support.[42] Many explain their support by arguing that such laws keep the abortion decision within the immediate family and give parents an appropriate amount of influence over an immature minor's actions. The argument is that parental input could be very important.

Unquestionably, the abortion decision has significant consequences for girls, and most parents would want to be a part of that decision. Still, there is much evidence that laws requiring either parental notification or consent do not add value to the minor's health or her well-being. There is solid evidence that forced parental involvement laws cause young women to delay reproductive health care, but not sexual activity.[43] While it is true that some girls mistakenly do not notify supportive parents when a pregnancy occurs, the implications of forcing a girl to notify a distant or violent parent is a public health concern in itself. To avoid such parental involvement laws, girls will sometimes resort to illegal procedures, or undergo procedures in other states.

The now famous case of Becky Bell is a classic example. Seventeen-year-old Becky avoided telling her parents about her pregnancy, and sought an illegal abortion rather than comply with her state's parental involvement law. Unsanitary instruments used during her procedure created a massive infection in Becky's body; one week later her veins collapsed and her heart stopped. Her actions and death indicate the length some girls will go to avoid involving their parents in their intimate decisions.

The Court has acknowledged the fact that for some girls, telling their parent or guardian about a pregnancy is dangerous for them physically. In *Belloti v. Baird II* (1979), the Supreme Court ruled that state notification and consent laws must offer a judicial bypass procedure that allows girls to avoid parental involvement by seeking an exception from a family judge.[44] Few girls use this route, however, because it has an intimidation factor of its own. Rather, many girls opt to cross state lines, seeking an abortion in a state without a parental involvement law. As discussed in chapter 4, Congress is considering a bill that would make the transport of a minor across state lines for the purpose of an abortion a felony when abortion is not allowed within her home state without parental consent.

The remaining barriers listed in Table 3.3 vary in their impact and severity. Some are so recent that they are poorly understood by the general public. Called TRAP (Targeted Restrictions on Abortion Providers) laws by their opponents, these barriers are a very new development. They are state-imposed restrictions on facilities that perform abortions; analogous restrictions are not found in regard to other health facilities. Supporters of TRAP legislation sometimes maintain that their purpose is to make abortion facilities safer; others admit the intent is to create obstacles to providers. Many of these provisions are minor architectural prohibitions that impose unnecessary business expenses on clinics; in other cases, the meaning of the requirement is unclear. Three examples reveal that although TRAP provisions create an economic disincentive to provide abortion, they do not make abortion in any way safer for women: The lone abortion clinic in Mississippi faces a new TRAP provision that requires abortion facilities to be in "attractive" locations, forcing the clinic's owners to incur additional landscaping expenses.[45] South Carolina requires that abortion clinics be free of grass outside that might attract pests; Arizona requires that physicians provide abortion in a way that raises a woman's self-esteem.

Another seemingly innocuous set of restrictions are the hospitals-only and physicians-only bills that limit where abortions may be performed and by whom. Given its commonness and low associated risks, abortion regulations like these further limit the type and number of locations where women might otherwise receive a safe abortion. Midwives, for instance, routinely performed abortions throughout the nineteenth century and continued to do so into the 1920s. During the 1960s when abortion was illegal, lay women formed a collective which called itself JANE and learned how to perform abortions for other women. And as historians Carole Joffe, Laura Kaplan, and Rickie Solinger demonstrate, many illegal "abortionists" during the 1940s and 1950s, although not licensed physicians, provided safe and compassionate abortions to many thousands of women.[46] Ruth Barnett of Portland, Oregon, provided forty thousand illegal abortions over three decades without a single patient death.

One of the great advantages of legalized abortion is that it can be regulated for safety. The hospital-only and physician-only requirements, however, are not necessary to maintain safety. In addition, because of the consolidation of hospitals in this country, some previously independent hospitals are now affiliated with the Catholic Church, which forbids the practice of abortion in their hospitals. By restricting abortions to hospitals (thereby eliminating the option of free-standing, independently owned clinics or Planned Parenthood affiliates) state legislatures whose hospital systems are church-owned are effectively making abortion obsolete. An example of this is the merger of St. Mary's Hospital, a Catholic facility, and Leonard Hospital in Troy, New York. All abortion services previously offered by Leonard ceased when the two institutions merged in the mid-1990s.[47]

Physician-only requirements create similar barriers. Several abortion physicians I spoke with admitted that a first-trimester abortion is a very simple procedure, usually performed using a sterilized mechanical suction device. As such, the procedure could arguably be performed by nurse practitioners or midwives at equally successful rates and in equally safe conditions as those found in hospitals or provided by licensed physicians.

Another common and effective way for states to limit access to abortion for low-income women is through facilities and funding restrictions. Gag rules prohibit those working in state-run health care facilities from even speaking of abortion as an option with patients; refusal clauses allow health care providers to deny abortion services if they morally object to them. Two types of state-initiated funding bans specifically curtail access to abortion for low-income women: state Medicaid funds, used to provide health care for low-income Americans, are banned from use for abortion services in thirty-three states. An additional fourteen states prohibit insurance companies from including abortion in their health coverage.

Of very recent interest is Missouri's state abortion law, which reads that "no state money, employees in the course of their employment, or facilities are to be used for abortions except abortions performed to save a woman's life." In 2005 the state's Department of Corrections, under pressure from pro-life legislators, interpreted that law as prohibiting its officers from transporting an inmate to a private abortion facility because such transportation would require the use of state resources. In the first abortion decision by the Supreme Court since John G. Roberts Jr. was sworn in as chief justice, the Court let stand a lower court's order to transport the prisoner to the facility, where she secured an abortion at her own cost. In a two-sentence ruling, the Court offered no substantive reason for its decision and gave no indication as to its vote. The federal district court will consider the constitutionality of the administrative rule in 2006.[48] The following section discusses funding bans, which are a serious obstacle to low-income women, and reflect the public's widespread discomfort with using public resources for abortion.

Barriers to Funding

Without access to funds, many low-income and young women find abortion services inaccessible or hard to obtain strictly on economic grounds. Following the Court's decision in *Roe,* abortions were routinely funded by the federal government through its Medicaid program, which provides health care to, among others, low-income Americans. One of the first actions taken by anti-abortion activists in the wake of that decision, however, was to eliminate this federal funding. The Hyde Amendment, named for its original author, Rep. Henry Hyde (R-Ill.), was first enacted in August 1977. It eliminated federal Medicaid funds for abortion for all cases except to save the life of the mother or when a pregnancy resulted from rape or incest. Since that time, the specific exceptions to the Medicaid ban have fluctuated. For instance, restrictions became more lenient during the Clinton administration, but then tightened once again during the Bush administration. As a rule, the federal government has not funded abortions in all but the most dire of instances since 1977.

Medicaid is a joint venture between the federal government and the states, however. The states may choose to extend their own resources to cover abortion expenses in additional circumstances beyond those required of them under the Hyde Amendment. As Table 3.4 indicates, however, few states offer additional resources for abortion services, although the procedure is far less costly than paying for childbirth. A state's decision to extend its own Medicaid coverage to expenses related to childbirth but not to those incurred for an abortion is not based upon economics, but rather indicates a state's moral preference for birth over abortion. This policy would seem to put some low-income women in the unenviable position of being able to afford to give birth (as this is covered by the state) but not to raise their children.

Two additional features of Table 3.4 are worth noting. First, many of the states that do provide generous abortion funding do so as a result of a court order, not as a consequence of affirmative legislative action. In these states, the courts have generally found that the state constitutions had more rigorous protections for the right to an abortion than the federal Constitution, and that this compels the state to assist women in acting upon their right. Notably, South Dakota is the only state in the nation whose law today is in flagrant violation of the Hyde Amendment; state law there provides abortion funding only to save the life of the woman.

While a few states extend more generous abortion funding than required by federal law, the Center for American Progress data indicate that only eighty-one women received federal funding in 2001 under the Hyde Amendment.[49] In response to the virtual elimination of public monies for abortion, 104 grassroots groups nationwide have formed the National Network of Abortion Funds. The group raises and contributes private donations for roughly twenty thousand abortions per year, including cases of abortion that would have fallen under the Hyde Amendment's narrow exceptions.

An examination of Idaho's distribution of funds helps illustrate why a woman would request private monies from the National Network of Abortion Funds before requesting public funds. In Idaho, a women who is pregnant as a result of rape or incest must provide a copy of the documentation that shows that the crime against her was reported to the appropriate law enforcement agency, a copy of court determination of rape or incest, or a written certification from her physician that she was unable to report the crime because of health conditions that precluded this action.[50] These intrusive and painful reporting requirements for a woman seeking public money for her abortion highlight not only the difficulty of obtaining state or federal Medicaid funding for abortion, but illustrate how low-income women are in a particularly difficult situation in securing access to the procedure.

TABLE 3.4

State Funding of Abortion under Medicaid

State	Life, Rape, and Incest	Other Exceptions	Funds All or Most Medically Necessary Abortions
Alabama	X		
Alaska			Court order
Arizona			Court order
Arkansas	X		
California			Court order
Colorado	X		
Connecticut			Court order
Delaware	X		
District of Columbia	X		
Florida	X		
Georgia	X		
Hawaii			Voluntarily
Idaho	X		
Illinois			Court order
Indiana	X	Physical health	
Iowa	X	Fetal abnormality	
Kansas	X		
Kentucky	X		
Louisiana	X		
Maine	X		
Maryland			Voluntarily
Massachusetts			Court order
Michigan	X		
Minnesota			Court order
Mississippi	X	Fetal abnormality	
Missouri	X		
Montana			Court order
Nebraska	X		
Nevada	X		
New Hampshire	X		
New Jersey			Court order
New Mexico			Court order
New York			Voluntarily
North Carolina	X		
North Dakota	X		
Ohio	X		
Oklahoma	X		

(Table continues on next page)

TABLE 3.4 *(continued)*
State Funding of Abortion under Medicaid

State	Life, Rape, and Incest	Other Exceptions	Funds All or Most Medically Necessary Abortions
Oregon			Court order
Pennsylvania	X		
Rhode Island	X		
South Carolina	X		
South Dakota	*		
Tennessee	X		
Texas	X		
Utah	x	Physical health/ fetal abnormality	
Vermont			Court order
Virginia	X	Fetal abnormality	
Washington			Voluntarily
West Virginia			Court order
Wisconsin	X	Physical health	
Wyoming	X		
Total	**32 + DC**		**17**

*State only pays for abortions when necessary to protect the woman's life.

Source: Alan Guttmacher Institute, "State Policies in Brief," as of March 1, 2005.

State Protections for Abortion

Some of the more liberal states in the country have taken affirmative steps to protect abortion access or to assist women in preventing the need for abortion in the first place. Table 3.5 indicates the range of protections presently offered by the states. Like the restrictions shown in Table 3.4, some of these abortion protections are more symbolic and potential than material. For instance, state statutory protection for abortion access is in place in California, Connecticut, Maine, Maryland, Nevada, Vermont, and Washington. In the event that *Roe* is overturned such legislation would maintain abortion's legality in these seven states. State constitutional protection is more binding on states than statutory protections simply because constitutional provisions, once enacted, are harder to remove; as with amendments to the U.S. Constitution, states generally require a supermajority vote to change their constitutions. Still, some states, including California, have chosen to enact both, either because people pushed for the changes through an initiative process or because lawmakers are seeking to please the pro-choice majority of their

TABLE 3.5
Abortion Rights Laws by State

State	Emergency Contraception	Insurance Coverage for Contraception	Public Funds for Abortion	Protection from Clinic Violence	State Constitutional Protection	State Statutory Protection
Alabama						
Alaska	X		X		X	
Arizona		X	X		X	
Arkansas						
California	X	X	X	X	X	X
Colorado				X		
Connecticut		X	X		X	
Delaware		X				X
District of Columbia				X		
Florida					X	
Georgia		X				
Hawaii	X	X	X			
Idaho	X					
Illinois		X	X		X	
Indiana					X	
Iowa		X				
Kansas				X		
Kentucky						
Louisiana						
Maine	X	X		X		
Maryland		X	X	X		X
Massachusetts		X	X	X		X
Michigan				X	X	
Minnesota			X	X	X	
Mississippi						
Missouri		X				

(Table continues on next page)

TABLE 3.5 (continued)
Abortion Rights Laws by State

State	Emergency Contraception	Insurance Coverage for Contraception	Public Funds for Abortion	Protection from Clinic Violence	State Constitutional Protection	State Statutory Protection
Montana			X		X	
Nebraska						X
Nevada		X		X		
New Hampshire		X				
New Jersey		X	X		X	
New Mexico	X	X	X	X	X	
New York	X	X	X	X		
North Carolina				X		
North Dakota						
Ohio						
Oklahoma						
Oregon	X		X	X	X	
Pennsylvania						
Rhode Island	X	X				
South Carolina						
South Dakota						
Tennessee					X	
Texas						
Utah						
Vermont		X	X		X	X
Virginia		X	X	X		
Washington	X	X	X			X
West Virginia					X	
Wisconsin		X		X		
Wyoming						

Source: *Who Decides? The Status of Women's Reproductive Rights in the United States*, 15th ed. (Washington, D.C.: NARAL Pro-Choice America, 2006).

state. State constitutional protection may also seem merely symbolic, but in fact, affirmative state constitutional protection of abortion rights is often interpreted by the courts to require state funding of abortion services.

There are those states that go beyond the Hyde Amendment's requirement to provide funding for a low-income woman when abortion is necessary to save her life or when the pregnancy is a result of either rape or incest. Moreover, a number of states responded to the grave instances of clinic violence by creating their own clinic access laws. As discussed earlier, most of these provide buffer zones that allow patients to enter and leave clinic facilities free of harassment. Finally, a small number of states require provision of emergency contraception, commonly known as Plan B or the morning after pill, which prevents the implantation of a fertilized egg. A larger number of states require contraceptive coverage in health plans as a means to reduce the single biggest cause of abortions: unwanted pregnancies.

PATTERNS OF RESTRICTION AND PROTECTION

In order to better understand the state patterns of abortion restriction and protection, Table 3.6 creates a measure of overall state support or suppression of abortion access. For each state, the number of enforceable statutory abortion barriers (restriction score), as well as the number of affirmative protections for abortion or contraception (protection score) have been tallied. The end result, the restriction score minus the protection score, equals the total restriction score. The higher the number, the more restrictive the overall picture of abortion access in a given state. Negative restriction scores denote the states with the most liberal abortion access.

These scores reveal the wide range of abortion environments women face across the country. Scores range from negative four in California and Vermont to ten in Mississippi, Ohio, Pennsylvania, and Virginia. Interestingly, a similar examination produced five years ago revealed largely the same patterns, but a narrower range of score outcomes, suggesting that the states are getting farther apart on the lenience-restriction scale with time.[51] Most important, these data reveal regional abortion policy patterns, which indicate that a woman's abortion right greatly depends upon her geographical location.

Regional patterns of abortion policy are best understood when viewed as a map. Map 3.1 illustrates stark geographical patterns of abortion support and opposition: while the coastal states are most likely to adopt very protective (from negative four to negative two) or protective (negative one through one) abortion policies, the South and Midwest are more likely to have restrictive (five through seven) or very restrictive (eight through ten) scores. Of note, there are more states in the very restrictive category (14) than in any other: restrictive (10), moderate (13), protective (8), or very protective (6). These patterns become essential to understanding the

TABLE 3.6
State Abortion Restriction Scores

State	Restriction Score	Protection Score	Total Restriction Score
Alabama	7	0	7
Alaska	5	−3	2
Arizona	5	−3	2
Arkansas	8	0	8
California	2	−6	−4
Colorado	5	−1	4
Connecticut	4	−5	−1
Delaware	5	−1	4
District of Columbia	2	−1	1
Florida	4	−1	3
Georgia	6	−1	5
Hawaii	4	−3	1
Idaho	8	0	8
Illinois	5	−4	1
Indiana	9	−1	8
Iowa	4	−1	3
Kansas	6	−1	5
Kentucky	9	0	9
Louisiana	8	0	8
Maine	4	−4	0
Maryland	3	−4	−1
Massachusetts	7	−4	3
Michigan	8	−1	7
Minnesota	8	−3	5
Mississippi	10	0	10
Missouri	8	−1	7
Montana	2	−2	0
Nebraska	8	−2	6
Nevada	5	−3	2
New Hampshire	1	−1	0
New Jersey	4	−2	2
New Mexico	2	−4	−2
New York	4	−4	0
North Carolina	6	−2	4
North Dakota	9	0	9
Ohio	10	0	10
Oklahoma	4	0	4
Oregon	1	−4	−3
Pennsylvania	10	0	10
Rhode Island	7	−1	6
South Carolina	10	−1	9

TABLE 3.6 (continued)
State Abortion Restriction Scores

State	Restriction Score	Protection Score	Total Restriction Score
South Dakota	8	0	8
Tennessee	6	-1	5
Texas	7	0	7
Utah	8	0	8
Vermont	0	-4	-4
Virginia	10	0	10
Washington	2	-5	-3
West Virginia	4	-2	2
Wisconsin	10	-2	8
Wyoming	4	0	4

Source: Compiled by the author.

partisan dimensions of abortion, a subject addressed in chapter 5. The items labeled X-3 in Table 3.3 (unenforceable barriers) are not included in the map calculations; if they were, there would be many more restrictive and very restrictive states.

STATE PROTECTIONS FOR THE FETUS

States have developed several additional fetal protections that do not bear immediately on abortion access, but have the potential to do so in the future. Laws surrounding prenatal drug exposure and third-party harm to the fetus have assisted states in the development of fetal citizenship status. Political scientist Jean Reith Schroedel documents the rise of state-level criminal statutes protecting fetal life (sometimes before viability) from either harm.[52] In a number of cases, women residing in states with these laws have been convicted of drug trafficking and other criminal acts when their babies are born addicted to or ill because of drugs. A South Carolina jury, for instance, convicted Regina McKnight of homicide in 2001 after her baby was stillborn, presumably because of McKnight's crack cocaine addiction.[53] Brown notes that in 1995, thirty-six states and the District of Columbia recognized wrongful death lawsuits involving fetal life. Missouri and West Virginia both have wrongful death laws that protect fetuses at any stage of development.[54] Elevating that protection to criminal status conveys a level of state protection to the unborn that implies citizenship. As states offer fetal life affirmative protection through wrongful death legislation and through increased barriers to abortion, the cumulative effect amounts to an incremental citizenship right. Laws are already in place to deal with child abuse, drug trafficking, and domestic

MAP 3.1
State Abortion Restriction Patterns

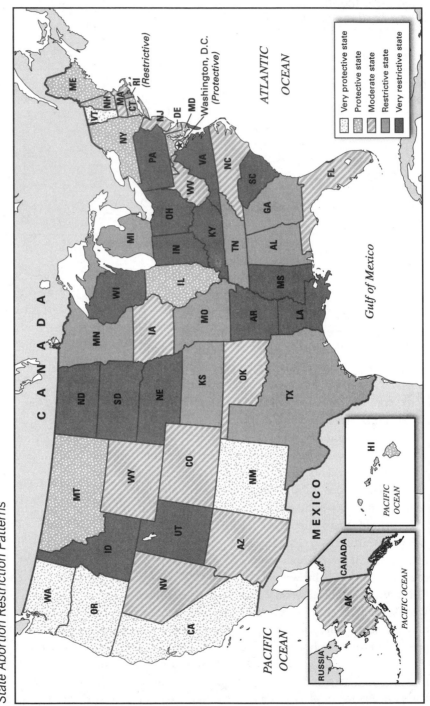

Source: Compiled by the author using NARAL Pro-Choice America data.

violence; some would argue that the double homicide provision says that a woman's life is worth more if she is pregnant—a sort of patriotic natalism.

CONCLUSION

This chapter illustrates the practical, local barriers that women seeking abortion services face in this country. Contrary to what some may suppose, abortion is not available "on demand," except for a select few adult women with the means to travel wherever they must to receive a safe and legal procedure. Even those women must navigate a series of obstacles. Today's women face a complex set of such obstacles—both statutory and practical—to their abortion "right." In addition, states are creating protections that raise the status of the fetus almost to that of full legal citizenship, leaving the full social citizenship of women hanging in the balance. Facing more restrictive abortion environments today than they have in thirty years, women in the United States have a choice, but not a right, to abortion. And for particular groups of women, namely the low-income, the young, and the geographically remote, access to abortion can be daunting. The nuances of state policy and contexts illustrate the tremendously varied status of abortion in the United States today; never in the years since *Roe* has a woman's right to an abortion depended so greatly on her physical location.

Based on the high degree of geographical variability, and the extent to which access is defined by financial means, abortion cannot honestly be considered the right of all women in the United States; it is the privilege of some. The preceding pages also indicate some of the costs to women of choosing to have an abortion. All women seeking the procedure must circumvent a web of legal restrictions and practical obstacles. Some women may experience a clinic frequented by protesters. Faced with protesters who may pity, harangue, berate, or harm them, women are challenged in securing an abortion; some may even risk their lives. As Dr. Newhall commented, "The more barriers you put up, the more risks people take to get there. It doesn't change anything." [55]

What is the federal government doing about this conundrum? Given that low-income women facing unwanted pregnancies live in every state of the nation, the federal government is in a unique position to assist them. The federal government has ceased paying for abortion in all but a few specific types of situations, however. The power it has to assist women in preventing unwanted pregnancies presents a possibility for cooperation between opponents and supporters of legal abortion. Is the federal government leading the way to prevention of unwanted pregnancy?

Chapter 4 addresses this and other questions about the role of the federal government in regulating abortion. The very recent explosion of federal intervention stands in stark contrast to its history. Only in the past three decades has every branch of the federal government become thoroughly invested in abortion policy—

often in ways that are quite unexpected. While this intervention is unanticipated, its direction—namely, on behalf of the fetus—has become predictable, with all three branches favoring increased fetal protection over women's health and social citizenship. And while the battery of state impediments (both statutory and practical) to abortion amounts to a growing protection of the fetus, federal protections provide a more ample opportunity to diminish women's social citizenship while simultaneously creating the citizen fetus.

DISCUSSION QUESTIONS

1. Is the decreasing number of abortion providers an issue that warrants a government solution? Why or why not?
2. In terms of freedom of speech, what do the actions of some clinic protesters suggest about abortion politics? What degree of public demonstration should or should not be acceptable under the law?
3. Should abortion training for ob-gyns and family physicians be mandated? Why or why not? What are some of the benefits? Drawbacks?
4. Should abortion provision be limited to licensed physicians? What ramifications would this have for abortion as a social regulatory policy? For the safety of pregnant women? What challenges does it present?
5. Are mandatory waiting periods a justified tool of public policy? Why or why not?
6. Should the right to an abortion be extended to minors to the same degree it is for adults? What role, if any, should parents or guardians play in their children's reproductive freedom?
7. Is a legitimate right to choose being provided if Medicaid funding for abortion procedures is denied to most lower-income patients?
8. If *Roe v Wade* is overturned, how do you believe the abortion debate will be transformed at the state level? Will abortion remain legal in most states?

SUGGESTED READING

Nosiff, Rosemary, *Before* Roe: *Abortion Policy in the States.* Philadelphia: Temple University Press, 2001.

Rose, Melody, "Social Policy," in Richard A. Clucas, Mark Henkels, and Brent S. Steel, eds. *Oregon Politics and Government: Progressives versus Conservative Populists.* Lincoln: University of Nebraska Press, 2005, 256–269.

Rozell, Mark J., and Clyde Wilcox. *God at the Grassroots: The Christian Right in the 1996 Elections,* 2nd edition. Lanham, Md.: Rowman and Littlefield, 1997.

Schroedel, Jean Reith. *Is the Fetus a Person?* Ithaca, N.Y.: Cornell University Press, 2000.

Segers, Mary C., and Timothy A. Byrnes, eds. *Abortion in the American States.* Armonk, N.Y.: M. E. Sharpe, 1995.

NOTES

1. Reprinted in Laurence H. Tribe, *Abortion: The Clash of Absolutes* (New York: W. W. Norton, 1990), 117.
2. The writings of Paul Hill are extensive, and can be found at his official Web site: www.armyofgod.com.
3. For an example of work on the impact of the Christian Right on state politics, see especially Mark J. Rozell and Clyde Wilcox, *God at the Grassroots: The Christian Right in the 1996 Elections,* 2nd ed. (Lanham, Md.: Rowman and Littlefield, 1997) and Jean Reith Schroedel, *Is the Fetus a Person?* (Ithaca, N.Y.: Cornell University Press, 2000).
4. Gina Kolata, "As Abortion Rates Decrease, Clinics Compete for Patients," *New York Times,* December 30, 2000.
5. My thanks to Dr. Peter Bours, who provides abortions in both rural and urban Oregon, for making this observation. He made an additional point about rural providers that deserves further investigation in future work: as a technical medical procedure, abortion requires practice like any other procedure. Those who provide the most abortions (typically in urban cores) develop a level of expertise that providers in sparsely populated areas may not. While not suggesting that rural providers are incompetent, Dr. Bours points out that with practice comes mastery; he maintains that in general, rural women are well served by traveling to urban providers. Dr. Peter Bours, personal interview with author, September 22, 2005, Bours Clinic, Portland, Oregon.
6. Alan Guttmacher Institute, "Get 'In the Know': 20 Questions about Pregnancy, Contraception and Abortion, 2004," www.guttmacher.org/in-the-know/.
7. Trans-state travel has piqued the interest of Congress, which is considering legislation to make cross-state travel illegal for minors. See chapter 5 for more information.
8. Dr. Peter Bours, personal interview with author, September 22, 2005, Bours Clinic, Portland, Oregon.
9. Stanley K. Henshaw and Lawrence B. Finer, "The Accessibility of Abortion Services in the United States, 2001," *Perspectives on Sexual and Reproductive Health,* 35, no. 1 (January–February 2003): 16–24.
10. Ibid.
11. Dr. Elizabeth Newhall, personal interview with author in her home in Portland, Oregon, October 21, 2005.

12. Dr. Siglinda Jacobsen, personal interview with author in her office at the Oregon Health Science University, March 28, 2005.

13. Joseph M. Scheidler, *Closed: 99 Ways to Stop Abortion* (Westchester, Ill.: Crossway Books, 1985).

14. Randall A. Terry describes his organization in *Operation Rescue* (Springdale, Pa.: Whitaker House, 1988).

15. Elliot Grossman, "Prosecutors Want Life Term for Waagner," *Allentown Morning Call,* June 26, 2004.

16. Dr. Warren Hern, quoted in Bob Herbert, "I Expect to be Shot Any Day," *San Jose Mercury News,* November 10, 1998.

17. Sandra G. Boodman, "The Dearth of Abortion Doctors: Stigma, Low Pay and Lack of Personal Commitment Erode Ranks," *Washington Post,* April 20, 1993, 7.

18. Paul Hill became the first U.S. abortion extremist sentenced to the death penalty; he was executed by lethal injection on September 3, 2003, in the state of Florida.

19. In Katherine Martin, *Women of Courage: Inspiring Stories from the Women Who Live Them* (Nowato, Calif.: New World Library, 1999), 132.

20. Dr. Elizabeth Newhall, personal interview with the author at her home in Portland, Oregon, October 21, 2005.

21. *Planned Parenthood of the Columbia/Willamette, Inc. v. American Coalition of Life Activists (ACLA),* 290 F.3d 1058, 1086 (921. Cir. 2002), cert. denied, 123 S. Ct. 2637 (2003).

22. Christiangallerynewsservice.com.

23. For the purposes of the graph, clinic violence is defined as the following acts: murder, attempted murder, bombing, arson, attempted bombing or arson, invasion, vandalism, trespassing, butyric acid attacks, anthrax threats, assault and battery, death threats, kidnapping, burglary, and stalking.

24. The *New York Times Magazine* did a cover story on the impact of clinic violence on Dr. Peter Bours of Oregon in 1985. See Dudley Clendinen, "The Abortion Conflict: What It Does to One Doctor," *New York Times Magazine,* August 11, 1985, 18–29, 42.

25. *National Organization for Women v. Scheidler,* 537 U.S. 393 (2003).

26. *Bray v. Alexandria Women's Health Clinic,* 506 U.S. 753 (1993). Curiously, the Court ruled this way by arguing that abortion protests did not amount to discrimination against women, because the protests were targeted at abortion provision, not women per se.

27. See *Madsen v. Women's Health Clinic,* 512 U.S. 5753 (1994), in which the Court ruled a discrete buffer zone appropriately protects women's right to a legal medical procedure; *Schenck v. Pro-Choice Network of Western New York,* 519 U.S.

357 (1997), in which the Court upheld fixed, but not floating, buffer zones; and *Hill v. Colorado*, 530 U.S. 703 (2000), in which the Court decided states may establish "bubble zones" around individuals entering or leaving clinics.

28. Sheryl Gay Stolberg, "Bankruptcy Bill Is Arena for Abortion Fight," *New York Times*, March 8, 2002.

29. Jody E. Steinauer et al., "Training Family Practice Residents in Abortion and Other Reproductive Health Care: A Nationwide Survey," *Family Planning Perspectives* 29 (September–October 1997): 222–227.

30. Stanley K. Henshaw, "Abortion Incidence and Services in the United States," *Family Planning Perspectives* 30, no. 6 (November–December 1998): 263–270, and 287.

31. Dr. Paula Bednarek, personal interview with author at Portland State University, May 19, 2005.

32. Ibid.

33. H. Trent MacKay and Andrea Phillips MacKay, "Abortion Training in Obstetrics and Gynecology Residency Programs in the United States, 1991–1992," *Family Planning Perspectives* 27, no. 3 (May–June 1995): 112–115.

34. Rene Almeling, Laureen Tews, and Susan Dudley, "Abortion Training in U.S. Obstetrics and Gynecology Residency Programs, 1998," *Family Planning Perspectives* 32, no. 6 (November–December 2000): 268–271, 320, and 271.

35. W. P. Metheny, F. W. Ling, and M. Mitchum, "What to Expect from a Residency Program: Answers from a Directory of Residency Programs in Obstetrics and Gynecology," *Obstetrics and Gynecology* 91, no. 2 (May 1998): 311–314.

36. E. S. Lazarus, "Politicizing Abortion: Personal Morality and Professional Responsibility of Residents Training in the United States," *Social Science and Medicine* 44, no. 9 (May 1997): 1417–1425.

37. Felicia H. Stewart and Philip D. Darney, "Abortion: Teaching Why as Well as How," *Family Planning Perspectives*, 35, no. 1 (January–February 2003): 37–39.

38. The full text of the Arkansas law is available online: www.arkleg.state.ar.us/ftproot/acts/2003/public/act1189.pdf.

39. To view the entire booklet, visit www.dshs.state.tx.us/wrtk/pdf/booklet.pdf. For text of the Texas law, see www.capitol.state.tx.us/cgibin/tlo/textframe.cmd?LEG=78&SESS=R&CHAMBER=H&BILLTYPE=B&BILLSUFFIX=00015&VERSION=5&TYPE=B.

40. Some of the work suggesting health implications of abortion can be found in Erika Bachiochi, ed., *The Cost of "Choice": Women Evaluate the Impact of Abortion* (San Francisco: Encounter Books, 2004). The research linking abortion to depression has largely been refuted by other studies. See, for instance, N. E. Adler et al, "Psychological Factors in Abortion: A Review," *American Psychologist* 47: 1194–1204; N. E. Adler, E. J. Ozer, and J. Tschann, "Abortion Rates among Adolescents," *American Psychologist* 58, no. 3: 208–217. More on the fed-

eral government's role in perpetuating the myth that abortion causes breast cancer in chapter 4.

41. Dr. Mark Nichols, personal interview with the author in his office at Oregon Health Science University, Portland, March 31, 2005.

42. The *New York Times* reported on a 2005 Pew Research Center Report that demonstrated wide majority support for minor consent laws. See Carol Eisenberg, "Abortion Still Supported; Despite Decades of Debate on Subject, Pew Poll Shows Majority of Americans Endorse It, with Restrictions," *New York Times*, August 4, 2005, A45. See also an article by Lydia Saad, "Americans Favor Parental Involvement in Teen Abortion Decisions," (Princeton, N.J.: Gallup News Service, November 2005).

43. Reddy, D. et al., "Effect of Mandatory Parental Notification on Adolescent Girls' Use of Sexual Health Care Services," *Journal of the American Medical Association*, 288, no. 6 (August 2002).

44. *Belloti v. Baird*, 443 U.S. 622 (1979).

45. PBS ran a *Frontline* program on Mississippi's last abortion clinic. See www.pbs.org/wgbh/pages/frontline/clinic/.

46. Carole Joffe, *Doctors of Conscience: The Struggle to Provide Abortion before and after Roe v. Wade* (Boston: Beacon Press, 1995); Laura Kaplan, *The Story of Jane: The Legendary Underground Feminist Abortion Service* (Chicago: University of Chicago Press, 1997); and Rickie Solinger, *The Abortionist: A Woman Against the Law* (Berkeley: University of California Press, 1994).

47. Patricia Donovan, "Hospital Mergers and Reproductive Health Care," *Family Planning Perspectives*, 28, no. 6 (November–December 1996).

48. Charles Lane, "High Court Allows Inmate's Abortion," *Washington Post*, October 18, 2005, A18.

49. Stephanie Poggi, "Abortion Funding for Poor Women: The Myth of Rape Exception," (Washington, D.C.: Center for American Progress, 2005), www.americanprogress.org/site/pp.asp?c=biJRJ8OVF&b=615981.

50. Idaho Code §56-209c; Idaho Admin. Code §16.03.09.095.

51. Melody Rose, "Social Policy," in *Oregon Politics and Government: Progressives versus Conservative Populists*, ed. Richard A. Clucas, Mark Henkels, and Brent S. Steel (Lincoln: University of Nebraska Press, 2005), 256–269.

52. Jean Reith Schroedel, *Is the Fetus a Person?* (Ithaca, N.Y.: Cornell University Press, 2000).

53. Lisa McLennan Brown, "Symposium: The Feminism and Legal Theory Project," *American University Journal of Gender, Social Policy, and Law* 13, no. 87 (2005): 95.

54. Ibid., 92.

55. Dr. Elizabeth Newhall, personal interview with author in her home in Portland, Oregon, October 21, 2005.

Abortion and the Federal Government

"One of the bills I am introducing today, the Sanctity of Life Act of 2005, reverses some of the damage done by Roe v. Wade. *The Sanctity of Life Act provides that the federal courts of the United States, up to and including the Supreme Court, do not have jurisdiction to hear abortion-related cases. Congress must use the authority granted to it in Article 3, Section 1 of the Constitution to rein in rogue federal judges from interfering with a state's ability to protect unborn life."*

—Rep. Ron Paul (R-Tex.)[1]

"No one likes abortion . . . but abortion will not go away until birth control always works, sex is always consensual, and human beings never make mistakes. We will improve on the first two, but the third is a hard fact of life. I accept it."

—Dr. Elizabeth Newhall, Portland, Oregon[2]

Unlike the states, the federal government is a relative newcomer to abortion policy. In the post-*Roe* era, however, it has quickly become a powerful, although sometimes subtle, player. A variety of federal abortion restrictions exist, including bans on the procedure on U.S. military bases, restrictions in federal prisons, and bans on federal employees' insurance coverage. These bans basically extend the Hyde Amendment funding ban beyond Medicaid, affecting other groups of vulnerable women.

In addition, and most interesting, is the documentation of more subtle forms of abortion barriers and affirmative fetal protections. These include fetal health insurance, federal money for zygote adoption, information published by the National Cancer Institute that informs women about a (hypothetical) link between abortions and breast cancer, refusals by the Food and Drug Administration (FDA) to extend new reproductive technologies to women, and a host of other regulatory changes that have largely gone unnoticed by the press or the public. This chapter, like the preceding one, builds the case for an emerging fetal citizenship at the expense of women's social citizenship.

The various phases of the federal abortion restriction illustrate how efforts to eliminate abortion have changed over time. Currently, all three branches of the federal government are entrenched in abortion policymaking, a phenomenon previously unseen in the history of social regulatory policy in the United States. And while the Supreme Court has permitted states to use policy to indicate a preference for birth over abortion, it has not explicitly done so for the federal government. The recent immersion of the federal government in abortion policy ultimately will provide the new Roberts Court the opportunity to judge whether the federal government in fact has a proper place in this policy arena. This chapter explores the three lines of strategy the federal government currently is employing to eliminate access to abortion in the United States. Although social regulatory policies share common techniques, abortion policy has developed some of its own unique patterns.

The first strategy is the effort to *persuade* American women seeking abortions that they should opt to give birth instead. As noted later, these restrictions do not ban particular activities, but rather provide patients with information designed to alter their opinion. This strategy is made possible by two trends in abortion jurisprudence. The first is the Court's recent acceptance of the government's interest in fetal life at all stages and an ancillary acceptance of the government's role in persuading women to choose birth over abortion. Second, persuasive policies are made possible by the Court's apparent disregard for the costs of abortion born by women.

The second effort is what I call the effort to *protect.* These are the policies that confer upon fetuses affirmative government protection or benefits of some kind—a patronage policy for the unborn. While most Americans would view these as benign and helpful to those women whose fetuses are wanted, protective policies carry with them the consequence of creating a fetal social citizenship. Additionally, these fetal benefits deny a woman her own full citizenship, by requiring her to "assist" her fetus in gaining the conferred social benefits while gaining none for herself. More and more, a woman's own citizenship appears ancillary to that of her fetus.

The other populations served by the protection policies are doctors, pharmacists, and institutions that might otherwise be called upon to provide abortion services or assist in its provision. Many Americans would argue that it is problematic to force individuals to engage in a practice that is morally reprehensible to them, and in fact it might not be in patients' interests to force such participation either. Still, most of the protection provisos in this area are redundant to other exceptions and protections that the medical industry enjoys, and serve mainly to send the symbolic message that government disapproves of abortion and those who participate in it.

Finally, the third contemporary restrictive effort in abortion policy is an outright attempt to *prohibit* particular practices. These policies are what would traditionally be viewed as social regulatory policy: they convey government's moral disapproval of a practice by removing it from the range of options available. As this chapter demonstrates, there are many more federal abortion prohibitions than are commonly known. They tend to target (as the state prohibitions do) those abortion practices with the lowest levels of public support and those vulnerable groups of women who don't have lobbyists to fight for them.

CONSTITUTIONAL AMENDMENT OR STATUTORY BAN?

The first federal reaction to the landmark court decision in *Roe v. Wade* was swift but ineffective. The ruling quickly mobilized a number of pro-life groups, including some that are still active today, such as the National Right to Life Committee (NRLC), to pressure Congress to ban abortion. Early opposition to the *Roe* verdict found vocal supporters in Congress who initially pursued a strategy to roll back *Roe*'s impact through constitutional amendment. Still, as the advocates of stripping abortion rights soon found, constitutional amendments are extremely difficult to pass, both because they require a supermajority vote from Congress, and because many in Congress are reluctant to make policy through constitutional change, sometimes in spite of their substantive sympathy with a cause. In 1974 and 1975, such amendments were considered within the Senate Judiciary Committee, but were never reported to the Senate floor. Only once did a constitutional amendment to ban abortion reach the floor of either chamber. On April 28, 1976, North Carolina Republican senator Jesse Helms proposed a fetal life amendment. Senator Birch Bayh, a Democrat from Indiana, offered a motion to table the amendment that passed 47–40.

While the constitutional amendment tactic failed to take hold, pro-life activists did take hope in their growing support in Congress. "The most important aspect of this entire thing is that the pro-life movement established itself as a major political force in this Congress," stated William Cox, executive director of the National Committee for a Human Life Amendment.[3] The Senate Judiciary Subcommittee on Separation of Powers and the Judiciary Subcommittee on the Constitution would consider the Human Life Amendment in future years; however, they would not send it on for full committee review.

In response to this stagnation, others in Congress advocated a federal statute to establish fetal protections. In 1981, Rep. Henry Hyde (R-Ill.) offered the Human Life Bill, which would have established that life begins at conception and would have offered Fourteenth Amendment protection to fetuses. His effort ended when the bill died in subcommittee. In 1983, his colleague Sen. Orrin Hatch (R-Utah) offered the Human Life Amendment in the Senate, where it received full floor consideration but split the pro-life supporters between those who preferred a constitutional amendment and those willing to accept statutory fetal protection in the process. The amendment was quite succinct, stating, "A right to abortion is not secured by this Constitution." The Senate rejected the amendment on June 28 by a 49–50 vote (well short of the 66 votes required for passage). Senator Helms, a proponent of the constitutional amendment strategy, indicated his dissatisfaction with the effort by voting "present."

Others who opposed the statutory effort were simply objecting to the use of federal authority in an area previously reserved for the states, still preferring, despite *Roe*, to allow the states to navigate the politically uncertain waters of abortion policy. However, the constitutionalists would receive some high-profile encouragement in 1985 when President Ronald Reagan endorsed the amendment in his State of the Union Address:

> The question of abortion grips our nation. Abortion is either the taking of a human life or it isn't. And if it is—and medical technology is increasingly showing it is—it must be stopped. It is a terrible irony that while some turn to abortion, so many others who cannot become parents cry out for children to adopt. We have room for these children. We can fill the cradles of those who want a child to love. And tonight I ask you in the Congress to move this year on legislation to protect the unborn.[4]

In spite of President Reagan's rhetorical support, the effort to protect fetuses directly through a federal ban has languished in Congress for more than twenty years.

BANNING FEDERAL FUNDING OF ABORTION

Although the blunt attempt to check the Supreme Court's decision of 1973 gained little traction, another, simultaneous effort enjoyed greater success. The language of the *Roe* ruling that described abortion as a woman's "choice" hurt attempts to create a full constitutional right to have an abortion through provision of federal funds to low-income women. For just as abortion rights advocates embrace the concept of a woman's right to choose, pro-life advocates voice their "choice" as taxpayers not to fund that decision with taxes. As opponents of abortion, they view the use of government funds to provide abortion services as immoral and as an implicit government endorsement of the procedure.

Presenting abortion as a choice suggests that it is a discretionary commodity rather than a right, and this invites detractors to choose alternatives.[5] A right, as described in the Introduction, inspires—in fact, it requires—affirmative government protection and provision. A choice that only women of means can actually act upon is in fact a liberty, not a right, and the government is not required to assure access. The pro-life movement very quickly identified this weakness in the *Roe* decision, and effectively moved to block all public funds for abortion provision. In practice, eliminating abortion funding has the potential effect of limiting the number of abortions performed, at least for specific groups of women. The success of this effort stands in stark contrast to the failure of a constitutional or statutory protection of the fetus.

It came as a surprise to many abortion opponents in the wake of *Roe* that the federal government had long funded that service for many groups of women. In the past, the federal government had offered some abortion funding through the Defense Department for service members and their dependents, women in federal prisons, and federal employees, but the main funding was through Medicaid, the federal program that provides health care for low-income Americans. Through this program, the government spent approximately $45 million in 1976 to cover the expenses of roughly three hundred thousand abortions in that year.[6] Thus, elimination of Medicaid abortion coverage became the first piece of a de-funding campaign by the pro-life organizations lobbying Congress.

This strategy partnered anti-abortion members of Congress with fiscal hawks and abortion moderates who found elimination of abortion spending an expedient way to walk the difficult political line emerging around the issue. The anti-funding campaign began in earnest in 1975, when the Senate attached an amendment to the Labor/Health, Education, and Welfare (Labor/HEW) appropriations bill that would deny Medicaid funding for an abortion, except in cases in which the woman's life was at stake. The House rejected the amendment handily, but Representative Bella Abzug (D-N.Y.) nevertheless lambasted her anti-abortion colleagues who had sided with the proposal for undermining the rights of low-income women.

The Hyde Amendment, named after its House sponsor, Henry Hyde, would resurface again the next year, and virtually every year after that. In 1976 an identical amendment was added to the Labor/HEW bill, an amendment Representative Hyde viewed as essential to "cut down on elective abortions."[7] The addition of this controversial measure stymied passage of the bill in the House for eleven weeks. Many members of Congress were simply not prepared to take a public stand on abortion, which had only recently become a topic of federal debate. Eventually the House version of the bill did include the ban on Medicaid funding for abortions, with no exceptions; the exception to save a woman's life was added in conference committee, where members of the Senate demanded it.

Still, confusion surrounded the new restriction. The exception added by the conference committee led many to question whether a woman's psychological health would be considered. Others wondered how the Department of Health, Education, and Welfare (HEW; currently the Department of Health and Human

TABLE 4.1
Medicaid Abortion Funding Exceptions by Year, 1977–Present

Year in Effect	Exceptions to Hyde Amendment
1977	Life of the woman
1978–1979	Rape, incest, health and life of the woman
1980–1981	Rape, incest, life of the women
1982–1993	Life of the women
1994–2001	Rape, incest, life of the woman
2001–present	Life of the woman

Source: Compiled by the author

Services) would interpret and implement the new restriction in order to meet the health standard expressed in *Roe.*

The confusion was compounded on October 22, 1976, when New York federal judge John F. Dooling Jr. ruled the restriction unconstitutional and forced HEW to continue abortion payments under the previous, unrestricted guidelines. On June 29, 1977, the U.S. Supreme Court informed Judge Dooling that he had twenty-five days to lift the injunction he had imposed on the Hyde Amendment in 1976. Abortion foes drew further hope for their Hyde Amendment from a June 20, 1977, Supreme Court decision that stated that local and state governments could legitimately refuse to pay for abortions with public dollars, even under *Roe.*[8] The Hyde Amendment was allowed to take effect August 4, 1977, virtually eliminating federal abortion coverage.[9] It has remained in place ever since, although the kinds of exceptions it contains have changed over time and have been a source of many legislative battles. Table 4.1 documents the many changes to the Hyde Amendment over the past three decades.

Abortion rights advocates have fought to loosen the restriction on Medicaid funding by supporting the extension of coverage to particularly vulnerable groups of women and to those who enjoy public support, such as victims of rape and incest. In 1977, for instance, the Hyde Amendment expanded its exceptions to include women whom two doctors had confirmed would face "severe and long-lasting physical health damage," as a result of their pregnancies, as well as those women whose pregnancies were the result of incest or a rape that had been properly reported. Congress eliminated the health exception in 1979, but left the rape, incest, and life exceptions intact. When in 1980 the Supreme Court validated the constitutionality of the Hyde Amendment in *Harris v. McRae,*[10] Congress maintained these same exceptions. Curiously, the Hyde Amendment was allowed to stand without providing an exception for women whose health would be endangered by a continued pregnancy—a protection central to the guiding principle of *Roe v. Wade* as well as *Planned Parenthood of Southeastern P.A. v. Casey* (1992).

Emboldened by the 1980 ruling and by a vocally pro-life president in the White House, Congress restricted Medicaid access further in 1981 by eliminating the exceptions for pregnancies that resulted from rape or incest. In 1988, abortion rights advocates in Congress attempted to add these exceptions back into the law. Upon hearing this, President Reagan wrote a letter to Senate leadership on September 7, indicating his disapproval and vowing to veto any bill that added rape and incest to the law.[11] In fact, President George H. W. Bush did veto the Medicaid bill in 1989 when it was expanded to include rape and incest exceptions, arguing that the addition of such exceptions would increase the incidence of "elective" abortions.[12] Congress would not seriously attempt any extension of Medicaid benefits under President Bush's tenure again.

A pro-choice president entered the White House in 1992, however, and Congress was quick to reattach the rape and incest exceptions to the Medicaid ban, which for twelve years had offered funding only to save a woman's life.[13] The Medicaid pendulum swung yet again when Republicans took control of the House in 1995. The House version of the Labor, Health and Human Services (Labor/HHS) appropriations bill for that year eliminated the rape and incest exceptions, allowed medical schools to get federal funding without requiring doctors to receive abortion training, and banned research on human embryos. The Senate version contained the same language as the 1993 bill signed by President Bill Clinton, which in the end prevailed, as pro-life forces were distracted from the funding issue by the Partial-Birth Abortion Ban Act. Still, in 1997 pro-life groups were satisfied when the Hyde Amendment was expanded to ban the use of Medicaid funds to pay for private health plans that covered abortions, and again in 1998 when the Hyde ban extended to trust funds of young women who receive Medicare because they are disabled. The Hyde Amendment has remained intact throughout the presidency of George W. Bush, allowing an exception only to save the life of the woman.

Of course the effort to eliminate federal spending on abortion did not end with Medicaid. A number of other smaller programs had allowed women, either directly or indirectly, to access abortion services with government assistance. The relative ease in passing the Medicaid ban therefore inspired anti-abortion activists to eliminate funds in the budgets of those agencies and departments that allowed abortion coverage. At present, the bans are so thorough that they extend to virtually all women who depend upon the federal government for their health care. Specifically, the bans include the following:

- military personnel and their dependents are prohibited from receiving abortions at overseas installations, even when they pay for the procedure with their own money;

- the District of Columbia may not use its own local monies for abortion provision;

- health care benefits of federal employees and their dependents may not cover abortion;

- the federal Native American health system may not cover abortion;

- federal prisoners may not receive abortions under their federal health care plan; and

- Peace Corps volunteers may not receive abortions under their federal health care plans.

All of these restrictions have been put into place within the last twenty years, and remain in effect as of summer 2006. The exceptions were passed separately under different bills and vary only slightly from bill to bill. They generally follow the pattern of exceptions seen in the Medicaid funding ban.

The prohibition on funding for abortion services was a highly successful early effort to eliminate government support of the procedure and to limit the scope of women's abortion right. Today, the avenues for unrestricted federal coverage of abortion are nonexistent. Although provision continues under the Medicaid program, it provides for a paltry number of abortions when compared to its pre-Hyde days.

In addition, these early efforts to deny funding to women seeking to fulfill their privacy right were upheld consistently at the Supreme Court level, and enforced informally through the court of public opinion. The de-funding strategy employed in early federal abortion politics remains a centerpiece of the anti-abortion strategy today. The effect of this strategy is that it targets the most vulnerable groups of women in society: those without an ability to pay for abortions also happen to be those who have no lobby in Congress fighting for their rights. Eliminating funding for abortion services effectively creates two classes of women: those with a right to have an abortion, based upon their ability to pay, and those with a liberty to *seek* an abortion.

THE PRO-LIFE MOVEMENT BEGINS TO ORGANIZE

Expectations for a rapid rollback of abortion access under President Reagan, the first president elected with help from the pro-life movement and the only U.S. president to write his own anti-abortion treatise, would be largely unmet.[14] Like any social movement, the pro-life movement in the 1980s faced organizational setbacks for a variety of reasons. First, disappointment was a natural outcome of the movement's strategy for sweeping change. Social movement organizations and their interest groups in Congress often collapse during prolonged periods of legislative defeat; given the early movement's ambitious congressional strategy to overturn *Roe*, legislative defeat was frequent and frustrating. The ambitious goals of the movement, aimed at dismantling *Roe*, won few friends in Congress, which is more suited to incremental change than sweeping policy swings.

Second, part of the explanation for the early movement's difficulty was related to its leadership. The movement suffered setbacks in public support when several of its most charismatic leaders hit stumbling blocks in their personal lives. A series of sex scandals and corruption charges against high-profile televangelists Jim Bakker and Jimmy Swaggart in the late 1980s discredited their movement's integrity. Even the Moral Majority, the largest of the groups, collapsed in 1989 under the weight of a scandal involving founder Jerry Falwell's personal life. Smaller groups were stagnating or disbanding altogether,[15] inspiring some scholars to prematurely predict the movement's demise.[16] Members of Congress understandably were even more reticent to advance the movement's legislative agenda under these conditions.

By the mid- to late 1980s, however, the conservative Christian movement was learning political sophistication and legitimacy through its earlier missteps. During Reagan's second term, the movement was rejuvenated by a consolidation of the remaining organizations and growing political experience in lobbying Congress. During the 98th Congress (1983–1984), the Christian Right organizations began to consider a more incremental strategy, and as a result enjoyed some legislative successes, such as Senate hearings on abortion legislation.

At the same time, the movement indicated its willingness to participate more directly in the Republican Party through participation in voter registration drives and candidate mobilization. The earlier movement had tried aligning with the Democratic Party, but this relationship was stymied when President Carter proved a disappointment to religious conservatives. As an evangelical Christian, Carter's very candidacy had assuaged some of their concerns regarding abortion and other social policy issues, but his performance in office enraged those who had hoped he would condemn abortion and roll back *Roe*. Carter won half the evangelical vote in 1976, a year dubbed the "Year of the Evangelical" by *Time* and *Newsweek*.

Still, in that year, Carter's interview with *Playboy* magazine, widely reported stories that he had gay individuals on his staff, his policy positions on abortion and school prayer, and his acceptance of both the Federal Communications Commission's decision to restrict religious broadcasting and the efforts of the Internal Revenue Service to revoke tax-exempt status for private religious schools that practiced racial discrimination led the fledgling Christian Right movement to distance itself from the administration. Carter's disappointing record on the abortion issue motivated many of these voters to look outside the Democratic Party for support. In 1980, the reverends Jerry Falwell and Pat Robertson supported the candidacy of Ronald Reagan—despite Robertson's endorsement of Jimmy Carter's campaign in 1976.

The relationship between the Christian Right movement and the Republican Party is considered more fully in chapter 5, but it is important to mention here. That emerging partnership gave the movement stability, endurance, and effectiveness by allowing it to gain political legitimacy and access it had not enjoyed previously. [17] Political scientist Matthew Moen characterizes the period up through the 1984 presidential election as one of movement expansion and partial cooptation by Ronald Reagan.[18]

The movement's effectiveness also was improved immeasurably by a savvy marketing and fund-raising strategy from within the Christian community,[19] and through secular interests as well.[20] Money had been a barrier to mobilization for the early anti-abortion movement, as it is for most movements. The one exception was Christian broadcasting. Although Christian radio had begun in the 1920s, it was not until the 1970s that the Christian Broadcasting Network, Trinity Broadcasting, Praise the Lord, and the Family Christian Broadcasting Network began. Indeed, one scholar argues that "Televangelism has been the single most important ingredient in the rise of the Christian Right." [21] By 1985, Pat Robertson's *700 Club* reported an annual budget of $230 million and could be seen on two hundred stations in the United States and in syndication in sixty countries worldwide.[22]

During his presidency, Reagan extended the bans on funding for abortion services by eliminating money going to agencies that either advised women about abortions or referred them to abortion providers. First, he announced his decision to ban international aid to overseas organizations that performed or advocated abortion while at a United Nations Population Conference in Mexico City in 1984. The "Mexico City" policy remained in place until President Clinton reversed it through executive order in January 1993; President George W. Bush reinstated the ban on January 22, 2001, the twenty-eighth anniversary of *Roe v. Wade*. Two months later the ban was added to the *Federal Register,* at which time it was extended to include overseas providers that prescribe mifepristone (RU-486), the drug used to induce early medical abortions. In 2003, Bush extended this "global gag rule" to all family planning agencies receiving funds from the State Department. Ronald Reagan may have been a disappointment to those who had wanted him to sign the Human Life Bill to extend Fourteenth Amendment protection to the unborn, but he was helpful to those same activists in that he effectively shifted the very terms of the abortion debate beyond the nation's borders.

In addition to this international action, Reagan took steps at home to prohibit domestic agencies from identifying abortion as one option within a range of reproductive choices. From 1970 until 1981, Title X had been the flagship of the federal government's sexual health and education program. Under Reagan, the program was underfunded—its budget cut by a quarter in 1981 alone—and stymied in Congress at every turn. Opponents claimed that the law's support for scientific sexual education encouraged promiscuity and the demand for abortions as a result of unwanted pregnancy, despite the evidence to the contrary. Reagan proposed an alternative vision: the Adolescent Family Life Program (AFLP). The AFLP funded programs taught abstinence, not the biology and science of sexual education. The program was essentially the predecessor to the current abstinence sex education programs favored by many elected Republicans, and was incorporated into school-based curricula nationwide. Reagan's apparent strategy was to discourage individuals—particularly teens—from becoming sexually active, and thus make the necessity for a ban on abortion moot.

In his first year in office, Reagan instructed the Department of Health and Human Services (HHS) that Title X recipients would be allowed to offer only "nondirective" abortion counseling, and could offer "referrals upon request" only. Then, on September 1, 1987, Reagan ordered the HHS to ban Title X organizations from making abortion referrals or mentioning abortion as an alternative to childbirth; in addition, no private money could be spent for abortions on physical premises funded through the federal government. The final draft of the order was due to take effect in 1988, but many wondered about its constitutional legitimacy in terms of free speech. In *Rust v. Sullivan* (1991), the high court ultimately settled the matter by upholding the "gag rule," arguing that the federal government could legitimately demonstrate its preference for birth in this manner, and the order took effect immediately. As with many other federal abortion restrictions, President Clinton rescinded the order in 1993. In 2001, President Bush reinstated the ban.

President Reagan's successor would deliver more assistance to the pro-life movement than he had. President H. W. Bush's pro-life accomplishments in part reflected the new, ever-evolving organizational approach of the movement, now based on a strategy of policy incrementalism, new social movement organization leadership, and a forthright commitment to helping elect pro-life Republican candidates.

Toward the end of the Reagan administration, in 1989, the pro-life movement had formed the Christian Coalition (CC), and turned an important organizational corner. With the birth of the CC, the mainstream anti-abortion movement committed to a plan to gradually roll back abortion access and build public sympathy for the fetus.[23] At the same time, the organization brought credibility to the movement through the selection of a young, dynamic leader. Highly educated and likeable, Ralph Reed built the CC into an organization prepared to fight for legislative change both through a gradualist strategy and by changing the membership of elected bodies. Reed's Christian Coalition became known for running candidates for presidential nominating conventions and for local political offices.[24] The impact of these strategies, while not initially felt in Congress, would come to fruition when the president's son, George W. Bush, took office years later. By the mid-1990s, many of the candidates the CC had helped elect to low-profile local offices had new offices in the nation's capitol as members of Congress. A large number rose to positions of leadership by 2000 and found themselves well positioned to move anti-abortion legislation forward.

President George H. W. Bush's legacy to the pro-life movement was his ability to check the pro-choice groups' own growing activism in Congress. Inspired by the 1989 ruling in *Webster v. Reproductive Health Services,* pro-choice forces mobilized during the 1990 midterm election, delivering a larger pro-choice class to the legislature that year. Buoyed by their results, the pro-choice members of Congress attempted to loosen a number of abortion funding restrictions, but to no effect. Bush vetoed each effort, keeping in place the pro-life legislation of the previous twenty-five years. In 1989 alone, Bush vetoed four bills because they included articles that eased funding bans. He vetoed the appropriations bill of Labor/HHS, for example, because Congress had extended coverage to women whose pregnancies were the result of rape or incest.

THE PRO-LIFE MOVEMENT SETS THE TERMS OF THE DEBATE

On January 22, 1993, on only his second full day in office, which coincided with the twentieth anniversary of *Roe v. Wade,* the first pro-choice president since that ruling issued five executive orders that rolled back restrictions accumulated during the previous twelve years. President Clinton's executive orders ended enforcement of the gag rule, rescinded the ban on funding fetal tissue research, lifted a 1988 ban that prohibited abortions in military facilities, directed HHS to study the ban on importation of RU-486 (mifepristone), and overturned President Reagan's 1984 Mexico City policy. Supported by renewed pro-choice activism resulting from *Casey* and by unified Democratic support in both chambers of Congress, many predicted that the Clinton presidency would fundamentally turn the tide of abortion politics.

Like the anti-abortion activists in the Reagan years, the pro-choice forces would experience disappointments equal to their expectations. For although those initial executive orders inspired the pro-choice community, they were the end, not the beginning, of Clinton's effective pro-choice campaign. His successes in that area would swiftly come to an end with the Republican Revolution of 1994, which brought a new wave of anti-abortion legislators to Washington. In his second term, Clinton would barely stem the tide of anti-abortion legislation. Not only did

Democrats never enact major pro-choice statutory change, they capitulated to the pro-life majority in a number of arenas.

Pro-choice members of Congress and the lobbies that supported them had sought a Freedom of Choice Act to codify the central holding in *Roe* since 1989; anti-abortion forces effectively stymied that legislation during Clinton's first term by adding amendments to kill the bill, such as parental notification and waiting periods for adult women. The closest the legislation came to passage was in 1993 when, riding a tide of successes, the movement pushed the legislation through both chambers of Congress, but it died in conference committee, where the two chambers could not agree on specifics. Some pro-choice organizations had advocated an effort to eliminate the Hyde Amendment altogether in 1994; still others hoped that radical changes to health care plans might create the same result with less public scrutiny. The demise of the Clinton universal health care plan meant the downfall of the pro-choice lobby's strategy for effectively reinstating federal assistance for abortion.

Still, the pro-choice lobby was able to rally enough support to pass the Freedom of Access to Clinic Entrances (FACE) bill in 1994. The legislation enjoyed wide support in Congress and was seen as a remedy to the actions of the increasingly violent extremist wing of the pro-life movement. Many legislators, not just pro-abortion rights members, supported legislation to make clinics safer by making clinic violence a federal offense.

It is fair to say that pro-choice forces lost control over the abortion agenda in Clinton's second term.[25] Although the Contract with America did not specify a Republican plan for abortion legislation, freshmen House members pursued new restrictions on the procedure in 1995. Due to their doggedness on the issue, in 1996 President Clinton signed a ban on abortions at military installations except in those cases in which the abortion was privately funded or was the result of rape or incest.[26] He also signed a ban on abortion coverage in the Federal Employees Health Benefits Program, which extended core pieces of the anti-abortion "prohibition" program.[27] The House attached a number of restrictions on additional bills, many of which were eliminated in the Senate.

The biggest challenge to the Clinton administration's abortion policy, however, was the 1996 passage of the Partial-Birth Abortion Ban. The ban criminalizes the dilation and extraction (D&X) method of abortion. Although Clinton vetoed the bill in 1996, and again in 1997, the debate around the legislation clearly changed the tenor of abortion politics, as chapter 1 of this text reveals.

The near successes of the pro-life movement over the D&X procedure, in addition to the extension of the military abortion ban led to new areas for federal intervention by 1998, when pro-life forces were confident that even with a pro-choice president in the White House, they controlled the terms of the debate. That year, the Senate fell a mere three votes short of overriding Clinton's veto of the Partial-Birth Abortion Ban. On the heels of this near victory, new efforts were launched to create federal support for state parental notification laws and to prevent the FDA from approving the use of RU-486. Although little happened in 1999 and 2000, the stage was set for a federal legislative revolution that would move beyond funding bans and other limitations on access.

A NEW STRATEGY FOR A NEW CENTURY: PERSUADE, PROTECT, AND PROHIBIT

Abortion rights supporters knew that the victory of George W. Bush in the 2000 election meant advancement of pro-life interests. What they might not have anticipated, however, was how swiftly policy would change. Also difficult to foresee was the singular strategy that would be employed by pro-life interest groups and members of Congress beginning in January 2001. Much of this strategy had been introduced in the late 1990s, when Clinton still had held some ground with his veto, but had capitulated in other areas of abortion policy. Anti-abortion forces implemented a three-prong approach: persuade, protect, and prohibit. They sought to persuade pregnant women to give birth, affirmatively build up the statutory protections and benefits of the fetus, and levy prohibitions against abortion practices with the lowest levels of public support. Prohibition efforts had been common dating back to the Hyde Amendment, but persuasion and protection techniques were elements of pro-life strategy first introduced in the 1980s. By the late 1990s, however, persuasion and protection techniques had gained momentum, becoming a centerpiece of the anti-abortion movement's legislative repertoire.

Persuade

Persuasion is a technique uncommon to social regulatory politics. It is more often associated with patronage politics, which generally entices particular actions through government giveaways or contracts. This technique is relatively new to abortion politics, and involves a deliberate effort to win over those who would make the abortion decision: women. It is a nuanced approach, because both fear and hope can be used to alter such decisions.

If abortion could be shown to detract from women's health or well-being, that information could be decisive to some women considering the procedure. The potential for fear to enter abortion politics is best understood through examination of a purported link between breast cancer and abortion. The National Council for Research on Women claims that the Bush administration advertised such a link.[28] While early studies on this subject in the 1950s proposed that abortion would become a risk factor for breast cancer, a 1997 study by the *New England Jour-*

nal of Medicine, the largest and most comprehensive of its kind, indicated no such link. Despite these findings, in November 2002 the Web site for the National Cancer Institute, a federal agency under the umbrella of the National Institutes of Health, posted a statement, over the objections from staff, that claimed that abortions were linked with higher rates of breast cancer.[29] The *New York Times* labeled the statement "an egregious distortion of the evidence." [30]

Moreover, another common pro-life assertion is that abortion leaves women psychologically unstable.[31] The anti-abortion movement has coined the phrase "post-abortion trauma syndrome" to describe the psychological damage women who have abortions reportedly experience. Although the "syndrome" is not acknowledged by medical or psychological texts, a number of states publish this perspective in their counseling guidelines for women seeking an abortion. If it were the case that women faced higher-than-usual rates of depression or anxiety as a result of the procedure, then that information would surely be of interest to women as a risk factor, but the support for this point is highly controversial. While anti-abortion Web sites declare the "fact" of psychological harm from abortion and point to a few studies as evidence, the largest studies to date do not support the claim and the major professional organizations within the field of psychology do not acknowledge such a syndrome.[32]

Claims of risks to women's health can be powerfully persuasive techniques in changing women's decisions, and so can similar claims about the fetus. With this in mind, Rep. Chris Smith (R-N.J.) and Sen. Sam Brownback (R-Kan.) introduced the Unborn Child Pain Awareness Act of 2005.[33] As written, the bill would amend the Public Health Services Act to define all fetuses at post-twenty weeks gestation as "pain-capable unborn children," and would require abortion providers to give the following statement to the abortion patient, unless she waived her right to hear the material:

> You are considering having an abortion of an unborn child who will have developed, at the time of the abortion, approximately XX [20] weeks after fertilization. The Congress of the United States has determined that at this stage of development, an unborn child has the physical structures necessary to experience pain. There is substantial evidence that by this point, unborn children draw away from surgical instruments in a manner which in an infant or an adult would be interpreted as a response to pain. Congress finds that there is substantial evidence that the process of being killed in an abortion will cause the unborn child pain, even though you receive a pain-reducing drug or drugs. Under the Federal Unborn Child Pain Awareness Act of 2005, you have the option of choosing to have anesthesia or other pain-reducing drug or drugs administered directly to the pain-capable unborn child if you so desire. The purpose of administering such drug or drugs would be to reduce or eliminate the capacity of the unborn child to experience pain during the abortion procedure. In some cases, there may be some additional risk to you associated with administering such a drug.

A number of interesting points emerge from this text. The first and most important is that not all physicians agree upon the pain perception of the fetus. In August 2005, the *Journal of the American Medical Association (JAMA),* one of the world's leading medical research journals, published a review of the evidence and concluded that "the functional pain perception in preterm neonates probably does not exist before 29 or 30 weeks," and that "little or no evidence addresses the effectiveness of direct fetal anesthetic or analgesic techniques" nor does "data exist on the safety of such techniques for pregnant women in the context of abortion." The review also concluded that such anesthetic techniques as are used in fetal surgery "are not directly applicable to abortion procedures." [34]

The authors of the Unborn Child Pain Awareness Act rely upon "expert testimony" given during the Partial-Birth Abortion Ban trials that refer to a fetus's increased heart rate, blood flow, and hormone levels as evidence of fetal pain. In a *New York Times* interview, Mark A. Rosen, a medical doctor and coauthor of the JAMA study, stated these responses were not evidence that the fetus feels pain but "was instead more likely to be a reflex." [35]

What is more, the bill appears to assume no confidence that physicians are giving their patients pertinent information prior to their abortion procedures; similarly, it assumes women are not considering all the implications of an abortion decision. Of concern with respect to the undue burden standard is the additional cost—both emotional and financial—that these hurdles would impose on the abortion patient.

While the Unborn Child Pain Awareness Act imposes on abortion recipients information that could possibly dissuade them from their decision, the Informed Choice Act is targeted at women visiting pregnancy crisis centers. HR 216/S755 would allow the secretary of Health and Human Services to grant money to non-profit organizations to purchase ultrasound equipment, provided they:

1. provide free ultrasound examinations to pregnant women;

2. show the visual image of the fetus from the ultrasound examination to each pregnant woman with a general anatomical and physiological description of the fetus;

3. give each pregnant woman the approximate age of the embryo or fetus;

4. provide information on abortion and alternatives to abortion, such as childbirth and adoption, and information concerning public and private agencies that will assist in those alternatives; and

5. obtain medical malpractice insurance.

Each grant would be limited to the lesser of 50 percent of the purchase price of the ultrasound machine involved or $20,000.

This bill provides possibly the best example of a federal strategy to support anti-abortion organizations by assisting them in making their services to clients more thorough and convincing. As imaging technologies improve, the very ability to see the fetus in detail becomes a tool in the power to persuade. The technique of persuasion may be recent, but it is not going away. Advancing technologies spell the future of incentive-based abortion policy. And since some of the federal money used to fund ultrasound machines would be allocated to faith-based organizations, concerns have been raised that the ultrasound may also come with a particular religious point of view.

Statutory Protection of the Fetus

Like his Democratic predecessor, in 2001 George W. Bush began his first term in the Oval Office with a series of executive orders related to abortion. Most of these simply reinstated abortion limitations lifted by President Clinton eight years earlier. For many anti-abortion activists, Bush, a born-again Christian, would be their best ally yet.

That hope would be delayed by the unexpected and tragic events of September 11, 2001. Not only would that day lead the United States to war and a focus on foreign policy, it would sideline the issue of abortion in Congress just as its opponents were anticipating the revival of the Partial-Birth Abortion Ban bill. For nearly two years they waited while Congress and the president channeled their energies into two wars and a rising national deficit. Not until 2002 would the issue of abortion fully reemerge within this presidency.

The momentum for fetal rights that began in 2002 would gain strength in the president's second term, which would produce surprisingly bold new initiatives to limit abortion. Not only has Bush had the opportunity to nominate two Supreme Court justices, he also has enjoyed solid support in Congress for his anti-abortion stance, allowing him an opportunity to advance the interests of anti-abortion forces.

One of the most provocative, albeit largely unnoticed, moves toward protection of the unborn came when the president approved allocation of federal money for the adoption of embryos. The Bush administration has approved more than two million dollars since 2002 to promote the "Snowflakes" program, a Nightlight Christian Adoptions agency in Fullerton, California, that seeks adoptive homes for embryos created through infertility treatments.[36] The president himself has lent his public support to this cause, appearing publicly with children born from adopted embryos.[37] Such embryos are typically the product of fertility treatments and are usually destroyed, stored through cryogenics, or used for scientific research.

One U.S. representative expressed his view of the adopted embryo by urging congressional protection of them:

> these human embryos are life and deserve our care and protection. There are thousands of embryos in existence, each one waiting in what some called frozen orphanages for a chance at life. . . . Embryo adoption affirms life while providing a family the opportunity to welcome a child into their family.[38]

Since 1997, eighty-one children have been born from adopted embryos.[39]

There are those who argue that embryo adoption is not as easy as it might seem. While the president and his supporters in Congress promote it as an effective protection of the emerging person, most embryos languish frozen in the laboratories in which they were created during in vitro fertilization procedures. The reason? The couples who created them simply are uncomfortable donating them to strangers, whose children they might someday become.[40] In any case, the use of federal dollars to support adoption over research indicates a view that the embryo is deserving of federal protection as the most elemental form of potential human life.

In January 2002, President Bush declared that January 18 would be established as National Sanctity of Human Life Day. Within the following year, his brother, Florida governor Jeb Bush, made legal history when he attempted to appoint a legal guardian to a fetus.[41] A twenty-three-year-old severely disabled woman, known in court documents only as J. D. S., became pregnant when she was raped in her group foster home. She had no capacity to consent to sex, and therefore seemed as in need of state protection as her fetus. The choice to appoint a guardian, and then to instruct lawyers to advance the fetus's legal rights, can be seen as particularly dismissive of the woman's special needs and delicate situation. That the governor chose to intervene in this case, and not that of a typical healthy woman appealing for an abortion, seems to suggest that disabled women have less right to end their pregnancies than other women. While Governor Bush's attempt to appoint a guardian ultimately failed, the legal wrangling over the question lasted so long that the woman eventually gave birth by cesarean section.[42]

Perhaps the most affirmative and materially substantial support offered for the fetus was Bush's September 2002 classification of the unborn as "children" under the State Children's Health Insurance Program (SCHIP), which extends health care benefits to some of the nation's poorest children. Under the new rules, then-secretary of Health and Human Services Tommy Thompson redefined the word "child" for purposes of Title 42 of the Public Health Law. Previously, the term, for purposes of SCHIP benefits, had meant all born children eligible for services, which would exclude all noncitizens, including legal and illegal immigrants.

Under Section 47.10 (3) of Title 42, however, "Child means an individual under the age of 19 including the period from conception to birth." [43] A fetus now qualifies for the same level of state benefits as a child, even when the fetus is within the womb of an illegal immigrant. While few would deny the importance of prenatal care to the health and well-being of all chosen pregnancies, this ruling has very little direct benefit to pregnant women and begs a whole host of administrative quandaries: How does one administer health care to the fetus independent of the woman? What if a medical procedure is necessary for the health of the (ineligible) woman, but not necessary for the (eligible) fetus—or even harmful to it? Having redefined the fetus as a child, can SCHIP rules be used to prosecute a mother whose actions injure the fetus? What if an (ineligible) woman has a miscarriage, requiring follow-up medical care? Since the fetus is no longer living, will that care be covered by SCHIP benefits?[44]

These questions of application go unanswered by the administration as the much larger issue of the slow accrual of affirmative state benefits—but not citizenship or personhood—for the fetus goes relatively unnoticed. The Bush administration has redefined childhood through this rule, extending material physical assistance to fetuses, even as many legal and illegal immigrants remain ineligible for such assistance. Some might argue that the rule is an effort to assist mothers-to-be with good prenatal care, which is widely understood to produce healthier babies. But the fact that the ruling offers no direct benefits to mothers, such as prenatal vitamins or other common prenatal products; it only offers them ancillary health benefits because they are carrying the benefits-eligible fetus.

On August 5, 2002, President Bush also signed the Born-Alive Infant Protection Act, which the House had passed earlier in 2000. The law provides legal support for fetuses born alive despite undergoing an abortion procedure.[45] The law has had very little practical effect because few experts can point to anything but anecdotal evidence that failed abortions happen, or that fetuses emerge still living.[46] In practice, the law would seem difficult to enforce. Should a fetus be born alive through an abortion, reporting a criminal end to that life would fall to someone attending the abortion. What is more, the law does not make any distinction between fetuses before and after the point of assumed viability, blurring the distinction in rights *Roe* once made clear.

The law's real impact is symbolic: it offers the same constitutional protections to fetuses as to citizens. Taken on its merits, it may have little effect, but when seen as a part of a larger picture, it becomes one more piece in the fetal citizenship jigsaw puzzle. The long-term political implication of the law is apparent to Professor Hadley Arkes of the National Committee for a Human Life Amendment, who calls the law "truly momentous," arguing that it is "a predicate that can be built into the foundation now of every subsequent act of legislation touching the matter of abortion: that the child marked for abortion is indeed a person who comes within the protection of law." [47]

In 2005 Bush expanded the act still further, issuing a directive that instructed doctors and hospitals to make every effort to save premature babies born from failed abortions. Secretary of Health and Human Services Michael O. Leavitt warned physicians that federal authorities would "aggressively enforce" the law. The fetus is now a person entitled to emergency care and protection from abuse or neglect. Bush stated upon signing the revised act, "This important legislation ensures that every infant born alive—including an infant who survives an abortion procedure—is considered a person under federal law."

The expansion of this law would be preceded by another, related action. On November 5, 2003, Bush signed the Partial-Birth Abortion Ban into law. This was a landmark that the pro-life movement had worked toward for nearly a decade, and solidified the movement's dominance in the abortion debate.[48] Unquestionably, it marked the success of their decade-long strategy of gradual policy change and election of pro-life legislators.

There is further evidence that President Bush's actions have not occurred in a vacuum. Abortion opponents in Congress also have attempted to protect fetuses from abortion in a more indirect way: by reducing the opportunities for medical school residents to learn the procedure. In the Abortion Non-Discrimination Act of 2003, abortion opponents were responding to the actions of the Accreditation Council for Graduate Medical Education (ACGME), which had proposed requiring "all teaching hospitals with obstetrics/gynecology residency programs to require abortion training." The ACGME's recommended rule change would have exempted physicians from such training only in cases in which they had religious or moral objections to abortion.[49]

The legislation would have amended the Public Health Service Act to prohibit any local, state, or federal government from discriminating financially against health care entities that refused to provide or pay for abortions. The bill, HR 4691, went to a vote in the House, where it passed 229–194 in September 2002. It has never come out of committee in the Senate, however, perhaps because the ACGME revised its recommendation to teaching hospitals, backing away from abortion training as a requirement by expanding the exceptions possible under its guidelines. In this case, the very threat of federal intervention produced the desired outcome: the ACGME backed down. The story of the Abortion Non-Discrimination Act indicates the power that politics (and the federal government) has over medicine in the arena of abortion provision.

Further expanding the idea that the human embryo requires legal protection, an advisory committee of HHS declared in October 2002 that any research conducted on fertilized eggs would invoke scrutiny and protection on the grounds that the eggs are "human subjects." Declaring the fertilized egg a human subject for purposes of scientific research renders most of that research illegal. For obvious ethical reasons, scientists face very strict limitations on research performed on human subjects; any research that causes pain, suffering, or duress is highly restricted and usually impermissible. Thus, by classifying embryos as humans, HHS essentially has extended the same protections to embryos, eliminating embryo research.

In 2003 the Unborn Victims of Violence Law (UVVL) extended legal status to fetuses in cases of assault or murder of the pregnant woman. Under the act, a perpetrator of a crime against a pregnant woman can be convicted and sentenced twice: once for harm to the woman, and again for harm to the fetus. The bill classified the fertilized egg as a "victim," and for the first time defined fetuses as crime victims—another step in creating a separate legal personhood for the unborn through a law and order framework. While the House passed the bill both in 1999 and 2001, it did not find sufficient support in the Senate to move forward, especially in light of the post–9/11 political climate. But the tipping point would come in the form of a horrific and highly publicized family tragedy.

Laci Peterson disappeared from her home in Modesto, California, on Christmas Eve 2002, one month before her first baby was due. Her husband, Scott, was the prime suspect in her disappearance, although he maintained his innocence while friends and neighbors searched for his wife. In April 2003, Laci's remains and that of her fetus, which the couple had named Conner, were found in San Francisco Bay. Scott was convicted in December 2004 of two murders—that of his wife Laci and that of the fetus—and now sits on death row.

The public and media attention of this crime allowed advocates of the Unborn Victims of Violence Act to draw enough additional support for the bill to get it passed in both houses. Informally dubbed "Laci and Conner's Law," it was signed into law in April 2004.[50]

The law does not require that the defendant have had knowledge of the woman's pregnancy or an intention to do harm to the fetus. Regardless of such knowledge or lack thereof, death or injury of a "child in the womb" is now a separate offense from the death or injury of the pregnant woman, and is punishable under federal law by the same measure. Much like the SCHIP rule, the act changes the very definition of childhood, extending protection to a "child in utero" at any stage of development. Both pieces of legislation confer federal protection to the fetus.

When signing the bill into law, President Bush made these remarks,

> Until today, the federal criminal code had been silent on the injury or death of a child in cases of violence against a pregnant woman. This omission in the law has led to clear injustices. The death of an innocent unborn child has too often been treated as a detail in one crime, but not a crime in itself. Police and prosecutors had been to crime scenes and have shared the grief of families, but have so often been unable to seek justice for the full offense.

The moral concern of humanity extends to those unborn children who are harmed or killed in crimes against their mothers. And now, the protection of federal law extends to those children, as well. With this action, we widen the circle of compassion and inclusion in our society, and we reaffirm that the United States of America is building a culture of life.

Pro-choice groups denounced this law while simultaneously decrying violence against women. NARAL Pro-Choice (formerly National Abortion Repeal Action League) argued that the law "elevates even a two-week-old embryo to the legal status of a person," and that it amounted to "a sneak attack on a woman's right to choose." [51] Although the legislation specifically exempts legal abortion from prosecution, it can be viewed as one step in the pro-life movement's staircase toward changing society's definition of childhood.[52] By creating greater public empathy for a fetus that dies as a result of violence against a pregnant woman and gradually extending protections to the fetus in non-abortion related policy areas, the movement can make the parallel argument that fetuses also ought to be protected from other kinds of violence: namely, abortion.

Prohibit

Following the 2004 election, the intensity and character of the anti-abortion movement fundamentally changed. Reelected president George W. Bush would make the moral mandate of the movement one of the mainstays of his platform (see chapter 5). In some ways, the approach first employed by activists in the early 1970s to criminalize abortion and establish fetal rights appears to be coming to fruition. Two thousand and five and early 2006 would prove watersheds for efforts to prohibit abortion under all circumstances.

Efforts to prohibit abortion access have been the most consistent and successful tool of the anti-abortion movement to date. Because the Court and abortion rights groups have characterized abortion as a "choice," Congress has effectively *chosen* not to support it by preventing federal funds and in some cases personnel monies from being used to subsidize the procedure. And while earlier attempts to prohibit abortion outright failed, there is some evidence that such a ban may once again be gaining momentum.

At the time of this writing, several prohibition measures are under consideration in Congress. The first of these continues the thread of prohibiting federal resources from being used in the practice of abortion. The Taxpayers' Freedom of Conscience Act 2005 would "prohibit any Federal official from expending any Federal funds for any population control or population planning program or any family planning activity." [53] Depending on the interpretation, the bill could go so far as to eliminate the funds presently used for sexual education and basic reproductive health services. The bill presently has only three co-sponsors, possibly because it is written so broadly.

A slightly different use of the prohibition technique is found in the RU-486 Suspension and Review Act of 2005, which would withdraw FDA approval of the drug mifepristone, commonly known as RU-486. The bill claims that since being approved, mifepristone has caused death and injury to women, despite its wide-spread acceptance and use by health care professionals worldwide. Introduced with eleven cosponsors in the Senate during the spring of 2005, it appears to be stuck in the Committee on Health, Education, Labor, and Pension.

As chapter 3 indicates, most states today have either a parental notification or consent law that presents a barrier to minors seeking abortions. For several years anti-abortion strategists have tried to stop the practice of teenage girls crossing state lines to avoid such laws in their own state. Advocates argue that these laws assist girls in getting the mature adult help they need when faced with a preg-nancy; abortion rights supporters are quick to argue that many girls tell a parent about their pregnancy without such a law, and that those who don't may face seri-ous safety issues in reporting their pregnancies to family members.

Congress has ratcheted up the teen access debate by crafting the Child Inter-state Abortion Notification Act, which would make it a crime for an adult other than the girl's parent or legal guardian—even a close family member or minister—to assist her in procuring an abortion outside her home state. The law also would make it a crime for a physician to provide the abortion—the current bill imposes both the possibility of jail time and up to a $100,000 fine. Once entitled the Child Custody Protection Act, the bill has passed in the House four times since 1998, the last time being April 27, 2005, but it has never passed in the Senate.

The effort to ban abortion through federal legislation or constitutional change has been revived in the wake of so many federal anti-abortion successes. This time, the effort comes in the form of the Sanctity of Life Act of 2005, which declares that:

1. human life shall be deemed to exist from conception, without regard to race, sex, age, health, defect, or condition of dependency; and

2. the term "person" shall include all such human life.

The act also recognizes that each state has the authority to protect the lives of unborn children residing in the jurisdiction of that state.[54]

As the language used here makes plain, the bill would establish fetal person-hood and extend rights to the unborn, functionally making abortion a criminal act. At the time of this writing, the bill sits in a House subcommittee with only five sponsors; still, it is not for nothing that abortion opponents have revived this approach. While the bill has lain dormant, the Supreme Court has taken on a new shape that will potentially change the legal context within which the bill would be debated and, if enacted, challenged.

NOMINATION POLITICS AND THE MAKING OF A NEW SUPREME COURT

No assessment of national abortion politics is complete without consideration of judicial and administrative nomination politics. Just as the revived pro-life movement of the late 1980s and early 1990s learned that congressional and local elections were opportunities to shape abortion policy gradually by changing the demographics of the policymakers themselves, so they have approached nominations to the judicial and executive branches. Such an approach is perhaps the most effective aspect of the current movement's strategy. In fact, a hallmark of social regulatory politics is that they are typically resolved in the judicial branch; hence, the identification by activists of nomination processes as places to influence is logical. Since Judge Robert Bork's highly controversial nomination to the Supreme Court in 1987, judicial nominations have received intense scrutiny from abortion activists of all stripes. Administrative appointments can be no less vitriolic. As seen in this chapter, administrative rulings and interpretations can have a dramatic effect on the implementation of abortion law.

A recent example is that of Dr. Lester Crawford's nomination to head the FDA. Senators Hillary Clinton (D-N.Y.) and Patty Murray (D-Wash.) stalled Crawford's nomination in 2005 when the agency refused to issue a decision on the application to sell Plan B (emergency contraception also known as the "morning after" pill) over the counter. As detailed in chapter 1, the pill, widely used in Europe, was approved for prescription in the United States in June 1999. Two committees recommended over-the-counter sales of the drug in December 2003, and the FDA was due to issue a decision in January 2005, but failed to do so. Given this highly unusual action on the part of the agency, the abortion rights community in Congress responded by preventing Crawford's nomination from moving forward, illustrating how politicized administrative nominations can become within the contemporary abortion debates.

As important as such administrative nominations are, however, 2005 and 2006 will be remembered better for a slate of judicial nominations. Upon the death of Chief Justice William Rehnquist and the retirement of Justice Sandra Day O'Connor, George W. Bush gained the opportunity to reshape the court and ensure his anti-abortion legacy. In the nomination of John Roberts to succeed Rehnquist, the president met with only modest resistance. Well regarded as a constitutional scholar and judge, Roberts was easily confirmed before the beginning of the 2005 term.

This was not to be the case with Bush's first choice to replace O'Connor. White House counsel Harriet Miers met with unexpected resistance from conservative groups. A born-again Christian, Miers has spent her legal career in corporate law, on the Texas state lottery commission, and most recently, in service to the president. A host of conservative activists claim to know her anti-abortion credentials, but Miers's career leaves no affirmative evidence of this position. This left many anti-abortion activists, who have long awaited the opportunity to remake the Court, nervous. Secular conservatives pointed to her lack of constitutional expertise as their source of concern. These concerns from the religious right largely eclipsed the objections from abortion rights groups, which were poised for a battle over the nomination. In the end, Miers withdrew her nomination in the face of mounting skepticism about her suitability to join the Court.

President Bush's second choice seemed a direct response to the concerns regarding his first. In the selection of Samuel J. Alito, the president nominated a highly regarded jurist, nominated to the Third Circuit of the U.S. Court of Appeals in 1990 by then-president George H. W. Bush. Before that service, Alito was a member of the Reagan administration, where he wrote several briefs for the president regarding abortion issues.

It is those briefs, as well as Alito's position on *Casey* when it was before his appeals court, that have caused concern in pro-choice organizations. In one brief, Alito refers to the "so-called" right of abortion; in another, which he did not disclose to the Senate Judiciary Committee but which was apparently leaked to the press, now-justice Alito gave President Reagan advice on the anti-abortion strategy of gradually undermining *Roe*. And when *Casey* came before him, Alito voted in favor of upholding Pennsylvania's husband notification law for married women seeking an abortion. These issues were central to Alito's Senate Judiciary Committee confirmation hearings. Yet despite the concerns expressed by some members of Congress, he was comfortably confirmed to the U.S. Supreme Court in January 2006.

But presidents have the opportunity to nominate judges to the entire federal bench, not just to the Supreme Court. Like his predecessor Bill Clinton, George W. Bush has put forward a group of jurists whose nominations have been stalled by detractors in the Senate. The practice of filibustering judicial nominees has been used for decades by the minority to stall nominations or encourage the nomination of more moderate individuals. In this instance, abortion rights supporters stalled the nominations of Judge Priscilla Owen of Texas and Judge Janice Rogers Brown of California. Judge Owen is of particular relevance to the abortion controversy, as she has interpreted Texas state law much more conservatively than even her compatriots in the state legislature advocate. By threatening to filibuster her nomination, Senate Democrats could have prevented her confirmation. With this in mind, Senate Majority Leader Bill Frist offered up what he called the "nuclear option": changing Senate rules to dismantle the filibuster so that only a simple majority vote ending filibuster on a judge's nomination would have been required.

The heightened intensity of this particular nomination battle was seen in the language used. Frist argued in May 2005 that the Democrats stalling Owen's nomination were seeking to destroy her. For their part, Democrats argue that dismantling the filibuster amounts to tyranny of the majority. A group of fourteen centrist senators—seven Democrats and seven Republicans—brokered a deal that allowed three controversial judicial nominees—Owen, Brown, and William Pryor—to move forward to a vote while two additional nominees—William Myers and Henry Saad—could be subject to filibuster. Owen was confirmed by a 54–43 vote on May 25, 2005; Brown was confirmed by a 56–43 margin on June 8, 2005.

The heightened pitch over judicial nominees will continue as long as the status of abortion hangs in the balance. With two new justices on the Supreme Court and abortion cases pending before it, all eyes will turn toward the Court for the next phase of abortion politics.

CONCLUSION

The national government is a powerful force in shaping abortion policy and politics in the twenty-first century. While the states continue to influence abortion policy, as chapter 3 illustrated, they are no longer alone in that endeavor. Congress, presidents, and the courts are now just as deeply entrenched in arbitrating abortion policy. And as seen in this chapter, the energy and direction of their attention is toward prohibiting some forms of abortion and persuading women to give birth.

Through the contemporary techniques of persuasion and fetal protection and the traditional technique of prohibition, the federal government is creating new avenues for fetal rights, while never addressing the implications for the full citizenship of women, socially and legally. This point would seem to pose a political risk for these very politicians: for while women have been voting for more than eighty years, the fetus makes a rather dubious constituent. If more than a million American women still have abortions every year, and polls indicate that the majority of Americans support some form of abortion access, should it not follow that at least one of the political parties would firmly support abortion rights? The role of partisanship in abortion politics will be examined in chapter 5.

DISCUSSION QUESTIONS

1. What has been the historic role of the federal government in social regulatory policy? What role do you think it should have? Are there particular policy areas that you think the government should have more control over than others? Why?

2. What were the early strategies of pro-life advocates? How were they successful? How were they not?
3. Define the strategies of prohibit, persuade, and protect. Which one seems to be most effective? Which is most effective as an instrument of federal policy?
4. What is the interest of pro-life advocates in changing medical terminology?
5. How do the federal prohibitions and protections described in this chapter change the overall availability of abortion in the United States? Do you think they achieve their goals? Have there been unintended ramifications?
6. Why has the pro-choice community been ineffective in preventing recent abortion restrictions?
7. What do you think is the likelihood that Congress will ban abortion in your lifetime? How will that affect you as a citizen? How do you think it will affect your life?

SUGGESTED READING

Critchlow, Donald T. *Intended Consequences: Birth Control, Abortion, and the Federal Government in Modern America,* New York: Oxford University Press, 1999.

Diamond, Sara. *Spiritual Warfare: The Politics of the Christian Right.* New York: Guilford Press, 1995.

Gorney, Cynthia. *Articles of Faith: A Frontline History of the Abortion Wars.* New York: Simon and Schuster, 1998.

Reed, Ralph. *Active Faith: How Christians are Changing the Soul of American Politics.* New York: The Free Press, 1996.

Terry, Randall A. *Operation Rescue.* Springfield, Pa.: Whitaker House, 1988.

Tribe, Laurence H. *Abortion: The Clash of Absolutes.* New York: W. W. Norton, 1990.

Risen, James, and Judy L. Thomas. *Wrath of Angels: The American Abortion War.* New York: Basic Books, 1998.

NOTES

1. Speech on the floor of the House of Representatives when introducing the Taxpayers' Freedom of Conscience Act of 2005, February 10, 2005, http://thomas.loc.gov/cgi-bin/query/D?r109:4:./temp/~r109vdhbCV.
2. *Women of Courage: Inspiring Stories from the Women Who Lived Them,* ed. Katherine Martin (Novato, Calif.: New World Library, 1999), 133.
3. *CQ Almanac,* (Washington, D.C.: Congressional Quarterly, 1977), 296.
4. Address before a Joint Session of the Congress on the State of the Union, February 6, 1985, www.reagan.utexas.edu/archives/speeches/1985/20685e.htm.

5. For more in-depth analyses of the problems of choice framing for abortion rights, see William Saletan, *Bearing Right: How Conservatives Won the Abortion War* (Berkeley: University of California Press, 2004). For an international perspective on abortion framing, see Myra Marx Ferree et al., *Shaping Abortion Discourse: Democracy and the Public Sphere in Germany and the United States* (Cambridge, UK: Cambridge University Press, 2002).

6. *CQ Almanac* (Washington, D.C.: Congressional Quarterly, 1976), 790.

7. *CQ Almanac* (Washington, D.C.: Congressional Quarterly, 1977), 295.

8. *Beal v. Doe, Maher v. Roe*, 432 U.S. 464 (1977); *Poelker v. Doe* 432 U.S. 519 (1977); *Williams v. Zbaraz* 448 U.S. 358 (1980).

9. *A bill making appropriations for the Departments of Labor, and Health, Education, and Welfare, and related agencies, for the fiscal year ending September 30, 1977,* Public Law 439, 94th Congress, 2nd sess. (June 1976).

10. *Harris v. McRae*, 448 U.S. 297 (1980).

11. *CQ Almanac* (Washington, D.C.: Congressional Quarterly, 1988), 706 and 96-H.

12. Ethan Bronner, "House Failes to Void Veto on Abortion; Medicaid Funding Remains Limited," *Boston Globe*, October 26, 1989, 1.

13. *Making appropriations for the Departments of Labor, Health and Human Services, and Education, and related agencies, for the fiscal year ending September 30, 1994, and for other purposes,* Public Law 112, 103rd Congress, 1st sess. (June 1993).

14. Ronald Reagan, *Abortion and the Conscience of the Nation* (Nashville, Tenn.: Thomas Nelson Publishers, 1984).

15. The movement's struggles led to the premature prediction of the Christian Right's demise. See in particular Steve Bruce, *Rise and Fall of the New Christian Right* (New York: Oxford University Press, 1988).

16. Ibid.

17. Sara Diamond, *Roads to Dominion: Right-Wing Movements and Political Power in the United States* (New York: Guilford Press, 1995).

18. Matthew C. Moen, *The Transformation of the Christian Right* (Tuscaloosa: The University of Alabama Press, 1992).

19. Connie Paige, *Right to Lifers: Who They Are, How They Operate, Where They Get Their Money* (New York: Summit Books, 1983), 31.

20. See Richard A. Viguerie, *The Establishment vs. the People: Is a New Populist Revolt on the Way?* (Falls Church, Va.: American Populist Institute, 1983).

21. Sara Diamond, *Spiritual Warfare: The Politics of the Christian Right* (Montreal: Black Rose Books, 1990), 1.

22. Ibid., 13.

23. Sara Diamond illustrates how the Christian Right has created staying power as a social movement by insulating its members in cultural organizations that support the movement's core values. See *Not by Politics Alone: The Enduring Influence of the Christian Right* (New York: Guilford Press, 1998).

24. For Reed's own description of his movement, see Ralph Reed, *Active Faith: How Christians Are Changing the Soul of American Politics* (New York: The Free Press, 1996).

25. For an article-length treatment on how the Clinton administration lost the war over framing abortion politics, see my article: Melody Rose, "Losing Control: The Intraparty Consequences of Divided Government," *Presidential Studies Quarterly* 31, no. 4 (December 2001): 679–698.

26. *Making appropriations for the Department of Defense for the fiscal year ending September 30, 1996, and for other purposes,* Public Law 61, 104th Congress, 1st sess. (July 1995).

27. *Making appropriations for the Treasury Department, the United States Postal Service, the Executive Office of the President, and certain Independent Agencies, for the fiscal year ending September 30, 1996, and for other purposes,* Public Law 52, 104th Congress, 1st sess. (July 1995).

28. *Summary Report: Early Reproductive Events and Breast Cancer Workshop* (Bethesda, Md.: National Cancer Institute, 2003), www.cancer.gov/cancerinfo/ere-workshop-report.

29. Union of Concerned Scientists, "Scientific Integrity in Policymaking: An Investigation into the Bush Administration's Misuse of Science," February 2004, http://go.ucsusa.org/global_environment/rsi/page.cfm?pageID=1641.

30. "Abortion and Breast Cancer," *New York Times* January 6, 2003.

31. See *The Cost of 'Choice': Women Evaluate the Impact of Abortion,* ed. Erika Bachiochi (San Francisco: Encounter Books, 2004).

32. N. E. Adler et al, "Psychological Factors in Abortion: A Review," *American Psychologist* 47, no. 10 (October 1992): 1194–1204; N. E. Adler, E. J. Ozer, and J. Tschann, "Abortion among Adolescents," *American Psychologist* 58, no. 3 (March 2003): 211–217.

33. *The Unborn Child Pain Awareness Act,* HR 356 109th Congress, 1st sess. (January 2005) and S 51 109th Congress, 1st sess. (January 2005).

34. "Abstract: Fetal Pain: A Systematic Multidisciplinary Review of the Evidence," *American Journal of the American Medical Association* 294, no. 8: (August 24–31, 2005).

35. Denise Grady, "Fetal Pain Challenged in Debate on Abortion," *New York Times,* August 24, 2005.

36. Angela Woodall, "Embryo Adoption Stokes Stem Cell Debate," *Washington Times*, May 30, 2005, http://washingtontimes.com/upi-breaking/20050525-081743-3754r.htm.

37. "Fact Sheet: Valuing Life through Embryo Adoption and Ethical Stem Cell Research," from the White House Web site, May 2005, www.whitehouse.gov/news/releases/2005/05/20050524-10.html#.

38. Republican Jim Ryun of Kansas, House of Representatives, July 17, 2001.

39. Stephanie Schorow, "Embryo Adoptions Give Rise to Lively Debates," *Boston Globe*, May 26, 2005.

40. Pam Belluck, "It's Not So Easy to Adopt an Embryo," *New York Times*, June 12, 2005.

41. Sherry F. Colb, "Governor Jeb Bush Sends Lawyers to Represent a Fetus: Targeting a Mentally Retarded Pregnant Woman for Pro-Life Intervention," http://writ.findlaw.com/colb/20030827.html, August 27, 2003.

42. "Disabled Rape Victim Gives Birth," CBSNews.com, www.cbsnews.com/stories/ 2003/09/01/national/printable570970.shtml, September 1, 2003.

43. *Code of Federal Regulations*, title 12, vol. 1, 42CFR457.10 (Washington, D.C.: Government Printing Office, 2003).

44. These and other relevant administrative questions were posed to the Department of Health and Human Services in May 2002 by Priscilla J. Smith, Acting Director of Domestic Programs, Center for Reproductive Rights, http://reproductiverights.org/hill_ltr_0506schip.html.

45. *Born-Alive Infants Protection Act of 2002*, Public Law 207, 107th Congress, 2nd sess (August 2002).

46. Dr. David Grimes, obstetrician-gynecologist and former abortion surveillance division researcher at the Centers for Disease Control and Prevention, has argued that, "The most significant impact of the 2002 law was a record-keeping change. Previously, a miscarriage before viability was classified as a spontaneous abortion. Under the new provision, it is recorded as a live birth followed by a neonatal death, and parents can claim the child as a tax deduction for that year." See Ceci Connolly, "Doctors Are Warned on Fetus Care; Guidelines Are Issued on Born-Alive Infants Protection Act," *Washington Post*, April 23, 2005., www.washingtonpost.com/wp-dyn/articles/A10411-2005Apr22.html.

47. National Committee for a Human Life Amendment, *Born-Alive Infants Protection Act*, www.nchla.org/issues.asp?ID=44).

48. *Partial-Birth Abortion Ban Act of 2003*, Public Law 105, 108th Congress, 1st sess. (November 2003).

49. Accreditation Council for Graduate Medical Education, *Program Requirements for Residency Education in Obstetrics and Gynecology*, www.acgme.org/acWebsite/downloads/RRC_progReq/220pr705.pdf.
50. *Unborn Victims of Violence Act of 2004*, Public Law 212, 108th Congress, 2nd sess. (April 2004).
51. NARAL Pro-Choice America, "The 'Unborn Victims of Violence Act' Is Not the Solution to Domestic Violence," January 1, 2004.
52. There are workplace protections afforded to the fetus that, while important, go beyond the scope of this work. For a complete analysis of fetal protection policies, see Rachel Roth, *Making Women Pay: The Hidden Costs of Fetal Rights* (Ithaca, N.Y.: Cornell University Press, 2000).
53. *Taxpayers' Freedom of Conscience Act of 2005*, HR 777, 109th Congress, 1st sess. (February 2005).
54. *Sanctity of Life Act of 2005*, HR 776, 109th Congress, 1st sess. (February 2005).

CHAPTER 5

Pro-Choice, Pro-Life, or *Pro-Birth*?

The Partisan Maneuverings of Abortion Politics

"We need to make population and family planning household words. We need to take the sensationalism out of this topic so that it can no longer be used by militants who have no real knowledge of the voluntary nature of the program but, rather are using it as a political steppingstone. If family planning is anything, it is a public health matter."

—George Herbert Walker Bush, 1969,
then a Republican member of Congress from Texas

"The promises of our Declaration of Independence are not just for the strong, the independent or the healthy. They are for everyone, including unborn children. . . . We share a great goal, to work toward a day when every child is welcomed in life and protected in law . . . to build a culture of life, affirming that every person at every stage and season of life, is created equal in God's image."

—President George W. Bush, 2001[1]

The number and severity of abortion restrictions today are higher than at any time since 1973, the year abortion became legalized. As the previous two chapters demonstrate, the provision of abortion is regulated in dozens of ways at both the state and national levels. In addition, women face a host of practical barriers, despite the fact that abortion procedures are safer than ever, and remain, at least ostensibly, legal. Yet activists on both sides of this debate now are faced with the reality that abortion is becoming increasingly inaccessible, particularly for the young and the poor. In fact, it is entirely possible that states and federal entities will continue to undermine abortion rights without ever toppling *Roe*. Given the present restrictions and obstacles, *Roe* appears increasingly obsolete. For many women in the United States, the fact that *Roe* still technically stands is cold comfort.

How did all these erosions to abortion access happen? Chapter 1 showed that a majority of Americans support legal abortion, albeit with some restrictions. How is it that in the face of relatively stable public opinion data, the policies of the last thirty years have consistently become more restrictive? The answer is found in the partisan shifts within abortion politics during that time. For while activists and average Americans might view abortion as a morally complex issue that affects real lives, many politicians see it as an opportunity to build constituency support, secure elections, and, ultimately, to implement their preferred policies. Because of the implications of politicized—and partisan—abortion policy, women's health and the science of reproduction are sometimes sacrificed for political expediency.

PARTY LINES CONVERGE

Any casual observer of contemporary abortion politics in this country might reasonably assume that Democrats have always embraced women's right to abortion access, while across the political aisle Republicans have consistently favored protection of the fetus. As with most policy debates in American politics, however, the devil is in the details. Closer scrutiny reveals that partisans on abortion politics are far from consistent in their stances over time, and far from principled or even logical. Of course, as a social regulatory policy, abortion politics has special features that motivate the political parties. Taking the "right" stance on the issue means representing morality itself; taking the "wrong" stance might mean you "stand up for sin."[2] Thus, the stakes are high for the parties as they settle on their official positions.

In point of fact, the two major parties have traded positions in the past forty years, effectively swapping stances to capture opposing voter groups. (See Appendix B for the party platforms statements on abortion.) There is evidence as well that as the parties' positions have grown more distinct, voters have shifted their loyalties to the party organization whose position best matches their own.[3] Most recently, the Republican Party has advanced a strong, clear anti-abortion position that alienates its moderates. For their part, Democrats take a rhetorical stand in favor of a pro-rights position but consistently compromise this principle when voting on abortion policies. As a result, the United States is presently bereft of a party that is effective in voicing a consistent abortion rights position, which explains how policy has grown more restrictive with time. If Republicans stand for fetal rights, and Republicans control the majority of elected positions in the state and national governments, then policies favoring fetal rights will dominate abortion politics.

It is not inconceivable that a third party could emerge to handle defections from one or both of the two main political parties. The United States has a long tradition of minor parties emerging to represent issues that the major parties have either avoided or not addressed satisfactorily. And in fact, the issue of abortion did inspire the creation of the Right to Life Party in New York State during the 1970s.[4] Still, as history also tells us, third parties in this country are faced with such institutional and practical barriers to success that their long-term viability is always doubtful.

Beginning in the 1970s the political parties grew more distinct in their rhetorical statements on abortion, reflecting the impact of shifting party interests and voter loyalties. Republicans were growing convinced of the strategic importance of the Christian Right, and therefore entertained a pro-life platform, and Democrats tentatively were endorsing *Roe*. In the 1980s, the parties took increasingly polarized positions, both rhetorically and in their voting patterns, entrenching the pro-life Republican and pro-choice Democratic stances, leaving many Americans feeling unrepresented by either party's official position. However, beginning with President Clinton's promise to make abortion "safe," "legal," and "rare," in the 1990s the meaning of "pro-life" and "pro-choice" grew increasingly complex and indistinct. In fact, the evolution of party politics from the Clinton administration through early 2006 is best reflected in statements made by Democratic senator Hillary Clinton and Democratic National Committee chair Howard Dean, both of whom insist that their party must "soften" its approach and reach out to pro-life interests.

This evolution indicates that the shift from abortion rights to fetal rights has come nearly full circle, with an inconsistent abortion rights position within the Democratic Party and a full embrace of fetal rights within the Republican Party. These positions must be understood for what they are: political maneuverings designed to attract interests and win voters. At the very least, the shifting of abortion policy control from doctors to politicians during a time of intense partisanship guarantees that abortion will become a political football; voters must ask whether an issue as deeply personal and moral should be left to the fluctuations and motivations of the party system.

In part the complexity of abortion partisanship must be understood as a reflection of the times, but as demonstrated in chapter 1, there has been only modest fluctuation in public opinion over time, and most Americans take a moderate position on the issue. So why the pendulum swing on official policy? Although it may be seen as a political "flip flop" for partisans to change their official stances, the truth is that individuals, even elected individuals, change their minds for a variety of reasons, both political and personal.

That said, there are some issues of partisanship that must be understood as specific to the United States and its political system. The political parties in this country are notoriously splintered, both because of federalism and because of a weak party system, in the sense that the requirements for membership are low. Federalism, the system of government established by the U.S. Constitution, divides government into three layers: local, state, and national. As a consequence, party organizations exist at all three levels. Sometimes they work in concert; other times they are notably disharmonious, as when local party needs conflict with those at the national level.

Federalism splinters the political parties, but so does the separation of powers at all levels into three branches. The partisans in Congress, elected by specific districts or states, might view any political issue differently than the president, who must serve the whole nation. Two further complications make it difficult to imagine party unity on such issues as abortion: the parties in the Senate and the House abide by different rules and answer to different constituencies, which has led one venerable political science scholar to argue that the United States has a "four party system." [5] Finally, to the extent that many members are elected today more often as individuals than as representatives of a particular political party, there is even less reason to expect party cohesion.

General Party Lines

Still, despite all evidence to the contrary, there are some generalizations that can be made about the party divide over abortion. Inarguably, these divides shift with time, and are evolving still today, but they do exist. Before these trends can be defined, however, it is necessary to first define what it means to be a "party."

One scholar elegantly breaks down party into three categories.[6] For the purposes of this text, this scheme is very useful. First, there is "party in the electorate," those citizens who identify with a political party. Next is "party organization," the institutional party apparatus. These are mostly unelected individuals in local, state, or national party institutions who create party policy and work toward getting party members elected. Last is "party in government," or those elected officials with a party label who represent the party's interests. Together, these three elements constitute political parties in the United States. The role of party in the electorate was considered when in the examination of public opinion data in chapter 1. What follows is a chronological assessment of the party organization and party in government evolutions on abortion policy.

The best indicator of how a party organization views an issue is its platform. National party organizations develop and refine a major party platform with each presidential election. Platforms attract electoral groups to the party, and studies indicate that party members in government do in fact pursue the promises they put forth.[7] With this in mind, it is critical to look more closely at the role of party members in the abortion debate. How well do they reflect their respective party's platform commitments? Can Democrats actually be expected to vote for abortion rights, and do Republicans really vote for fetal rights? Scrutiny of the historical voting patterns of partisans in Congress allows an assessment of the consistency between party organizations and their platforms and parties in government, mainly Congress, and reveals the partisan interests underpinning abortion politics and policy.

THE PARTIES ORGANIZE TO WIN ELECTIONS

Activists in abortion politics may genuinely view the issue purely in terms of values or principles, but partisans see additional, ancillary benefits to embracing the issue. Like other issues, abortion has the power to bind voter groups to political parties. Given that parties win or lose elections based upon their ability to construct winning coalitions, abortion serves a distinctly partisan role. Of course partisans also have values and beliefs, but issues can complement personal beliefs while simultaneously serving a more utilitarian end. As the following paragraphs reveal, the two major parties in the United States have carved out abortion positions that allow them to attract particular voters to the ballot booth. Still, only the Republicans have ridden their position to party dominance and claim the moral high ground on the issue. This fact is not lost on Democrats, who appear to be reconsidering their pro-choice commitment in light of their recent electoral defeats.

The 1960s: The Parties of Lincoln and Douglas

In the 1960s, the two major political parties were largely remnants of the Civil War. Because President Abraham Lincoln was viewed as responsible for ending slavery, Republicans still had very little presence in the South—until the party began taking a states' rights approach on racial issues.[8] For their part, Democrats historically had been the party of local control on issues of race and business. Still, both parties were experiencing significant internal debates over their roles in American politics.

On issues related to women specifically, the Republican Party had taken the lead on progressive public policy since before women gained the federal right to vote in 1920, embracing women's suffrage and supporting the Equal Rights Amendment before Democrats.[9] Democrats appeared consistently late in supporting women's rights position, but clearly saw the electoral advantages in doing so, as evidenced by their inclusion of the Equal Rights Amendment in their own platform.[10]

The party organizations remained officially silent on abortion throughout the decade. The issue at that point was roiling in the states, but the national party organizations had no precedent for becoming involved or for making policy pronouncements on this issue. In fact, they were making a strategic decision to stay clear, preferring instead to allow local party organizations and social movements to take the issue to state legislatures. This silence allowed the parties to remain ostensibly neutral on this controversial subject. National party organizations often choose this course to avoid offending voting groups that might otherwise be supporters. And while a number of Republican officials, including Rep. George H. W. Bush (R-Tex.) and President Richard Nixon made positive statements about the need for contraceptive planning on the heels of the 1965 *Griswold v. Connecti-*

cut decision and growing concern about rising global population rates, the parties themselves took no firm stance.[11]

The 1970s: New Coalitions for New Positions

The absence of national party involvement in abortion politics would end with *Roe*. In fact, the issue gained some momentum in the party organizations just before that ruling during the 1972 presidential nominating conventions, and that momentum would continue unabated throughout the 1970s. As one scholar notes, a fledgling pro-life party organization emerged during the 1972 elections, and attempted to align itself with the Democrats.[12] This effort met with little success prior to *Roe*. However, once fueled by interested presidential candidates, the landmark Supreme Court ruling, and the abortion de-funding movement in Congress, the issue would gain a foothold in both the national party organizations and national government institutions in the mid-1970s. The party organizations at the national level, the Republican National Committee (RNC) and the Democratic National Committee (DNC), have offered official abortion positions in their presidential platforms consistently since 1976. A post-*Roe* political climate had forced them out of their complacency.

For contemporary observers it often comes as a surprise that the parties ever debated the abortion issue at all. Given the Grand Old Party's (GOP) embrace of women's concerns ahead of its rival; many in the abortion rights movement viewed the GOP as the natural party home for their cause. A few years later, when the Republicans' anti-abortion position became clear, some longtime abortion rights supporters within the party were stunned.[13] Others expected that their party would take a rhetorical position in favor of fetal rights, but doubted that party actors would pursue those promises through policy change.[14]

In 1976, both parties ultimately chose to straddle the abortion debate. This should not be surprising, given that the political parties in the United States have a widely acknowledged tendency toward issue avoidance. In part, this tendency stems from the peculiarity in this country of having a *two*-party system in a plurality voting system. Most advanced democracies have three or more viable political parties; this allows each to appeal to a narrower set of interests. With just two parties typically vying for a vast and diverse electorate, the parties tend toward moderation to capture the largest number of voters. When the issue is one of social policy, like abortion or slavery, the parties may have an even greater incentive toward moderation because of the intensity with which many voters approach the question.

The platforms of each party in 1976 confirm this view of national party trends. Both adopted rather tepid statements suggesting divergent positions but acknowledging differences within their parties. By refusing to take absolutist positions, the parties maintained a "big tent"—a centrist position with room enough for reasonable people within each party to disagree.[15] Democrats offered a rather succinct statement to "recognize the religious and ethical nature of the concerns which many Americans have on the subject of abortion," but ultimately argued that overturning *Roe* would be unwise. Calling the issue of abortion "one of the most difficult and controversial of our time," Republicans objected to the Court's intervention in abortion policy and endorsed a constitutional amendment to protect fetal rights, but also encouraged an ongoing civic dialogue.

The Democratic platform appears the more ambiguous of the two, but the Carter administration years did little to distinguish the party organization's position. A self-proclaimed evangelist, President Carter explained his opposition to abortion as an outgrowth of his faith's beliefs. Despite this, there were those who still viewed the Democratic Party as a possible friend to women's progressive interests, and continued to advocate for abortion rights there.

Meanwhile, rights advocates were finding less support than they had anticipated within the RNC, which was growing increasingly discomfited by its minority status. By the mid-1970s, Democrats had controlled the House of Representatives consistently for two decades, and had dominated political office—state and national—as well. As chapter 4 indicated, the emergence of the Christian Right was serendipitous for Republicans anxious to find new constituencies to help them regain majority status. Partnering with the Christian Right would allow the GOP to claim a superior moral stance on many issues, not the least of which is abortion.

The 1980s: The Parties Change Sides

The 1970s might be characterized as the decade of indecision; the 1980s, in contrast, is the decade of decisive party organization mobilization around abortion. Both parties embraced strong positions, characterized by their party platforms, their emergent voting patterns in Congress, and their interest group affiliations. Most surprising to students of political party history, the Democrats and Republicans effectively switched sides on the larger issue of women's rights. All parties go where the voters are; as the minority party in the early 1980s, GOP party leaders were well aware that they needed to make changes. The party's decision to disavow its longtime advocacy of progressive women's causes was made politically possible by the growing Christian Right and its pro-life activists. It had done its math and calculated that the burgeoning movement could deliver more voters than could the older women's movement. A side benefit? Pro-life voters are highly committed and often choose candidates based solely on their abortion stance. The effect of pro-choice voters, on the other hand, is diluted because they are more prone to select candidates and vote based on a larger range of issues.

At the 1980 presidential nominating conventions, Democrats embraced a vague rights position, still acknowledging public disagreement on abortion while objecting to a constitutional amendment designed to overturn *Roe*. For their part, Republicans took a much bolder stance, both in abandoning their forty-year commitment to the Equal Rights Amendment, and in taking up a clear anti-abortion position by endorsing the Hyde Amendment and "protest[ing] the Supreme Court's intrusion into the family structure through its denial of the parents' obligation and right to guide their minor children." While still acknowledging the existence of diverse opinion within its own ranks, the 1980 Republican platform supported a constitutional amendment to protect fetal life.

The Christian Right organizations that were becoming ever more important to the Republican Party experienced some setbacks during this time, as indicated in chapter 4. Although many of their issues made it onto the congressional agenda (a success in itself), the religious lobby won few of these legislative battles. The period up through 1984 might be considered one of trial and error; by the mid- to late 1980s, however, the conservative Christian movement was gaining political sophistication and legitimacy. During Ronald Reagan's second term, the movement was rejuvenated by streamlined organizations and growing political experience. During the 98th Congress (1983–1984), it began to see some legislative success, such as Senate hearings on abortion legislation, and the movement indicated its willingness to participate more fully in the GOP through voter registration drives. National Christian interest groups, including Christian Voice (through its "Christians for Reagan" program) and the American Coalition for Traditional Values, registered voters for Reagan in 1984. In fact, political scientist Kenneth Wald indicates that all together, the Christian Right had registered somewhere between two hundred thousand and three million voters, depending on the study, by 1984.[16]

As a result, the Republican Party in 1984 demonstrated a real change in its abortion commitment. The Republicans wrote an unequivocal fetal rights platform, abandoning the conciliatory tone of the 1970s and promising both to nominate pro-life judges and to eliminate all abortion subsidies because, "The unborn child has a fundamental individual right to life which cannot be infringed." For their part, Democrats also rejected any hint of compromise, articulating the abortion rights position as a matter of protecting the rights of low-income individuals by including a commitment to abortion funding because, "The Democratic party recognizes reproductive freedom as a fundamental human right." They also lamented rising clinic violence, claiming an aspect of abortion politics in which many pro-life and pro-choice activists could find agreement.

By 1988, these divergent positions were solidified, marking the commitments to distinct interests and defying the wisdom that American political parties converge on the centrist position. The Democrats opted for a succinct statement that "The fundamental right of reproductive choice should be guaranteed regardless of ability to pay." The Republicans kept their 1984 language intact, which clearly "opposes the use of public revenues for abortion." Moving into the 1990s, the party lines on abortion had been forged, clearly and indelibly. On its face, the Democrats' strategy may appear the savvier of the two; after all, a majority of the nation supports moderate abortion rights. Still, Republicans were willing to test the limits of that commitment by forcing the most controversial aspects of abortion onto congressional and state agendas. Add to that the greater willingness of pro-life voters to focus their election choices on the abortion issue, and the Republican strategy emerged as the more sanguine of the two.[17]

The 1990s: Republican Loyalty and Democratic Disunity

The language of the 1992 Democratic platform marked a new energy within the pro-choice community. Responding to *Webster v. Reproductive Health Services* (1989) and boasting a pro-choice candidate in Bill Clinton, the Democrats included support for a national law to protect abortion rights in their platform, and most important, embraced "the right of every woman to choose, consistent with *Roe v. Wade*, [and] regardless of ability to pay." Republicans, on the other hand, remained stalwart in their fetal rights statement through their commitment to a human life amendment, the ban on federal funding, and the appointment of pro-life judges. In 1992, the Republican Party also "commend[ed] those who provide alternatives to abortion," indicating their emerging call for "compassionate conservatism."

The language changed measurably in both platforms during the 1996 election. Democrats appeared defensive in the wake of *Planned Parenthood of Southeastern P.A. v. Casey* (1992), and advocated fewer abortions and more comprehensive family planning to prevent unwanted pregnancies: "Our goal is to make abortion less necessary and more rare, not more difficult and more dangerous." Whether this shift represented the fact that socially conservative Republicans had taken control of Congress midway through Clinton's first term, or that Democrats were nominating a pragmatic centrist, the 1996 Democratic abortion plank was a temporary retreat from earlier language that had resolutely supported a woman's right to have an abortion.

For their part, the Republicans faithfully embraced their pro-life position, as well as the party's continued dedication to the nomination of pro-life judges and the enactment of a constitutional amendment for fetal rights. Emboldened by electoral successes in 1994, Republicans extended their platform statement to more broadly include sexuality and contraception. The party articulated a commitment to abstinence education, to the extension of the anti-abortion position to international programs, and to "chastity until marriage as the expected standard of behavior," the last indicating a deeper partisan divide on family planning than had been previously revealed. Overall, the 1996 Republican statement was a bold affirmation of pro-life values.

On one point, however, the Republican platform struck a surprisingly defensive tone, revealing some internal dissent within the party. In explaining that "We oppose abortion, but our pro-life agenda does not include punitive action against women who have an abortion," the party reveals a concern about pushing their position so far as to lose moderate voters. Thus, the platform carefully balances the interests of affirming their base of support (Christian Right voters) while not alienating other potential supporters (moderate Republicans and Democrats). This tension is in part a reflection of the party's nominee in 1996; as a moderate in the Senate, Bob Dole had articulated a softer abortion stance through the early phases of his campaign. In addition, widespread media attention of the "gender gap" postulated that women would defect from the party over abortion.[18] Although the statistics in chapter 2 reveal that women and men do not disagree measurably over abortion, the media attention to this argument may have persuaded some Republicans to soften their message.

2000 and Beyond: Party Platforms Dictate Policy

Vice President Al Gore, anxious to affirm his pro-choice credentials, accepted a Democratic platform that returned to the earlier promise to endorse the right to choose "regardless of ability to pay." Still, the Democratic Party opted to balance a rights principle with a prevention strategy, maintaining the promise to make abortion less necessary through contraceptive research, family planning, and contraception education that had been introduced during the Clinton administration. In their 2000 statement, the Democratic Party made the connection between platform promises and voting outcomes clear: "This year's Supreme Court rulings show to us all that eliminating a woman's right to choose is only one justice away. That's why the stakes in this election are as high as ever." By 2004 the Democratic platform had become more direct than it had been since 1988:

> Because we believe in the privacy and equality of women, we stand proudly for a woman's right to choose, consistent with *Roe v. Wade*, and regardless of her ability to pay. We stand firmly against Republican efforts to undermine that right. At the same time, we strongly support family planning and adoption incentives. Abortion should be safe, legal, and rare.

For their part, Republicans in 2000 maintained a consistent policy, reiterating previous statements as well as the idea of "compassionate conservatism," which was central to candidate George W. Bush's campaign message. It is significant to note that in their 2004 platform, Republicans for the first time listed a number of abortion policy successes, congratulating President Bush for signing the Partial-Birth Abortion Ban in 2003. In addition, in language openly reflecting the Christian Right base of the party, the platform declared, "We praise him for signing the Born Alive Infants Protection Act."

The evolution of party platforms described here reveals the two major parties' philosophical and policy commitments to abortion reform. The significance of these commitments lies both in their predictive possibility, because members of the parties would be expected to generally pursue these positions once elected, and in their symbolic value: platforms can be seen as gestures toward supportive interest groups or those interests that parties would like to attract. Democrats in government are reasonably expected to try to extend abortion rights to low-income women, and likewise, Republicans in government are expected to pursue fetal rights legislation and the nomination of pro-life federal judges.

Of course, parties pursue policy change within a challenging context. In modern America, it has become rare for a political party to control both the White House and the Congress, both of which are necessary for policy change. Moreover, each party can have a fair amount of philosophical and policy disagreement within them. The following paragraphs give an overview of the national political environment over the past thirty years to help readers better understand which perspectives have enjoyed the better opportunity for success.

PARTY IN GOVERNMENT

At the state and federal levels, Republicans have gained majority status with the help of the Christian Right movement, whose primary interest lies in abortion policy. It is no coincidence then that as state legislatures have swung to Republican control, they have increased restrictions on abortion access and explicit protections for the fetus. Chapter 3 documented the number and kind of state-level impediments to abortion access originating at the state level. Figure 5.1 shows that whereas Republicans controlled a mere four state legislatures in the year following *Roe*, they controlled twenty-one—the largest number they had controlled since 1950—after the 2004 election.

Figure 5.2 illustrates a similar transfer of party power in the governors' mansions: whereas in 1974, Republicans could claim only eighteen governorships, by 2004 they controlled twenty-eight. The evolution of Republican Party dominance at the state level, when viewed next to the party's platforms on abortion, explains the tremendous transformation of abortion law during the past thirty years.

There is evidence that the transformation of federal law mirrors this same partisan change of power. The Republican Revolution of 1994 produced the first Republican majority in the House of Representatives in forty years. Since that time, Republicans have maintained that control, and extended it to the Senate in 2002. Legislative dominance, when combined with a two-term Republican president, puts the party in a position of policy dominance it has not enjoyed since President Dwight Eisenhower's first term fifty years ago. Add to these congres-

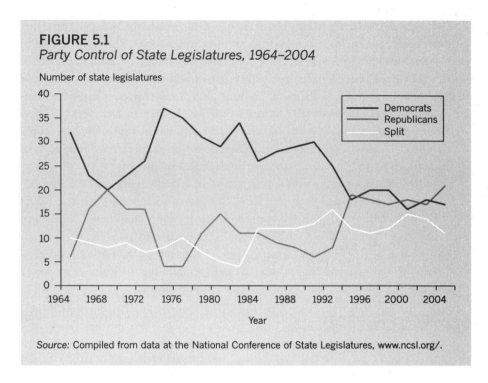

FIGURE 5.1
Party Control of State Legislatures, 1964–2004

Number of state legislatures

Source: Compiled from data at the National Conference of State Legislatures, www.ncsl.org/.

sional successes the observation that by 2008 a Republican will have occupied the White House in twenty-four of the past thirty-six years since the *Roe* ruling, the swing of the pendulum toward abortion restriction is not surprising.

When viewed from this macro level, the parallel takeover by Republicans of the federal government and the shifting tide of abortion politics is understandable. Within these broad strokes, however, are more nuanced shades of opinion within the ranks of both major political parties. For while the elected Republicans have succeeded in moving abortion policy toward the goals of their platform, analysis of congressional voting demonstrates two additional trends: first, abortion voting in Congress complicates the facile definitions of pro-choice and pro-life, which illustrates that abortion invokes a host of other, sometimes competing, ideologies and policy positions. Second, and despite these complexities, it is evident that Democrats are far more likely to break ranks and vote with Republicans on abortion bills than vice versa. Republicans demonstrate much greater party unity on this issue. In the wake of the 2004 general election, several prominent and socially liberal Democrats made nods toward the Republican position on abortion, illustrating a significant shift in the ranks of the party.

What it means to be pro-choice or pro-life may be crystal clear to activists on either side of the abortion debate, but it is not always clear within the context of

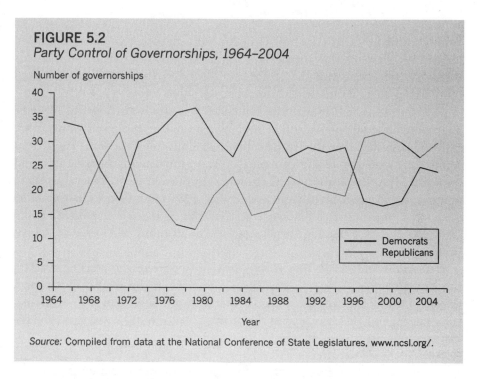

FIGURE 5.2
Party Control of Governorships, 1964–2004

Number of governorships

Year

Source: Compiled from data at the National Conference of State Legislatures, www.ncsl.org/.

congressional voting. In broad terms, Republicans voting in Congress lean toward protection of the fetus, while Congressional Democrats lean more cautiously toward protection of a woman's right to choose to have an abortion. Still, such votes do not occur within a political vacuum. Some abortion policies invoke other ideologies, like freedom of speech, as in the case of the Freedom of Access to Clinic Entrances (FACE) law or the suppression of information on abortion (the "gag" rule). In other instances, adherence to a philosophy that protects women's ability to choose to have an abortion is in conflict with a member's theories of fiscal responsibility, the scope of government involvement in abortion, or both. The lesson of this chapter may be that Congress, of all places, reveals the nuances in Americans' thinking on abortion as much as it reveals the politicking around the issue. A look at a few congressional votes illustrates the point.

Crossing Party Lines on Funding

Voting patterns over the past thirty years show Democrats deeply divided over their promises, while Republicans are consistently unified and committed to their platform. One window into party unity on abortion voting is the Hyde Amendment, the oldest federal abortion restriction. Viewing abortion platform loyalty through the Hyde prism is particularly illuminating because the Democrats have at times promised explicitly through their platform to protect the abortion access of low-income women. In the 1977 Hyde Amendment vote, 103 Democrats joined 98 Republicans in the House to pass the legislation. For their part, 21 Republicans voted against it, along with 134 Democrats. The vote reveals nearly complete party unity among Republicans, while Democrats were split nearly in half.[19]

In all fairness, the 1977 vote may not be the best test of party unity. The issue was new to national politics, and neither party had a deeply committed platform. By 1988, however, when the House considered a bill to let the Hyde restrictions stand, there is an even clearer example of Democratic disunity. In their 1984 and 1988 platforms, the Democrats had announced their desire to protect access to abortion for low-income women. Still, in the 1988 House final floor vote, 90 Democrats joined 126 Republicans to reaffirm the Hyde restriction on Medicaid-funded abortions. While 136 Democrats voted to abandon Hyde, only 30 Republicans agreed.[20]

Democrats were equally split during the unified government years of the Clinton administration. Despite a pro-choice Democrat in the White House and a majority Democratic stronghold in both chambers of Congress in 1993, 98 Democrats voted to uphold Hyde, against their party's platform; 161 voted to rescind the ban. For their part, Republicans illustrated greater party unity than ever: 157 Republicans voted to maintain Hyde; a mere 16 voted against.[21]

The consistent success of the Hyde Amendment prompted Republicans to pursue additional funding restrictions in the 1990s and into the twenty-first century. Looking at the previous vote counts, the Republicans had every reason to expect Democratic support for extending funding bans to other government programs besides Medicaid. Of course, the fact that Republicans gained control of the House in 1995 allowed them to chair committees and set the legislative agenda. And while they have indeed extended the ban to virtually every woman who depends on the federal government for health care, they did so with less help from Democrats than they might have anticipated.

Two votes make the point best. First, a vote to strike a provision that banned funding for abortion under the federal employee health program in the fiscal 2001 Treasury Appropriations bill was supported by 155 Democrats and 28 Republicans. An impressive 185 Republican Representatives rejected the amendment along with 44 Democrats. Nearly 25 percent of Democrats voted against their party platform, but that number is far shy of the nearly 50 percent defection rate that occurred on earlier Hyde votes.[22]

Similarly, roughly 25 percent of Democrats voted with Republicans when the issue before them was federal funding for abortion in federal prisons. The vote concerned an amendment to strike the prohibition of funding in the fiscal 2002 Commerce, Justice, State Appropriations bill. In this instance, 198 Republicans voted with 54 Democrats to retain the ban, whereas 151 Democrats were joined by a mere 17 Republicans (13 percent) to remove the restriction from the bill.[23]

There are several possible explanations for this reduction in Democratic defections from their party's platform. Were there simply fewer Democrats in the House by 1995, as Republicans had gained control of that body through the 1994 election? Were the Democrats in the House at that time from fairly safe Democratic districts, and so voting for restrictions on abortion funding would not hurt them? Or, did Democrats discover by 2000 that voting against funding abortions for low-income and vulnerable groups of women did not hurt their electoral prospects, because these women rarely are represented by congressional lobbies? Citizens against funding for abortions did have congressional lobbies, however, and so those Democrats in competitive districts may have felt that a vote to uphold funding bans was the easier electoral decision. Whatever the reason, it is striking that on the clearest aspect of the Democratic abortion platform—funding—a sizable plurality of Democrats consistently vote to uphold the *Republican* position.

Partisan Loyalty in Prohibition and Fetal Protection

Recently, congressional voting on abortion has gone beyond funding bans and has included prohibitions on procedures and practices, as well as affirmative fetal protections, as chapter 4 demonstrated. This might be considered a "front door" attack on abortion access. It is not surprising to find that here too Democrats are defecting from their party organization's pro-choice stance in record numbers and assisting Republicans in rolling back abortion access.

Table 5.1 illustrates this trend. Overall, of the four major pieces of restrictive abortion legislation to reach the House floor in recent years, most are supported overwhelmingly by Republicans and by what could be seen as a surprising number of Democrats. The exception to this rule was the FACE bill of 1994, which sought to curb the rising clinic violence of the 1980s and early 1990s. An unusually high percentage of Republicans joined Democrats in sending this legislation to President Clinton for his signature. Still, as a matter touching upon concerns of both abortion and crime, this vote should be viewed less as an embrace of abortion access per se, and more as a law-and-order provision. Republicans could object to abortion provision and to clinic violence simultaneously in casting a supportive vote for FACE.

The Democratic defection rates exhibited in Table 5.1 exceed their rates of party-line defection on recent funding issues. These bills perhaps clearly challenge the depth of support among Democrats for abortion rights and access, although they also can be seen as reaching beyond the traditional scope of support for abortion access. Both the Parental Notification Bill of 1998 and the Child Interstate Notification Abortion Act of 2005 invoke frames of parental rights and child

TABLE 5.1

Recent Examples of Party-Line Abortion Voting in the House of Representatives

Bill	Political Party	Ayes	Nays	Present	Not Voting	% Party Voting in Unity
Freedom to Clinic Access Act of 1994	Republicans	35	133	0	8	68
	Democrats	201	36	0	19	79
Parental Notification Bill of 1998	Republicans	209	14	0	4	92
	Democrats	67	135	0	4	66
Partial Birth Abortion Ban Act of 2003	Republicans	208	9	0	4	94
	Democrats	65	141	1	4	67
Child Interstate Abortion Notification Act of 2005	Republicans	216	11	0	4	94
	Democrats	54	145	0	3	72
Average Party Unity Score, across Four Abortion Votes	Republican					87
	Democrats					71

Source: Data compiled from *CQ Almanac* (Washington, D.C.: Congressional Quarterly), relevant years.

safety in addition to abortion rights per se. Furthermore, the Partial-Birth Abortion Ban was widely viewed as stretching the Democrats' commitment to abortion rights. Nevertheless, the 2004 Democratic platform was among the most assertive statements of the pro-choice position articulated by the party to date. Actual party in government votes, however, illustrate a precipitous decline within elected Democrats' commitment to abortion rights and access, signaling future encroachments as well as extended protections for fetuses. As the last row in Table 5.1 demonstrates, Republicans can boast an average party unity score of 87 percent across these four bills, while Democrats produce a much lower unity score of 71 percent.

Democratic Disunity, Republican Unity

A pivotal shift in the Democratic Party began in the 1990s under the leadership of President Clinton, who famously intoned that abortion should become "safe," "legal," and "rare." With these words, the president gave a nod to those who believe abortion to be fundamentally wrong, and offered cover for conservative Democrats to vote in a way that would be discordant with their party platform. Since gaining the majority in 1995, Republicans have become expert at identifying the aspects of abortion policy that divide the Democratic Party, such as late-term abortion and abortion for minors, and pushing forward those issues to challenge the Democrats' commitment to the pro-choice position and to lay bare their internal divisions on abortion.

According to one prominent scholar, "Being pro-choice means being in favor of contraception's and abortion's being legal, available, and accessible to those who want to use them, no matter what their circumstances might be and what decision they want to make."[24] Given this definition, it is not entirely clear how pro-choice the Democrats in government are today.

Still, for their part, Republican voting is not wholly consistent either. Democrats' abortion votes appear incongruous with their platform commitments; however, Republicans offer inconsistency of a different sort: Much of the Republican commitment to the pro-life position in abortion votes appears incompatible with their votes on other life-related policies and quality of life issues. Sister Joan Chittister, a Benedictine prioress and social psychologist, describes the discontinuity:

> But I do not believe that just because you're opposed to abortion that that makes you pro-life. In fact, I think in many cases, your morality is deeply lacking. If all you want is a child born but not a child fed, not a child educated, not a child housed, and why would I think that you don't? Because you don't want any tax money to go there. That's not pro-life. That's pro-birth. We need a much broader conversation on what the morality of pro-life is.[25]

For their part, Republicans in Congress are consistently voting to protect fetal interests. Those protected fetuses, presumably, will become children. So what kind of protection do Republicans extend to children? A short overview of recent welfare and health care reform demonstrates a striking lack of concern for fetuses after birth.

The Personal Responsibility and Work Opportunity Reconciliation Act of 1996, illustrates the point.[26] This legislation, which President Clinton promised would "end welfare as we know it," is widely understood to have decreased federal spending on welfare recipients while simultaneously increasing the role of states in welfare administration. One seldom-mentioned aspect of the law is its relationship to abortion practice. Welfare today creates a curious incentive for low-income women to have abortions; this fact may in part account for the increased abortion rates among low-income women noted earlier in this book. The law creates a financial incentive to abort by allowing states the option to deny welfare benefits to infants whose mothers became pregnant while receiving welfare.[27] This provision seems incompatible with the Republicans' fetal protection policy.

Some might argue this point further: the United States ranks quite low among industrialized nations for child health and quite high for infant and child mortality rates. And while the Republicans are responsible for extending State Children's Health Insurance Program (SCHIP) benefits to fetuses, these benefits do not ostensibly include prenatal care for the mother, despite the fact that prenatal care is widely understood as a key component to preventing, premature births, low birth weight, and sickly babies.

Looking to the other resources that children need to lead healthy lives, we find additional lapses within Republican policy. Inaction on health care insurance for America's forty-five million uninsured, especially during a period of unified Republican government, seems out of step with a pro-life stance. Support for K–12 education has declined nationwide, just as Republicans gained control of state and federal legislative and executive bodies. So while Democrats can be criticized for decreasing support of abortion access and rights despite their rhetorical commitment to these policies, the Republicans' defense of the fetus sits uncomfortably with the lack of policy commitments to children's health and education.

The 2004 Election: Abortion as a Wedge Issue?

Pundits and politicians alike from all political stripes proclaimed 2004 as a victory for social conservatives. From the passage of eleven state referenda banning gay unions[28] to the triumph of Republican candidates at all levels, the media touted 2004 as the year of the values vote. "Three days after the presidential election, it is clear that it was not the war on terror, but the issue of what we're calling moral values that drove President Bush and other Republicans to victory this week," proclaimed Tucker Carlson, then-host of CNN's political program *Crossfire*.[29]

The profile of abortion in the 2004 election was elevated when some Catholic bishops in the Northeast announced John Kerry, a Catholic candidate, should not receive communion as a result of his pro-choice position. Other church leaders declared that a vote for pro-choice candidates would amount to a sin. Colorado Archbishop Charles J. Chaput proclaimed that Catholics voting for pro-choice candidates were "cooperating in evil." [30] Other church officials, including Washington, D.C.'s Archbishop Theodore Cardinal McCarrick, distanced themselves from these statements, possibly indicating some tension within the church hierarchy on this question.

A more nuanced appraisal of the election, however, reveals thin evidence for this "values vote" claim. Some Democrats were quick to counter that there is more to morality than gay marriage and abortion. Not only do many Democrats and liberals more broadly view their positions on poverty, Social Security, war, and education to be matters of morality, there is little evidence that the electorate ranked the "moral" issues of abortion or gay rights high on their list of voting priorities. One exit poll of nearly seven thousand voters on November 2, 2004, asked, "Which one issue mattered most in deciding how you voted for president?" The poll found that 22 percent of those surveyed responded "moral values." [31]

Pundits were quick to assume that the result indicated wide support for President Bush's reelection bid; however, that question was so broadly worded it is hard to discern what the respondents meant by "moral values." [32] The question did not define moral values, which means that voters most concerned with gay marriage and voters most concerned with candidate honesty could have been lumped together in the result. A later poll conducted by Harris found that for the 22 percent who ranked morality high on their list of concerns, there was little consensus about they thought the term meant.[33]

Recent scholarship on the issue suggests media claims of a moral vote in 2004 were hasty and overblown.[34] The most thorough analysis of the exit polling for that year reveals that abortion had "no significant effect on presidential vote choice when party identification, ideology, and demographics are taken into account." [35] Other issues, like the war and the economy, were far better predictors of voters' candidate selections. In addition, early analysis suggests that the voter turnout of religious conservatives, long acknowledged as a mainstay of the Republican Party's electoral success,[36] did not increase in 2004 from previous elections.[37]

Even so, Democratic politicians took note of the impact that the moral vote could have had on the election. Their failure to wrest control of either chamber of Congress or the White House from the Republicans for the past decade may pressure the party to reexamine policy positions and strategy. Combined with the success at the federal and state levels of legislation that protects the fetus and restricts women's access to abortion services, the electoral struggles of the Democratic Party has led some Democrats in government to question their commitment to abortion access.

The increased pressure on Democrats to redefine their abortion position was most evident in the election for DNC chair in 2005. A number of Democratic loyalists announced their intention to run for the position. Most interesting was the short-lived candidacy of former representative Tim Roemer of Indiana. Roemer identifies himself as a pro-life Democrat, and indicated his interest in moderating the party's official abortion position. On the heels of that announcement, former Vermont governor and 2004 presidential aspirant Howard Dean, in running for the position, announced his view that "We ought not turn our back on pro-life people, even though the vast majority of people in this party are pro-choice. . . . I don't have any objection to someone who is pro-life, if they are really dedicated to the welfare of children." [38] Dean's statement startled some observers and angered pro-choice organizations, who viewed it as strategic pandering to a vocal minority.

Dean went on to win the chair, and has remained relatively quiet on the subject of abortion since his election.

Signs of internal dissent within the party were seen in the comments of a few high-profile Democrats in January 2005, when supporters and opponents alike marked the thirty-second anniversary of the *Roe* ruling. Most notably, liberal senator Ted Kennedy of Massachusetts reaffirmed former president Bill Clinton's safe, legal, and rare slogan at a press club speech. Like her colleague, Sen. Hillary Rodham Clinton of New York also struck a compromising tone in her speech at a New York State Family Planning Providers conference: "reducing unwanted pregnancy [is] an issue we should be able to find common ground on with people on the other side of this debate." Acknowledging the implicit morality in the abortion decision, Clinton angered many in her audience by intoning that "we can all recognize that abortion in many ways represents a sad, even tragic choice to many, many women." [39] Senator Clinton went on to emphasize the centrality of family planning in solving the incidence of unwanted pregnancy, the largest reason for abortion in the United States. She bashed the Bush administration's reapplication of the international gag rule, arguing that only through thorough family planning could unintended pregnancy rates, which are higher in the United States than in most of the industrialized world, be reduced.

Given Clinton's long record of supporting abortion rights, the media and pro-choice groups nationwide pronounced these comments inspired by political maneuverings, not ideological convictions. A rumored 2008 presidential bid may have been the cause, and her remarks might be viewed as a capitulation to pro-life interests to some, but her emphasis on abortion prevention also appears to be a sincere effort to find common ground with those interests. While pro-life and pro-choice activists cannot agree on the proper outcome for unintended pregnancies, the most likely place for any agreement at all is in preventing those pregnancies in the first place.

Senator Clinton and many of her colleagues have adopted a strategy of pregnancy prevention as a way to move the country toward fulfillment of her husband's avowal of safe, legal, and rare abortions. But in practice, this effort has met with great resistance from pro-life interests. As chapter 4 illustrated, funding for Title X, which provides family planning services to roughly 4.5 million people per year, has lost funding just as the nation's population has increased. In 2005, Clinton and her colleagues drafted the Equity in Prescription Insurance and Contraceptive Coverage Act of 2005 (S 1214), which would require private insurance plans to cover FDA-approved prescription contraceptives and related medical services. That legislation, as well as the House version of the bill, remains in committee at the time of this writing. [40]

Still, there appears to be little possibility for the expansion of family planning programs; in fact, the Bush administration has chosen instead to increase funding for abstinence-only programs. In 2005, the federal government will spend an estimated $170 million on such programs for youth, more than double the amount spent in 2001. The trend toward abstinence instruction over sexual education in schools once again reflects the growing influence of the Christian Right within the federal government. Federally funded abstinence programs are prohibited from teaching any method of pregnancy prevention other than abstinence before marriage, despite little scientific evidence that such programs reduce teen pregnancy or the incidence of sexually transmitted diseases.[41]

Ineffectiveness may not deter lawmakers from funding abstinence-only programs, but a study of these programs, prepared for Rep. Henry A. Waxman (D-Calif.), may. Released in December 2004, *The Content of Federally Funded Abstinence-Only Education Programs* uncovered a series of errors, distortions, and scientific misrepresentations in the curricula. The report found that more than 80 percent of SPRANS (Special Programs of Regional and National Significance Community-Based Abstinence Education) grantees' curricula in 2003 contained information that was factually incorrect. Among the errors were spurious claims about a connection between abortion and future sterility, an admonition regarding the negative psychological effects of abortion, such factual errors as a claim that fetuses are formed through the combination of twenty-four chromosomes from each parent, and a host of dangerously erroneous claims about birth control methods.[42]

References to religious values were common throughout the curricula. The SPRANS program declares that sex within marriage "is the expected standard of human sexual activity," and that "Conception, also known as fertilization, occurs when one sperm unites with one egg in the upper third of the fallopian tube. This is when life begins." The programs routinely refer to blastocysts and fetuses as "babies." In all, these programs reinforce the religious values of some Americans while jeopardizing scientific fact and public health. Within this context, it is hard to envision a compromise that Democrats and Republicans could forge through pregnancy prevention.[43]

In addition, there seems to be little political will on the Republican side of the aisle to provide emergency contraception to prevent abortions. When the Department of Justice's Office of Violence against Women released a new 130-page protocol for sexual assault treatment, it contained no message about "Plan B," the morning after pill that can prevent unwanted pregnancy if taken shortly after intercourse.

Likewise, the Prevention First Act of 2005 (HR 1709; S20), which would increase Title X monies to expand Medicaid family planning; fund emergency contraception public education for doctors, nurses, and women; and require emergency health workers to stock Plan B for survivors of sexual assault, works to reduce the need for abortion. Sponsored in the Senate by pro-life Senate minority leader Harry Reid (D-Nev.) and more than one hundred representatives in the House, this legislation has also languished in committee since April 2005.

Democrats like Howard Dean and Hillary Clinton have challenged their party's official abortion platform by suggesting a softening of it. Likewise, in 2005, former head of the Environmental Protection Agency and Republican governor of New Jersey Christine Todd Whitman has publicly distanced herself from her party's stance on abortion and contraception, among other policies. Whitman's statement is worth including at length below, because it may indicate a schism within the Republican Party over the abortion position:

> I frankly find the so-called debate about abortion counterproductive and the tactics of the social fundamentalists offensive. I don't know anyone who is proabortion. Every person I've ever known or worked with who supports the right of the woman to make the choice about whether or not to continue a pregnancy has wished that no one ever had to confront that choice. I consider myself to be pro-life, but I also understand that there are times when a woman may face that terrible decision. I believe the truly conservative view is that it is a woman's choice to make for herself, not government's to dictate. The suggestion by some in the antiabortion movement that most women who undergo the trauma of an abortion are simply indulging themselves in a form of cosmetic surgery or birth control is insulting to all women. Even though there are some women who abuse their freedom of choice, they are in the distinct minority. Most Americans see this just the way I do; they're neither proabortion nor antichoice, but are somewhere in the middle.[44]

The two party organizations in this country have clearly diverged in their abortion statements since 1976, when those statements first appeared in party platforms. Since then, a powerful Christian Right movement committed to the pro-life position has effected significant change in aligning the Republican Party's agenda with its own. Democrats have diverged too, although very recently there is evidence that they are in retreat. In response to shifting public policy and a perceived values vote in 2004, Democratic leadership has been making more efforts at conciliation through pregnancy prevention efforts. The 2008 presidential election may provide some clarity about the parties' future strategies regarding the abortion issue.

CONCLUSION

The Republican and Democratic party organizations have embraced polarized positions on abortion rights to capture particular groups of voters. For anyone who cares deeply about abortion as either a moral or scientific issue, the fact that abortion policy reflects political maneuverings should be reason for concern. The current party positions and voting patterns do not reflect long-held philosophical commitments, but rather the strategy of collecting together enough votes to win elections. For their part, Republicans have made policy promises that have amassed a powerful coalition that includes members of the Christian Right. Republicans who have elected to enact those promises have consistently done so since being in the majority.

Democrats, meanwhile, maintain a real platform commitment to abortion rights, but waffle when confronted with abortion policy. They are well aware that many Americans are pro-choice, but they also are not single-issue voters, and Democrats have lost their way in protecting women's rights. Because Democratic voters are less likely to be single-mindedly concerned about abortion policy, Democratic officeholders can easily stray from the path of pro-rights abortion lawmaking. As a consequence, the United States today lacks a party that reliably and consistently pursues policies that protect women's access to abortion, which could ultimately affect their social citizenship. Furthermore, the reality that women affected most by abortion restrictions, the young and the poor, either cannot vote or do so in low numbers allows the two parties to ignore the impact these advancing restrictions have: unless the consequence of abortion restrictions are felt at the ballot box, the two parties are unlikely to change course.

Whether this restrictive trend sits comfortably within the larger Republican ideology and policy commitments is another question. It is not unreasonable to assume that the party of fetal rights would become the party of children's rights to wellness and education. Curiously, while Democrats are busy fighting with each other over the depth of their commitment to abortion, Republicans have forged a fetal rights agenda that appears to end at birth.

DISCUSSION QUESTIONS

1. Why have the abortion positions of the two major political parties changed over time? What forces caused the abortion stances of the two major parties to shift? Which groups of voters does each party hope to attract? Who will each party alienate as a result of its platform?
2. What are the logical and practical weaknesses in the Democratic and Republican abortion positions?
3. How does the issue of contraception complicate the abortion positions of the two major political parties?
4. Does contraception policy provide any opportunity for collaboration between the pro-rights and anti-abortion positions? Why or why not?

5. Why are the parties not coming together to provide federally funded contraception and sex education? Wouldn't the demand for abortion decline if the federal government increased access to contraception?
6. Do shifts in party positions over time change your view of recent Supreme Court decisions that give more authority to politicians in the arena of abortion?
7. What would you say is the future of the Republican Party's view on abortion? The Democratic Party's view?
8. Are there aspects of abortion not being articulated by either party? Why?
9. What inconsistencies, if any, exist within each party's abortion position or voting patterns?

SUGGESTED READING

Fiorina, Morris P., with Samuel J. Abrams and Jeremy C. Pope, *Culture War? The Myth of a Polarized America,* New York: Pearson Longman, 2005.
Frank, Thomas, *What's the Matter with Kansas? How Conservatives Won the Heart of America,* New York: Owl Books, 2005.
Melich, Tonya, *The Republican War against Women: An Insider's Report from behind the Lines,* New York: Bantam Books, 1996.
Miller, Zell, *A National Party No More: The Conscience of a Conservative Democrat,* Atlanta: Stroud and Hall, 2003.
Spitzer, Robert J., *The Right to Life Movement and Third Party Politics,* Westport, Conn.: Greenwood Press, 1987.
Wallis, Jim, *God's Politics: Why the Right Gets It Wrong and the Left Doesn't Get It,* San Francisco: HarperSanFrancisco, 2005.
Whitman, Christine Todd, *It's My Party Too: The Battle for the Heart of the GOP and the Future of America,* New York: Penguin Press, 2005.
Wilcox, Clyde, *Onward Christian Soldiers: The Religious Right in American Politics,* 3rd ed., Boulder, Colo.: Westview Press, 2005.

NOTES

1. Ann Blackman, "Bush Act on Abortion 'Gag Rule'," *Time* magazine online, January 22, 2001, www.time.com/time/nation/article/0,8599,96275,00.html.
2. Elizabeth Anne Oldmixon, *Uncompromising Positions: God, Sex, and the U.S. House of Representatives* (Georgetown University Press, 2005), 37.

3. Greg D. Adams, "Abortion: Evidence of an Issue Evolution," *American Journal of Political Science* 41, no. 3 (July 1997): 718–737.

4. Robert J. Spitzer, *The Right to Life Movement and Third Party Politics* (Westport, Conn.: Greenwood Press, 1987).

5. James McGregor Burns, *The Deadlock of Democracy: Four-Party Politics in America* (Englewood Cliffs, N.J.: Prentice-Hall, 1963).

6. Marjorie Randon Hershey, *Party Politics in America*, 11th ed. (New York: Pearson Longman, 2005). Hershey owes this framing of party politics to the great political scientist V. O. Key, *Politics, Parties, and Pressure Groups*, 5th ed. (New York: Crowell, 1964).

7. Gerald Pomper argued in 1968 that party changes that allowed new interests into the conventions would increase the chances that the parties might adopt divergent planks on hotly contested issues. See *Elections in America* (New York: Dodd, Mead, and Company, 1968), in which he also documents the pursuit of platform promises by members of Congress. Others confirmed this view. See, for instance, Paul T. David, "Party Platforms as National Plans," *Public Administration Review* 31 (May–June 1971): 303–315; Jeff Fishel, *Presidents and Promises* (Washington, D.C.: CQ Press, 1985); Michael G. Krukones, *Promises and Performance: Presidential Campaigns as Policy Predictors* (Lanham, Md.: University Press of American, 1984); and Alan D. Monroe, "American Party Platforms and Public Opinion," *American Journal of Political Science* 27 (February 1983): 27–42.

8. For an examination of how race and taxes changed the Republican Party in the mid-twentieth century, see Thomas Byrne Edsall and Mary D. Edsall, *Chain Reaction: The Impact of Race, Rights, and Taxes on American Politics* (New York: W.W. Norton, 1991).

9. Jo Freeman, "Whom You Know versus Whom You Represent: Feminist Influence in the Democratic and Republican Parties," in *The Women's Movements of the United States and Western Europe: Consciousness, Political Opportunity, and Public Policy* ed. Mary Fainsod Katzenstein and Carol McClurg Mueller (Philadelphia: Temple University Press, 1987), 215–244.

10. Nancy F. Cott, *The Grounding of Modern Feminism* (New Haven, Conn.: Yale University Press, 1987).

11. Paul Ehrlich, *Population Bomb* (New York: Ballantine Books, 1968).

12. Spitzer, *Right to Life Movement.*

13. Longtime party loyalist and Republican delegate Mary Dent Crisp remarked during a personal interview with the author in 1993 that she was stunned by her party's embrace of the pro-life position, arguing that her party had "moved away from me." Mary Dent Crisp, director of Republican Coalition

for Choice. Personal interview with author, at home in Washington, D.C., March 21, 1993.

14. Ann Stone, director of Republicans for Choice. Personal interview with author, Republicans for Choice headquarters, Fairfax, Virginia, March 20, 1995.

15. The term "big tent" was coined in the early 1980s by Republican strategist and RNC chair Lee Atwater, who urged his party to take an inclusive abortion position so as not to alienate voters.

16. Kenneth D. Wald, *Religion and Politics in the United States* (Washington, D.C.: CQ Press, 1992), 195.

17. For a recent discussion of single-issue voting and abortion, see Ted G. Jelen and Clyde Wilcox, "Causes and Consequences of Public Attitudes toward Abortion: A Review and Research Agenda," *Political Research Quarterly* 56, no. 4. (December 2003): 489–500.

18. For an example of these works, see Bella Abzug with Mim Kelber, *Gender Gap: Bella Abzug's Guide to Political Power for Women* (Boston: Houghton-Mifflin, 1984).

19. *CQ Almanac* (Washington, D.C.: Congressional Quarterly, 1977).

20. *CQ Almanac* (Washington, D.C.: Congressional Quarterly, 1988).

21. *Congressional Quarterly Weekly Report,* June 30, 1993, HR 2518.

22. *Congressional Quarterly Weekly Report,* July 21, 2000, HR 4871.

23. *Congressional Quarterly Weekly Report,* July 17, 2001, HR 2500.

24. Alexander C. Sanger, *Beyond Choice: Reproductive Rights in the 21st Century* (New York: PublicAffairs, 2004) 5.

25. Sister Joan Chittister, interview by Bill Moyers, *NOW: With Bill Moyers,* PBS, November 12, 2004, www.pbs.org/now/printable/transcript346_full_print. html.

26. *Personal Responsibility and Work Opportunity Reconciliation Act of 1996,* Public Law 193, 104th Congress, 2nd sess. (August 1996).

27. The law reads as follows: "Under the new law, states have the option to implement a family cap. HR 4 required states to deny cash benefits to children born to welfare recipients unless the state legislature explicitly voted to provide benefits," http://thomas.loc.gov/cgi-bin/query/z?c104:H.R.3734.ENR:htm.

28. The states that had gay marriage ban ballot initiatives were Arkansas, Georgia, Kentucky, Michigan, Mississippi, Missouri, North Dakota, Ohio, Oklahoma, Oregon, and Utah.

29. See Dick Meyer, "The Anatomy of a Myth: How Did One Exit Poll Answer Become the Story of How Bush Won?" *Washington Post,* December 5, 2004.

30. Joseph Cardinal Ratzinger, "Vote God: Worthiness to Receive Holy Communion," www.st-thomascamas.org/votegod2004/worthiness.htm and Jaimal Yogis and Nicole LaRosa, "Voting Is Not a Sin: The Catholic Church Divided,"

Columbia Journalism online, www.jrn.columbia.edu/studentwork/election/2004/catholic_vote.asp.

31. Meyer, "Anatomy of a Myth."

32. Linda Feldmann, "For Democrats, Abortion Revisited," *Christian Science Monitor,* January 21, 2005, www.csmonitor.com/2005/0121/p03s01-uspo.htm.

33. Fiorina argues that the culture war is a myth concocted by partisans to win elections. See Morris P. Fiorina, with Samuel J. Abrams and Jeremy C. Pope, *Culture War? The Myth of a Polarized America* (New York: Pearson Longman, 2005).

34. D. Sunshine Hillygus and Todd G. Shields, "Moral Issues and Voter Decision Making in the 2004 Presidential Election," *PS: Political Science and Politics,* 38, no. 2 (April 2005), 201–209.

35. www.harrisinteractive.com/harris_poll/index.asp?PID=529.

36. Clyde Wilcox, *Onward Christian Soldiers: The Religious Right in American Politics,* 3rd. ed. (Boulder, Colo.: Westview Press, 2005).

37. Barry C. Burden, "An Alternative Account of the 2004 Presidential Election," *The Forum* 2, no. 4, article 2, www.bepress.com/forum/vol2/iss4/art2.

38. Adam Nagourney, "Democrats Weigh De-emphasizing Abortion as an Issue," *New York Times,* December 23, 2005, www.nytimes.com/2004/12/24/politics/24abortion.html?oref=login&page.

39. "Remarks by Senator Hillary Rodham Clinton to the NYS Family Planning Providers," January 24, 2005, http://clinton/senate.gov/~clinton/speeches/2005125A05.html or www.nytimes.com/2005/07/13/nyregion/13hillary.ready.html?ei=5090&en=ca200c39b840ad53&ex=1278907200&partner=rssuserland&emc=rss&pagewanted=all.

40. *Equity in Fertility Coverage Act of 2005,* HR 2759, 109th Congress, 1st sess. (June 2005).

41. There have been two major studies: Douglas Kirby, *Do Abstinence-Only Programs Delay the Initiation of Sex among Young People and Reduce Teen Pregnancy?* (Washington, D.C.: National Campaign to Prevent Teen Pregnancy, 2002), 6; and Debra Hauser, *Five Years of Abstinence-Only-Until-Marriage Education: Assessing the Impact,* (Washington, D.C.: Advocates for Youth, 2004), 2–3.

42. House Committee on Government Reform—Minority Staff Special Investigation Division, *The Content of Federally Funded Abstinence-Only Education Programs,* 108th Congress, 2nd sess. (December 2004), www.democrats.reform.house.gov.

43. Ibid.

44. Christine Todd Whitman, *It's My Party Too: The Battle for the Heart of the GOP and the Future of America* (New York: Penguin Press, 2005), 81.

CHAPTER 6

Conclusion: The Pendulum Swings

He was an obstetrician; he delivered babies into the world. His colleagues called
this "the Lord's work." And he was an abortionist; he delivered mothers, too.
His colleagues called this "the Devil's work," but it was all the Lord's work to
Wilbur Larch.

—*The Cider House Rules*, by John Irving

"I am pro-choice because I'm a mother, I'm a Christian, and I'm a doctor."

—Dr. Siglinda Jacobsen, obstetrician-gynecologist

INTRODUCTION: WHERE COULD WE GO FROM HERE?

In February 2006, South Dakota set aside the familiar practice of limiting abortion
in favor of the tactic preferred by early anti-abortion organizations: ban it. In taking this tack, the state is deliberately challenging *Roe v. Wade* (1973). The law makes
abortion illegal in all cases except to save the life of the mother, including instances
in which pregnancy is the result of rape or incest, or when a woman's health is at
risk. Although the legislation would not punish a woman for procuring an abortion, it would penalize anyone providing one with a fine and possible jail time.

Many abortion rights activists in this country fear the possibility that with the
addition of new justices on the Supreme Court, *Roe v. Wade* will be overturned,
either through consideration of the South Dakota statute, the federal Partial-
Birth Abortion Ban, or some similar provision. In fact, some organizations are
preparing for that inevitability.[1] More likely than legal prohibition is the possibility that abortion may become functionally *unavailable,* even while remaining ostensibly legal and medically safe. Faced with ever more hurdles and the fewest number of abortion providers since abortion first became legal, women may find
themselves with a legal *right* to abortion, but no access to the procedure, particularly if they are poor or young.

This book has chronicled the sweeping abortion changes both at the state and
federal levels since 1973. The central argument here is that abortion today is less
accessible than it has been since it was illegal prior to the *Roe* ruling. Through
both statutory and practical barriers, abortion is becoming inaccessible to those

without resources, much as it was before *Roe* limited a state's ability to restrict access. These restrictions, now commonplace across the nation, are the result of intense social regulatory politics and demonstrate all the typical characteristics of this policy type.

Beyond the evidence of the erosion of abortion access, this text has made a case for emerging fetal citizenship. As defined in the Introduction, social citizenship implies state-sponsored programs, benefits, and protections. While they are not yet protected to the extent that pro-life activists would prefer, fetuses are better protected today that at any time since *Roe*. The accumulation of these affirmative protections and abortion restrictions weights the state's interest in favor of fetal life. The U.S. Supreme Court has maintained in recent years that states have a right to favor fetal life over abortion, and may indicate this preference through state law so long as the law does not create an undue burden to the woman seeking to end her pregnancy.

The greatest danger to the pro-abortion rights cause, however, is that most Americans are unaware of the incremental protections for the fetus at the expense of the rights of the mother. Americans need to understand the real consequences of limited abortion access. Abortion may be available "on demand" for adult women who can travel to find a clinic or other appropriate facility, or who have the advantage of a private physician willing to perform the procedure, but it is certainly less accessible to the young, those with low incomes, and the geographically remote. For these groups of women, abortion may remain a right, but little else.

Given the preponderance of evidence the reality must be faced that there are two classes of abortion patients: those with the resources to surmount the barriers to fertility control, and those without them. One thing, however, binds all abortion patients together: they face mounting social and statutory pressures to continue their pregnancies, reflecting the weight of moralism at play in the abortion debate. Society is increasingly sending the message that abortion is first a moral issue, and only becomes a medical issue when there is a crisis.

What might offset these growing trends? As is the case with other public policies, even social regulatory policies, the pendulum may yet swing in the other direction. The catalysts that will provoke such action are unforeseeable. Nevertheless, three trends, quiet and subtle, may reaffirm women's rights in the area of reproductive health. In the interstices of these movements lie possibilities for change and new understandings of how seeking an abortion is a right of citizenship.

THE PHYSICIANS RETURN

A number of signs point to the possible re-emergence of physicians as a political lobby in the abortion policy arena, not the least of which is history. As University of California, Berkeley, sociologist Kristin Luker and others have demonstrated, doctors in this country have played a pivotal role in shaping abortion policy, sometimes by restricting it, sometimes by liberalizing it. Today's physicians have fresh reasons to become involved: both their occupations and their lives are at risk.

To a person, the physicians I spoke with in preparing this book talked about the barriers to career-entry and advancement when becoming an abortion provider. Those affiliated with a major institution are perhaps the more fortunate: their work is insulated within a large infrastructure, tucked away from protesters and protected institutionally from any discrimination they might face in contracting for malpractice insurance, medical waste removal, or rent. Still, the large institutions that house physicians performing abortions are growing scarce. As hospitals merge to cut costs, previously independent institutions have come to be owned by Catholic organizations that do not permit abortion. This macro trend also has an impact at the local level, causing more doctors to take their abortion practices to freestanding clinics.

For any woman who has sought an abortion, organizations such as Planned Parenthood and smaller, independent facilities, are viewed as a haven of respectful gynecological care. This is not always the case, as the examples in the previous chapters illustrate. Issues of security and privacy should embolden abortion providers—as well as their colleagues in other specialties—to act. Protesters stake out the comings-and-goings of the women and doctors who visit these clinics. The radical Advocates for Life Ministries—best known for their "Deadly Dozen" Web site that targeted abortion providers for violence—even operated a Web cam in front of small clinics.

Increasing regulations on abortion providers could also inspire political mobilization. The physicians I interviewed made it clear that abortion is more often regulated in ways that are unhelpful to women's health than any other medical procedure. Regulation of this well-trained group of professionals might engender future political outcries, much as the rubella outbreaks in California discussed in chapter 1 did half a century ago.

There are recent indications that there may be growing unrest among doctors in the abortion community.[2] Medical Students for Choice, founded in 1993, is an example of emergent organization among younger doctors. This organization advocates better training and mentoring of medical students, interns, and residents interested in abortion care. Through annual meetings, an externship program, and leadership training, Medical Students for Choice is offering new abortion providers with the support and resources they need to succeed. What is more, their mission is decidedly political: part of the Leadership Training Program that the organization offers is directly geared toward teaching abortion providers grassroots organizing skills. By 2005, Medical Students for Choice had grown from a fledgling organization to one with 10,000 members on 123 medical school campuses nationwide.[3]

Like Medical Students for Choice, the National Coalition of Abortion Providers (NCAP) is a relatively new organization. Formed in 1990, the NCAP is a national trade organization representing and lobbying on behalf of abortion providers. It tackles the political aspects of abortion provision and offers expert testimony when states consider new abortion restrictions. In addition, it addresses some of the hurdles to the business of abortion provision. By recently assisting member physicians in purchasing medical malpractice insurance as a group, the NCAP has lowered the cost of business to some of the small, independent providers who otherwise had to rely on the open market and going rates.[4]

Both of these organizations indicate the emergent mobilization and agitation of the medical community providing abortions. Some I spoke with, however, are disappointed in the lack of support for abortion providers among physicians not performing abortions. Nonetheless, one of the most interesting contributions to the abortion debate that physicians (both providers and non-providers) contribute is their scientific language.

Americans are accustomed to contemporary, politicized abortion language. In fact, one of the great challenges of this book has been to choose language that allows for objective analysis. This task becomes nearly impossible in the current political environment. Physicians, however, whose voices are rarely heard in the contemporary debate, use distinct medical language to describe the abortion practice. Where pro-life activists refer to "unborn babies," and pro-choice advocates refer to "fetuses," physicians speak of the "products of conception." For doctors, abortion is neither "murder," nor an abstract "right," but is instead a simple medical process of "emptying the uterus." These are but examples of the unique framework that scientists and physicians bring to the abortion debate, which has become so fraught with the signals and messages of the political world that the public mostly hears about abortion through a black-and-white lens instead of situated within the rich complexities of the health and medical necessity of both women and fetuses. Given physicians' recent lobbying efforts and mobilization, the neutral language they have to offer can potentially enlighten participants and onlookers in the abortion debate with new understandings.

WOMEN'S SELF-HELP MOVEMENT

Women themselves could propel the abortion rights movement forward, of course. In recent years, the mainstream pro-abortion rights organizations in the United States have maintained their positions, but a number of journalists and scholars have noted the ineffectiveness of their message. Journalist William Saletan, for one, argues that the pro-rights position, best represented by NARAL Pro-Choice America (formerly National Abortion Repeal Action League), has lost the public relations war for abortion rights because it chooses to frame the issue of abortion within a choice-based discourse that plays into the hands of the pro-life movement. The "choice" framing sends the message that abortion is not a *right* per se, but rather something of a whim—a whim the pro-life movement, and a sizeable segment of the American public, would rather not indulge.[5]

Still, this is not the only way to understand abortion rights. At other times in American history, access to abortion has been justified through the language of women's health or women's rights. So it may be beneficial for women's groups that advocate abortion access to reframe the public discourse within a context that better reflects their experience and reasons for abortions and the impact that restrictions have on women's self-determination and social status.[6]

Historically, women have largely understood abortion as a private practice associated with their personal health. Recall that in the nineteenth century, women secured abortions through their midwives, free of the political spotlight and the regulation of "regular" medicine. In the 1920s, Ruth Barnett and others provided women with illicit, but safe, abortions through private associations. Most recently, JANE, the women's abortion collective of the 1960s, taught women to perform safe, respectful abortions outside of the medical establishment when the establishment refused to carry them out.

While these periods should not be glamorized—many women suffered at the hands of some less-than-ethical providers—sweeping demonization does an injustice to those who were committed to women's health. While various political interests manipulate the images of the "back alley" abortionist, too seldom are the humane acts of medical intervention during the periods when abortion was illegal acknowledged. Recalling these stories points to the possibility that the illegal provider—careful or cavalier—may rise again as fewer women have access to legal procedures.

One recent book, Ninia Baehr's *Abortion without Apology*, recounts the story of JANE and independent women abortionists in the 1960s, reminding women that early abortion is a simple procedure that many have learned without medical degrees.[7] The possible dangers of self-conducted abortions cannot be taken lightly, but neither should the long history of women's assertiveness in securing their own health care needs despite regulations to the contrary.

Whether the self-care movement takes hold, or whether there is a more conventional assertion of women's authority to demand and receive the health care they require within traditional medicine, it is quite plausible that new forms of women's activism will arise in response to further encroachments on their social citizenship. Either through more vocal legislative strategies and political framing via the nation's pro-abortion rights organizations (NARAL, NOW), or through grassroots activism and street theatre akin to the 1960s women's movement, women in this country will eventually reach a point of demanding access.

THE RELIGIOUS LEFT

Perhaps the most unexpected reinvigoration of the abortion rights movement is occurring within the religious community. While younger students of politics know only the dominance of the conservative religious within contemporary political culture, the progressive faithful have a long and venerable history in American political development. The apparent absence of that interest in today's abortion politics is a notable exception to an otherwise rich history of activism in social policy debates.

Religious progressives have been a consistent, driving force in American politics within the abolition movement, the anti-vice movements at the turn of the twentieth century, and more recently within the Civil Rights movement of the 1950s and 1960s. The current period spells but a lapse in vocal, organized activism. What do progressive religious people say in the face of further restrictions on abortion access? There are stirrings within that community that point to answers.

The most notable response to date from Christian progressives comes from Jim Wallis, evangelist and Christian liberal. Wallis has authored many books on such subjects as politics, faith, and the political parties. He recently argued in *God's Politics* that the religious communities addressing abortion are missing the larger moral issue that should capture their attention: poverty. In that book, Wallis is most famous for pointing out that the Bible has more than three thousand references to poverty, but not a single direct reference to abortion. For him, one of the most prominent evangelists on the political left, abortion should not be the focus of the religious community. In fact, he argues that the demand for many abortions would be alleviated through more holistic poverty programs.

A recent article by Bill McKibben, environmental writer for *Harper's*, argues that the modern Christian Right movement fundamentally misunderstands and misrepresents the core teachings of Jesus, and that this has misinformed the religious community's policy concerns. McKibben argues that the movement is flawed in overlooking the central call of the Christian faith to love and serve others. Quoting John Giles, the president of the Christian Coalition of Alabama, "You'll find most Alabamians have got a charitable heart. They just don't want it coming out of their pockets." McKibben argues that the conservative Christian movement has undercut the central, radical proposal of Christianity by avoiding poverty as a moral problem and that this signals a coming debate within the Christian community about its priorities.[8]

Other progressives argue that contemporary religious communities should focus their political efforts on the environment. According to the *New York Times,* the National Association of Evangelicals has circulated a policy proposal that would encourage members of Congress to restrict carbon emissions in an effort to limit global warming. Those religious leaders concerned for the environment point to biblical passages that charge humans with caring for the earth.[9] This example and the examples of Wallis and McKibben indicate the policy interests of the nation's religious leaders and lay people may eventually shift away from abortion.

Still, it would be an overstatement to suggest that there is unanimity among the Christian Left regarding its mission or response to the Christian Right. Frances Kissling, the president of Catholics for a Free Choice, suggests that the Christian Left may be no better at representing the needs of women than conservative Christians. Calling the progressive religious movement "amorphous," Kissling claims the nascent movement has "not yet articulated an agenda or even a mission statement or set of values." As a consequence, she argues that women theologians should take up a prominent place in the emergent movement. Although Wallis articulates the needs of the poor, Kissling maintains that his position is deeply rooted in the views of Catholic bishops, and as such offers a "classically patriarchal beneficence." [10] This feminist critique of Wallis's version of progressive Christianity reveals the debates within the Christian Left that perhaps have prevented a unified response to the conservative religious community, which for years has been able to construct a concerted effort around abortion, gay rights, and other social policy issues.

In fact, even vague biblical references to abortion are cause for debate within the Christian community. A recent *New York Times* article documents three such references, as well as the various theological interpretations of them.[11] In surveying the major theologians on their interpretations of Psalm 139:13-16, Exodus 21:22-25, and Luke I: 41-42, they disagreed in fundamental ways about the symbolic and literal meanings of those passages.

Exodus 21:22-25 provides the most direct statement regarding abortion

> If men who are fighting hit a pregnant woman and she gives birth prematurely but there is no serious injury, the offender must be fined whatever the woman's husband demands and the court allows. But if there is serious injury, you are to take life for life, eye for eye, tooth for tooth, hand for hand, foot for foot, burn for burn, wound for wound, bruise for bruise.

In one view, this passage gives equal value to the woman and her fetus. This view might be used to argue for the Laci and Conner law, which provides for double sentences for someone harming a woman and her fetus. On the other hand, some argue that "life for life" refers only to the woman's injury. Under that reading, a fetus born dead justifies only an additional fine, indicating a greater biblical respect for the woman's life than for that of the fetus. A California jury struck a compromise between these views by differentiating between the lives of Laci Peterson and her fetus. Scott Peterson was convicted of first-degree murder for the death of wife Laci, but second-degree murder for the death of the fetus.

Other passages speak about the connection between fetal life and God. Psalm 139: 13–16 proclaims:

> For you created my inmost being; you knit me together in my mother's womb. I praise you because I am fearfully and wonderfully made; your works are wonderful, I know that full well. My frame was not hidden from you when I was made in the secret place. When I was woven together in the depths of the earth, your eyes saw my unformed body.

To some, this passage indicates the holiness of the fetus from conception; to others, the psalms are understood as poetic symbolism that celebrates a relationship between God and human, allowing for a more scientific definition of the beginning of life.

Finally, Luke I: 41–42 offers yet another puzzle over the status of the fetus: "When Elizabeth heard Mary's greeting, the baby leaped in the womb, and Elizabeth was filled with the Holy Spirit." [12] Again, two interpretations of the passage are possible: one, that the verse indicates fetal personhood, and another, that Elizabeth clearly was in the late stages of pregnancy, making late abortion morally questionable. While these examples of differing biblical interpretation might breed further public confusion, the debate itself might inspire a more nuanced plurality of interpretations that would allow abortion to be defined as a moral choice within particular religious communities.

Such is the argument of Daniel C. Maguire, author of *Sacred Choices*, a book that argues that each of the world's major religions provides fuel for a pro-abortion rights position. Within each of the major religions, Maguire argues, is a complex history around contraception and abortion perspectives. Using the academic research of some of the country's leading religious scholars, Maguire contends that the contemporary perception that traditional religions are per se opposed to abortion is incorrect, and that eventually, the alternative views rooted in these religions will make themselves heard again.[13]

Certainly the forthcoming book by Rabbi Michael Lerner, *The Left Hand of God*, which purports to presage and inspire a reinvigorated religious left movement designed to return the White House to Democratic control, would suggest so. Lerner is the editor of *Tikkun* magazine, a progressive Jewish publication that seeks to inspire interfaith progressive political activism. Whether this movement, inspired by a Jewish rabbi but marketed as an opportunity for progressive religious cooperation across faiths, can spark a new spiritually-grounded movement for abortion access remains to be seen.

CONCLUSION

For now, the dominant policy trend on abortion favors restriction, in large part because of the influence that the conservative religious wield in the debate. That abortion has grown harder to access, while becoming ever safer and no less legal, is a policy and political accomplishment of the religious conservatives active in American politics today, and their effectiveness within morality politics. Still, history reveals that the pendulum of social regulatory policy—and abortion policy specifically—swings in two directions. Given the current debates over late-term abortions and parental notification, there are numerous potential catalysts for a swing toward increased abortion rights.

The current limits on abortion access hit the most vulnerable women in society the hardest. The costs of abortion restrictions to these women are financial, emotional, medical, and societal. Eventually, concern for the health and well-being of the young and the poor will mobilize the interests that purport to care for them. In the meantime, their rights and well-being hang in the balance, caught in the crosshairs of an intense moral debate that has lost sight of the science of abortion and the inherent worth and morality of the individual woman who chooses it.

DISCUSSION QUESTIONS

1. Will abortion continue to become less available? Given the justices appointed by President George W. Bush to the Supreme Court, what do you think the Court is most likely to decide in future cases?
2. Of the pro-rights movements described in this chapter, which do you think is the most likely to succeed? Why?
3. How might the religious right respond to a counter-movement from the religious left? How might the religious right respond if the language of the debate shifted from that of "choice" to that of "rights"?
4. Why do you think the religious right focuses so much attention on abortion when other issues, such as poverty and the environment, affect more people and seem to be addressed more directly and specifically in Christian scripture?
5. In your view, what is the future of abortion policy in the United States? Do you imagine the Supreme Court overturning *Roe v. Wade* in your lifetime? What would be implications for public policy? For women's citizenship?

SUGGESTED READING

Baehr, Ninia, *Abortion without Apology: A Radical History for the 1990s,* Boston: South End Press, 1990.

Lerner, Michael, *The Left Hand of God: Taking Our Country Back from the Religious Right,* San Francisco: HarperSanFrancisco, 2006.

Maguire, Daniel C., *Sacred Choices: The Right to Contraception and Abortion in Ten World Religions,* Minneapolis, Minn.: Fortress Press, 2001.

McDonagh, Eileen, *Breaking the Abortion Deadlock: From Choice to Consent,* New York: Oxford University Press, 1996.

Saletan, William, *Bearing Right: How Conservatives Won the Abortion War,* Berkeley: University of California Press, 2004.

Wallis, Jim, *God's Politics: Why the Right Gets It Wrong and the Left Doesn't Get It,* San Francisco: HarperSanFrancisco, 2005.

NOTES

1. *What If Roe Fell? The State-by-State Consequences of Overturning* Roe v. Wade (New York: Center for Reproductive Rights, 2004),www.reproductiverights.org/pdf/bo_whatifroefell.pdf.

2. For more on this trend, see Carole Joffe, Patricia Anderson, and Jody Steinauer, "The Crisis in Abortion Provision and Pro-Choice Medical Activism in the 1990s," in "Regendering the U.S. Abortion Debate," in *Abortion Wars: A Half Century of Struggle, 1950–2000,* ed. Rickie Solinger (Berkeley: University of California Press, 1998), 320–333.

3. Medical Students for Choice, www.ms4c.org/history.htm.

4. National Coalition of Abortion Providers, www.ncap.com/index.html.

5. William Saletan, *Bearing Right: How Conservatives Won the Abortion War* (Berkeley: University of California Press, 2004). For a cross-national examination of the framing of abortion politics, see Myra Marx Ferree et al., *Shaping Abortion Discourse: Democracy and the Public Sphere in Germany and the United States* (Cambridge, UK: University of Cambridge Press, 2002).

6. Alison M. Jaggar makes a similar argument in "Regendering the U.S. Abortion Debate," in *Abortion Wars,* 339–355.

7. Ninia Baehr, *Abortion without Apology: A Radical History for the 1990s* (Boston: South End Press, 1990).

8. Bill McKibben, "The Christian Paradox: How a Faithful Nation Gets Jesus Wrong," *Harper's Magazine* August 2005, 31–37.

9. Michael Janofsky, "When Cleaner Air Is a Biblical Obligation," *New York Times,* November 7, 2005, www.nytimes.com/2005/11/07/politics/07air.html?ei= 5070&en=b2a9f0a13a9a4847&ex=1132203600&oref=login&emc=eta1&page- wanted=print.

10. Frances Kissling, "A Cautionary Tale: Has Progressive Religion Moved Far Enough Away From Patriarchy to Do Women and Democracy Much Good?" *Conscience,* Autumn 2005, www.catholicsforchoice.org/conscience/archives/ c2005autumn_acautionarytale.asp.

11. Michael Luo, "On Abortion, It's the Bible of Ambiguity," *New York Times,* November 13, 2005.

12. All three passages are taken from the New International Version translation of the Bible; interpretations are adapted from Michael Luo, "On Abortion."

13. Daniel C. Maguire, *Sacred Choices: The Right to Contraception and Abortion in Ten World Religions* (Minneapolis, Minn.: Fortress Press, 2001).

APPENDIXES

APPENDIX A
Landmark Contraception and Abortion Cases

Name and Citation	Nature of Case
1917 *People v. Sanger,* 179 App. Div. 939, 166 N.Y.S. 1107	Challenged a New York State prohibition against the sale and provision of contraceptive devices.
1936 *United States v. One Package of Japanese Pessaries,* 86 F.2d 737	Challenged the federal Comstock Law that made it illegal to distribute contraceptive materials.
1965 *Griswold v. Connecticut,* 381 U.S. 479	Challenged a Connecticut law that banned the sale of contraceptives to married couples.
1973 *Roe v. Wade* 410 U.S. 113	Challenged a Texas law that prohibited abortion except to save a woman's life.
1973 *Doe v. Bolton* 410 U.S. 179	Challenged a Georgia law, which was based on the model proposed by the American Law Institute, that prohibited abortions except in cases of medical necessity, rape, incest, and fetal abnormality. The law also required that all abortions be performed in accredited hospitals, that two doctors and a committee concur in the woman's abortion decision, and that only Georgia residents may obtain abortions in that state.
1975 *Connecticut v. Menillo* 423 U.S. 9	Appealed the conviction of a nonphysician for performing an abortion.
1976 *Planned Parenthood of Central Missouri v. Danforth* 428 U.S. 52	Challenged Missouri law that required – parental consent to a minor's abortion, – husband's consent to a married woman's abortion, – a woman's written informed consent, – no second-trimester abortions by saline amniocentesis, and

Holding

The New York Supreme Court upheld Sanger's conviction but interpreted the law broadly enough to protect physicians who prescribed contraception for medical reasons.

U.S. Court of Appeals overturned the Comstock Law.

The Court held that the law was unconstitutional and acknowledged a constitutional right to privacy that encompassed contraception issues.

The Court found the law unconstitutional and ruled that the right to privacy extends to the decision of a woman, in consultation with her physician, to terminate her pregnancy. During the first trimester of pregnancy, this decision may be effectuated free of state interference. After the first trimester, the state has a compelling interest in protecting the woman's health and may reasonably regulate abortion to promote that interest. At the point of fetal viability (capacity for sustained survival outside the uterus), the state has a compelling interest in protecting potential life and may ban abortion, except when necessary to preserve the woman's life or health.

The Court found the unconstitutional as a violation of a woman's right to choose abortion as recognized in *Roe v. Wade*. In addition, the residency requirement violated the Privileges and Immunities Clause of the Constitution.

The Court ruled that states may require that only physicians provide abortions.

The Court found the parental and spousal consent requirements unconstitutional because they delegated to third parties an absolute veto power over a woman's abortion decision that the state does not itself possess. The requirement that the woman certify that her consent is informed and freely given was found constitutional, as were the record keeping and reporting requirements. The ban on saline amniocentesis was later struck down because this was the most commonly used abortion method after the first twelve weeks of pregnancy and was shown to be less

APPENDIX A *(continued)*
Landmark Contraception and Abortion Cases

Name and Citation	Nature of Case
	– specific record keeping and reporting by abortion providers.
1976 *Bellotti v. Baird (Bellotti I)* 428 U.S. 132	Challenged a Massachusetts law that required the consent of both parents to a minor's abortion, but allowed the requirement to be waived by a judge if "good cause shown."
1977 *Maher v. Roe* 432 U.S. 464	Challenged Connecticut's limitation of state Medicaid funding to medically necessary abortions and the state's refusal to fund elective abortions.
1977 *Poelker v. Doe* 432 U.S. 519	Challenged a St. Louis, Missouri, municipal policy in which publicly financed hospitals were closed to the provision of elective abortions.
1979 *Colautti v. Franklin* 439 U.S. 379	Challenged provisions of Pennsylvania law that required a physician intending to perform an abortion to determine that the fetus is not viable. If the physician found that fetus "is or may be viable," he or she was required to exercise the degree of care in performing the abortion that would have been exercised if a live birth were intended.
1979 *Bellotti v. Baird (Bellotti II)* 443 U.S. 622	The Massachusetts law challenged in *Bellotti I* (1976) arrived before the Court definitively interpreted by the Massachusetts Supreme Judicial Court. The Massachusetts court found that the law would require that – a minor first attempt to obtain her parents' consent and be refused before approaching a court for permission for her abortion, – the parents be notified when a minor files a petition for judicial waiver, and – the judge hearing the minor's petition may deny the petition if the judge finds that an abortion would be against the minor's best interests.

Holding

dangerous to the woman's health than other available methods; the Court determined that the choice of method must be left to the physician. (Currently, dilatation and evacuation—D&E—is the most common method of mid-trimester abortion.)

The Court ruled that the statute may be constitutional, depending on the meaning of "good cause" and the exact procedure that will be utilized. Case was remanded for definitive interpretation of meaning of the statute by the Massachusetts state courts (see *Bellotti II*).

The Court found the law constitutional; the state need not fund a woman's abortion.

The Court found the law constitutional for the reasons stated in *Maher v. Roe.*

The Court found that the provisions were "void for vagueness" because the meanings of "viable" and "may be viable" were unclear. Decision on viability must be left to the good-faith judgment of the physician. Provisions were also unconstitutional because they imposed criminal liability on physicians regardless of their intent to violate the law.

The Court found the law unconstitutional and ruled that all minors must have an opportunity to approach a judge without first consulting their parents, and that the proceedings must be confidential and expeditious. A mature minor must be given permission for an abortion, regardless of the judge's view as to her best interests; even an immature minor must be permitted to have a confidential abortion, if the abortion is in her best interests.

APPENDIX A *(continued)*
Landmark Contraception and Abortion Cases

Name and Citation	Nature of Case
1980 *Harris v. McRae* 448 U.S. 297	Challenged the Hyde Amendment's ban on the use of federal Medicaid funds for medically necessary abortions except those necessary to save the woman's life.
1980 *Williams v. Zbaraz* 448 U.S. 358	Challenged an Illinois version of the Hyde Amendment.
1981 *H. L. v. Matheson* 450 U.S. 398	Challenged a Utah law that required a physician to notify the parents of an unemancipated minor prior to an abortion.
1983 *City of Akron v. Akron Center for Reproductive Health* 462 U.S. 416	Challenged an Akron, Ohio, ordinance that required that – a woman wait twenty-four hours between consenting to and receiving an abortion; – all abortions after the first trimester be performed in full-service hospitals; – minors who were fifteen years of age or younger have parental or judicial consent for an abortion; – the attending physician personally give the woman information relevant to informed consent; – specific information be given to a woman prior to an abortion, including details of fetal anatomy, a list of risks and consequences of the procedure, and a statement that "the unborn child is a human life from the moment of conception"; and – fetal remains be "humanely" disposed of.

Holding

The Court found the Hyde Amendment constitutional, ruling that the government has no obligation to provide funds for medically necessary abortions.

The statute was found constitutional for the same reasons the Hyde Amendment was upheld in *Harris v. McRae.*

The Court found the law constitutional, ruling that the plaintiff is a dependent minor, living at home, who has made no claim that she is mature enough to give informed consent to an abortion or that she has any problems with her parents that make notice inappropriate.

The Court found that all of the challenged portions of the ordinance were unconstitutional:
- the twenty-four-hour waiting period served neither the state's interest in protecting the woman's health nor in ensuring her informed consent;
- the post-first trimester hospitalization requirement interfered with a woman's access to abortion services without protecting her health, because the dilatation and evacuation (D&E) method of mid-trimester abortion may be performed as safely in out-patient facilities as in full-service hospitals;
- the minors' consent requirement failed to guarantee an adequate judicial alternative to parental involvement (see *Bellotti II*);
- the counseling requirement would have made abortions more expensive and was not necessary to ensure informed consent, because physicians can delegate the counseling task to another qualified individual;
- the informed consent script intruded on the physician's judgment as to what is best for each individual woman and contained information designed to dissuade the woman from having an abortion; and
- the requirement for "humane" disposal of fetal remains was too vague to give fair warning of what the law required.

In 1992, the Supreme Court overruled parts of this case (see *Planned Parenthood v. Casey*).

APPENDIX A *(continued)*
Landmark Contraception and Abortion Cases

Name and Citation	Nature of Case
1983 *Planned Parenthood of Kansas City, Missouri, v. Ashcroft* 462 U.S. 476	Challenged a Missouri law that required that – all post-first-trimester abortions be performed in hospitals, – minors younger than the age of eighteen have parental consent or judicial authorization for their abortions, – two doctors be present at the abortion of a viable fetus, and – a pathologist's report be obtained for every abortion.
1983 *Simopoulos v. Virginia* 462 U.S. 506	The criminal conviction of a physician for violating a Virginia law that required all post-first trimester abortions be performed in hospitals.
1986 *Babbitt v. Planned Parenthood of Central and Northern Arizona* 789 F. 2nd 1348 (9th Cir. 1986); affirmed 479 U.S. 925 (1986)	Federal Court of Appeals for the Ninth Circuit ruled an Arizona law unconstitutional for prohibiting grants of state money for family planning to organizations that provided abortions or abortion counseling and referrals. The law would be valid, the appeals court said, only if the state could prove it was the only way to stop its money from being used to pay for abortions and abortion-related activities. Since the state could not prove this, the law was struck down.
1986 *Thornburgh v. American College of Obstetricians and Gynecologists, Pennsylvania* Section 476 U.S. 747	Challenged Pennsylvania's 1982 Abortion Control Act that required that – a woman be given specific information before she has an abortion, including state-produced printed materials that describe the fetus; – physicians performing post-viability abortions use the method most likely to result in fetal survival unless it would cause "significantly" greater risk to a woman's life or health; – a second physician be present at post-viability abortions; – providers give the state detailed reporting on each abortion, with these reports open for public inspection; and

---

Holding

The Court ruled that
- the hospitalization requirement was unconstitutional for the reasons stated in *City of Akron v. Akron Center for Reproductive Health*;
- the parental consent requirement was constitutional because the judicial bypass alternative contained in the statute conforms to the standards set out in *Bellotti II*;
- the presence of two doctors at late-term abortions served the state's compelling interest in protecting potential life after viability and was, therefore, constitutional; and
- the requirement of a pathology report was constitutional because it poses only a small financial burden to the woman and protects her health.

The Court upheld the physician's conviction, finding that the Virginia law provided for licensing of freestanding ambulatory surgical facilities as "hospitals." Consequently, the law was not as restrictive as those struck down in *City of Akron v. Akron Center for Reproductive Health* and *Planned Parenthood of Kansas City, Missouri v. Ashcroft*, and was, therefore, constitutional. The justices stated that Dr. Simopoulos could have avoided criminal prosecution by having his clinic licensed.

The Supreme Court summarily affirmed the Ninth Circuit Court ruling without issuing an opinion. Compare to *Rust v. Sullivan*.

The Court found
- the informed consent provision invalid because it interfered with the physician's discretion and required a woman to be given information designed to dissuade her from having an abortion;
- the provision restricting post-viability abortion methods invalid because it required the woman to bear an increased risk to her health in order to maximize the chances of fetal survival;
- the second physician requirement invalid because it did not make an exception for emergencies; and
- the reporting requirement unconstitutional because it could lead to disclosure of the woman's identity.

The parental consent issue was remanded to the lower court for consideration in light of newly enacted state court rules.

APPENDIX A *(continued)*
Landmark Contraception and Abortion Cases

Name and Citation	Nature of Case
	– one parent's consent or a court order be provided for a minor's abortion.
1989 *Webster v. Reproductive Health Services* 492 u.s. 490	Challenged Missouri's 1986 Act that – declared that life begins at conception, – forbid the use of public funds for the purpose of counseling a woman to have an abortion not necessary to save her life, – forbid the use of public facilities for abortions not necessary to save a woman's life, and – required physicians to perform tests to determine the viability of fetuses after twenty weeks gestation.
1990 *Ohio v. Akron Center for Reproductive Health* 497 u.s. 502	Challenged a 1985 Ohio statute that required a physician performing an abortion on a minor to give notice to her parent or guardian twenty-four hours prior to the procedure. Although the law provided a judicial bypass mechanism, the Sixth Circuit Court of Appeals found several aspects of it unduly burdensome to minors and constitutionally deficient.
1990 *Hodgson v. Minnesota* 497 u.s. 417	Challenged a 1981 Minnesota statute that required notification of both biological parents, followed by a waiting period of at least forty-eight hours, prior to a minor's abortion. No exception to the notification requirement was provided for divorced parents or for couples who were not married. A second section of the statute provided for a judicial bypass if the two-parent notification provision without a waiver procedure were enjoined. The plaintiffs challenged the second section based on evidence gathered during the five years that the parental consent requirement and judicial bypass were in effect.

Holding

In 1992, the Supreme Court overruled portions of this case in *Planned Parenthood v. Casey.*

The Court
– allowed the declaration of when life begins to go into effect because five justices agreed that there was insufficient evidence that it would be used to restrict such protected activities as choices of contraception or abortion; should the declaration be used to justify such restrictions in the future, the affected parties could challenge it at that time;
– unanimously declined to address the constitutionality of the public funds provision, accepting Missouri's representation that this provision was not directed at the conduct of any physician or health care provider, private or public, but solely at those persons responsible for expending public funds, and that the provision would not restrict publicly employed health care professionals from providing full information about abortion to their clients;
– upheld the provision that barred the use of public facilities for abortion procedures, ruling that the state may implement a policy that favors childbirth over abortion by allocations of such public resources as hospitals and medical staff; and
– upheld the provision that required viability tests, interpreting it as not requiring tests that would be "imprudent" or "careless" to perform.

Without deciding whether a law that requires notice to only one parent requires a judicial bypass, the Court held that the bypass provided by the Ohio law met constitutional standards. It rejected the argument that the judicial bypass was flawed because it required the minor to sign her name on court chapters, prove her entitlement to avoid parental involvement by clear and convincing evidence, and wait as long as three weeks to obtain a court ruling. The Court also upheld a requirement that the physician personally notify the parent.

The Court held that the two-parent notification with no judicial bypass alternative posed an unconstitutional burden on a minor's right to abortion. A different majority of the Court allowed the second section of the Minnesota law to stand, however, because of the addition of a judicial alternative. In addition, the Court upheld the validity of the forty-eight-hour waiting period.

APPENDIX A *(continued)*
Landmark Contraception and Abortion Cases

Name and Citation	Nature of Case
1991 *Rust v. Sullivan/State of New York v. Sullivan* 500 U.S. 173	Challenged 1988 federal regulations that forbade counseling and referral for abortion or advocacy of abortion rights in programs that receive funds under Title X of the federal Public Health Service Act (1970). In addition, the regulations required clinics to "financially and physically" separate Title X-funded activities from privately funded "abortion-related activities."
1992 *Planned Parenthood of Southeastern Pennsylvania v. Casey* 505 U.S. 833	Challenged Pennsylvania's 1989 Abortion Control Act that required that, except in medical emergencies, – a woman wait twenty-four hours between consenting to and receiving an abortion; – the woman be given state-mandated information about abortion and be offered state-authored materials on fetal development; – a married woman inform her husband of her intent to have an abortion; – minors' abortions be conditioned upon the consent, provided in person at the clinic, of one parent or guardian, or upon a judicial waiver, and – physicians and clinics that performed abortions provide to the state an annual statistical report on abortions performed during the year, including the names of referring patients.
1993 *Bray v. Alexandria Women's Health Clinic* 506 U.S. 753	Anti-abortion demonstrators, including the leadership of Operation Rescue, challenged an injunction against their activities, including blocking access to health care facilities in the Washington, D.C., area. The injunction was based on an 1871 civil rights statute that forbids private conspiracy to violate constitutional rights. The demonstrators claimed their activities did not violate the statute.
1994 *National Organization for Women v. Scheidler* 510 U.S. 249 (*Scheidler I*)	The National Organization for Women (NOW) sought to use the federal Racketeer Influenced and Corrupt Organizations (RICO) Act of 1970 to sue anti-abortion organizations engaged in unlawful blockades and other harassment against reproductive health clinics. NOW

Holding

The Court held that the regulations did not violate the Title X statute because they are a reasonable interpretation of the statutory prohibitions against the use of Title X funds in programs "where abortion is a method of family planning." The Court further held that the regulations do not violate the First Amendment or the right to choose abortion, ruling that the government has no obligation to pay for the exercise of constitutional rights, and that the government's decision not to fund the provision of information did not directly interfere with the rights of doctors, clinics, or patients, since providers were free to offer abortions and abortion-related information in separate programs, and women who wish unbiased medical information and services were free to seek them elsewhere.

The Court reaffirmed the validity of a woman's right to choose abortion under *Roe v. Wade,* but announced a new standard of review that allowed restrictions on abortion prior to fetal viability so long as they did not constitute an "undue burden" to the woman. A restriction is an "undue burden" when it has the purpose or effect of placing a substantial obstacle in the path of a woman seeking an abortion. Under this standard, only the husband notification provision was considered an undue burden and, therefore, unconstitutional. All the other provisions were upheld as not unduly burdensome. In upholding the Pennsylvania restrictions, the Court overturned portions of *City of Akron v. Akron Center for Reproductive Health* and *Thornburgh v. American College of Obstetricians and Gynecologists.*

The Court held that the demonstrators' activities did not violate the civil rights statute because their actions were not motivated by "class-based discriminatory animus against women," as the statute requires, but rather by opposition to the practice of abortion. It further held that the demonstrators' incidental impact on the right of women to travel interstate for the purpose of securing an abortion was not the kind of violation of a right for which the 1871 statute was enacted.

The Court overturned the appeals court decision and allowed the lawsuit to proceed using RICO as its basis. It held that RICO could be used in the absence of an economic motive, and that the term "enterprise" could include any individual or group of individuals, partnership, corporation, association, or other legal entity.

APPENDIX A *(continued)*
Landmark Contraception and Abortion Cases

Name and Citation	Nature of Case
	argued that RICO was applicable because the unlawful actions constituted a nationwide conspiracy to eliminate access to abortion services by using extortion and intimidation to drive clinics out of business. The U.S. Court of Appeals for the Seventh Circuit had ruled that the case could not go forward because RICO applies only to activities motivated by economic gain, which could not be demonstrated in this case.
1994 *Madsen v. Women's Health Center* 512 U.S. 5753	Anti-abortion protesters sought to overturn, on First Amendment grounds, an injunction against their activities at a Melbourne, Florida, clinic. The injunction prohibited demonstrations within thirty-six feet of the clinic's property line; banned noise and visual displays that could be heard and seen inside the clinic; prohibited approaching any person seeking services within three hundred feet of the clinic, unless the person indicated a desire to communicate; and established a three-hundred-foot buffer zone around the residences of clinic physicians and staff.
1997 *Schenck v. Pro-Choice Network of Western New York* 519 U.S. 357	Challenged, on First Amendment grounds, an injunction aimed at protecting access to reproductive health care clinics. Three elements of the injunction were challenged – a "fixed" buffer zone that prohibited all demonstration activity within fifteen feet of clinics doorways, driveways, and parking lot entrances; – a "floating" zone that prohibited all demonstration activity within fifteen feet of any person or vehicle entering or leaving the clinics; and – "cease and desist" provisions, which allowed no more than two "sidewalk counselors" to approach patients within the buffer zones, but required them to stop "counseling" and withdraw outside the zones upon request.
1997 *Mazurek v. Armstrong* 520 U.S. 968	Challenged a Montana law that requires only physicians, not physician assistants, provide abortion services.

Holding

The Court held that the thirty-six-foot buffer zone that protected the clinic entrances and driveways was a content-neutral measure that did not infringe on the First Amendment rights of abortion opponents, and that the ban on disruptive noise was also constitutional. The majority indicated that Florida's interests include "protecting a woman's freedom to seek lawful medical or counseling services in connection with her pregnancy." But the Court limited the scope of its ruling by striking portions of the injunction as broader than necessary to protect the state's interests, including the application of the buffer zone to certain private property adjoining the clinic, the three-hundred-foot no-approach zone and residential buffer zone, and the prohibition against "images observable to" patients inside the clinic.

The Court found that the government's interests in ensuring public safety and protecting a woman's freedom to seek pregnancy-related services justified properly tailored injunctions to secure unimpeded physical access to clinics. It upheld the "fixed" buffer zone as necessary to ensure safe access to the clinics in light of the demonstrators' previous behavior. The Court, however, struck down as unconstitutional the "floating buffer zone," because it burdened more speech than was necessary to achieve the government's interest. It upheld the "cease and desist" provision, because it allowed demonstrators to espouse their message outside of the zone and was necessary to address their previous behavior. As the Court struck down the "floating" zone, it did not rule on the "cease and desist" provisions as applied to that zone.

The Court found that the law had neither the purpose nor the effect of placing a substantial obstacle in the path of a woman seeking an abortion. It therefore did not create an undue burden on a woman's right to abortion and was constitutional. The

APPENDIX A *(continued)*
Landmark Contraception and Abortion Cases

Name and Citation	Nature of Case
2000 *Hill v. Colorado* 530 u.s. 703	Challenged, on First Amendment grounds, a Colorado statute that forbade individuals from knowingly approaching closer than eight feet another person who was within on hundred feet of the entrance of a health care facility, without that person's consent, in order to offer a leaflet, display a sign, or engage in protest, education, or counseling.
2000 *Stenberg v. Carhart* 530 u.s. 914	Challenged Nebraska's abortion ban.
2003 *National Organization for Women v. Scheidler* 537 u.s. 393 (*Scheidler II*)	The National Organization for Women (NOW) sought to use the federal Racketeer Influenced and Corrupt Organizations (RICO) Act of 1970 to sue anti-abortion organizations that engage in unlawful blockades and other harassment against reproductive health clinics. NOW argued that RICO was applicable, because the unlawful actions constituted a nationwide conspiracy to eliminate access to abortion services by using extortion and intimidation to drive clinics out of business. After the Supreme Court held the suit could proceed even if the anti-abortion groups were not economically motivated (see *Scheidler I*'s 1994 ruling), the case was

Holding

Court reiterated its position that "the performance of abortions may be restricted to physicians."

This statute was later ruled unconstitutional by the Montana Supreme Court in *Armstrong v. Montana,* 989 P.2d 364 under the Montana Constitution.

The Court found that the statute did not violate the First Amendment, because it did not regulate speech on the basis of content or viewpoint. The justices concluded that it was a reasonable time, place, and manner restriction that left open ample alternative means of communication, and reasoned that
- the eight-foot distance of separation required by the statute would not adversely affect the regulated speech, because this is a normal conversational distance;
- the statute only bans "approaches," so protesters were not liable if they stood still and others came within eight feet of them; and
- the protester must "knowingly" approach, and this requirement protects against accidentally or unavoidably coming within eight feet of someone who is in motion.

The Court also addressed the question of the legitimacy of the state's interest in enacting this type of restriction and found the state's interest in protecting the unwilling listener from persistent and dogged intrusions, particularly in situations that the listener cannot choose to avoid, to be legitimate.

The Court found the statute unconstitutional because it lacked an exception for situations in which the procedure was necessary to protect the woman's health. The exception must allow the banned procedure both because the woman's medical condition requires it and because the banned procedure is less risky than others. In addition, the statute created an undue burden on a woman's right to abortion, because it had the effect of outlawing the dilation and evacuation (D&E) procedure, the most commonly used method for performing second-trimester abortions.

The Supreme Court reversed the lower court's ruling, finding that because defendants did not acquire property, their actions were not extortion. Therefore, the jury's finding of a RICO violation was erroneous and the injunction was reversed.

APPENDIX A *(continued)*
Landmark Contraception and Abortion Cases

Name and Citation	Nature of Case
	remanded to the lower courts for further proceedings. A jury found that the defendants had violated RICO by committing extortion, and the district court entered a permanent nationwide injunction that prohibited defendants from threatening clinics, their employees, or their patients. The defendants appealed on the basis that they did not commit extortion because they did not obtain anything of value for themselves by interfering with the provision of medical services.
2006 *Ayotte v. Planned Parenthood of New England* No. 04-1161	The ACLU of Northern New England sought a declaratory injunction against the enforcement of New Hampshire's Parental Notification Law. The law requires that the parents of a minor be notified before an abortion can be performed, with an exception for those situations in which an abortion is necessary to prevent the death of the girl. Parental notification also can be forfeited if a court holds that the minor in question is mature and capable of giving informed consent, or if abortion without consent would be in her best interests. The proceedings are to take place in secret, and a court must make a decision within seven days of the time the petition was filed. The decision of the court can be appealed, at which time the appeals court has seven days to make a finally ruling. The law also establishes a forty-eight-hour waiting period for minors after their parents have been notified. Physicians who perform abortions in violation of the law can face misdemeanor changes and are civilly liable to the parents of the minor. Federal District Judge Joseph A. DeClerico Jr. issued an injunction against the law on December 29, 2003, two days before the law was set to take effect. The First Circuit Court of Appeals upheld DeClerico's ruling in November 2004.

Holding

In a unanimous decision, the Supreme Court refused to consider the constitutional issues at stake in this case. It instead returned the case to the lower courts on technical grounds for reconsideration.

Source: Adapted from www.naral.org

APPENDIX B
National Political Party Platforms Statements on Abortion

Year	Democrat	Republican
1976	We fully recognize the religious and ethical nature of the concerns which many Americans have on the subject of abortion. We feel, however, that it is undesirable to attempt to amend the U.S. Constitution to overturn the Supreme Court's decision in this area.	The question of abortion is one of the most difficult and controversial of our time. It is undoubtedly a moral and personal issue but it also involves complex questions relating to medical science and criminal justice. There are those in our Party who favor complete support for the Supreme Court decision which permits abortion on demand. There are others who share sincere convictions that the Supreme Court's decision must be changed by a constitutional amendment prohibiting all abortions. Others have yet to take a position, or they have assumed a stance somewhere in between polar positions. We protest the Supreme Court's intrusion into the family structure through its denial of the parents' obligation and right to guide their minor children. The Republican Party favors a continuance of the public dialogue on abortion and supports the efforts of those who seek enactment of a constitutional amendment to restore protection of the right to life for unborn children.
1980	We fully recognize the religious and ethical concerns which many Americans have about abortion. We also recognize the belief of many Americans that a woman has the right to choose whether and when to have a child. The Democratic Party supports the 1973 Supreme Court decision on abortion rights as the law of the and opposes any	There can be no doubt that the question of abortion, despite the complex nature of its various issues, is ultimately concerned with equality of rights under the law. While we recognize differing views on this question among Americans in general—and in our own Party—we affirm our support of a constitutional amendment to restore protection of the right to life for unborn children. We also support the Congressional efforts to restrict the use of taxpayers' dollars for abortion.

APPENDIX B *(continued)*
National Political Party Platforms Statements on Abortion

Year	Democrat	Republican
	constitutional amendment to restrict or overturn that decision.	We protest the Supreme Court's intrusion into the family structure through its denial of the parents' obligation and right to guide their minor children.
1984	The Democratic party recognizes reproductive freedom as a fundamental human right. We therefore oppose government interference in the reproductive decisions of Americans, especially government interference which denies poor Americans their right to privacy by funding or advocating one or a limited number of reproductive choices only. We fully recognize the religious and ethical concern which many Americans have about abortion. But we also recognize the belief of many Americans that a woman has a right to choose whether and when to have a child. The Democratic Party supports the 1973 Supreme Court decision on abortion rights as the law of the land and opposes any constitutional amendment to restrict or overturn that decision. We deplore violence and harassment against health providers and women seeking services, and will work to end such acts. We support a local family planning and family life education programs and medical research aimed at reducing the need for abortion.	The unborn child has a fundamental individual right to life which cannot be infringed. We therefore reaffirm our support for a human life amendment to the Constitution, and we endorse legislation to make clear that the 14th Amendment's protections apply to unborn children. We oppose the use of public revenues for abortion and will eliminate funding for organizations which advocate or support abortions. We commend the efforts of those individuals and religious and private organizations that are providing positive alternatives to abortions by meeting the physical, emotional, and financial needs of pregnant women and offering adoption services where needed. We applaud President Reagan's fine record of judicial appointments, and we reaffirm our support for the appointment of judges at all levels of the judiciary who respect traditional family values and the sanctity of innocent human life.

APPENDIX B *(continued)*
National Political Party Platforms Statements on Abortion

Year	Democrat	Republican
1988	The fundamental right of reproductive choice should be guaranteed regardless of ability to pay.	See 1984 language.
1992	Democrats stand behind the right of every woman to choose, consistent with *Roe v. Wade*, regardless of ability to pay, and support a national law to protect that right. It is a fundamental constitutional liberty that individual Americans—not government—can best take responsibility for making the most difficult and intensely personal decisions regarding reproduction.	We believe the unborn child has a fundamental individual right to life that cannot be infringed. We therefore reaffirm our support for a human life amendment to the Constitution, and we endorse legislation to make clear that the 14th Amendment's protections apply to unborn children. We oppose using public revenues for abortion and will not fund organizations that advocate it. We commend those who provide alternatives to abortion by meeting the needs of mothers and offering adoption services. We reaffirm our support for appointment of judges who respect traditional family values and the sanctity of innocent human life.
1996	Our goal is to make abortion less necessary and more rare, not more difficult and more dangerous. We support contraceptive research, family planning, comprehensive family life education, and policies that support healthy childbearing. For four years in a row, we have increased support for family planning. The abortion rate is dropping. Now we must continue to support efforts to reduce unintended pregnancies, and we call on all Americans to take personal responsibility to meet this important goal.	Human nature and aspirations are the same everywhere, and everywhere the family is the building block of economic and social progress. We therefore will protect the rights of families in international programs and will not fund organizations involved in abortion.

APPENDIX B *(continued)*
National Political Party Platforms Statements on Abortion

Year	Democrat	Republican
		The unborn child has a fundamental individual right to life which cannot be infringed. We support a human life amendment to the Constitution and we endorse legislation to make clear that the Fourteenth Amendment's protections apply to unborn children. Our purpose is to have legislative and judicial protection of that right against those who perform abortions. We oppose using public revenues for abortion and will not fund organizations which advocate it. We support the appointment of judges who respect traditional family values and the sanctity of innocent human life. Our goal is to ensure that women with problem pregnancies have the kind of support, material and otherwise, they need for themselves and for their babies, not to be punitive towards those for whose difficult situation we have only compassion. We oppose abortion, but our pro-life agenda does not include punitive action against women who have an abortion. We salute those who provide alternatives to abortion and offer adoption services. Abstinence education in the home will lead to less need for birth control services and fewer abortions. We support educational initiatives to promote chastity until marriage as the expected standard of behavior. This education initiative is the best preventive measure to avoid the emotional trauma of sexually-transmitted diseases and teen pregnancies that are serious problems among our young people. While

APPENDIX B *(continued)*
National Political Party Platforms Statements on Abortion

Year	Democrat	Republican
		recognizing that something must be done to help children when parental consent or supervision is not possible, we oppose school-based clinics, which provide referrals, counseling, and related services for contraception and abortion.
2000	The Democratic Party stands behind the right of every woman to choose, consistent with *Roe v. Wade,* and regardless of ability to pay. We believe it is a fundamental constitutional liberty that individual Americans—not government—can best take responsibility for making the most difficult and intensely personal decisions regarding reproduction. This year's Supreme Court rulings show to us all that eliminating a woman's right to choose is only one justice away. That's why the stakes in this election are as high as ever. Our goal is to make abortion less necessary and more rare, not more difficult and more dangerous. We support contraceptive research, family planning, comprehensive family life education, and policies that support healthy childbearing. The abortion rate is dropping. Now we must continue to support efforts to reduce unintended pregnancies, and we call on all Americans to take personal responsibility to meet this important goal.	We say the unborn child has a fundamental right to life. We support a human life amendment to the Constitution and we endorse legislation that the 14th Amendment's protections apply to unborn children. Our purpose is to have legislative and judicial protection of that right against those who perform abortions. We oppose using public revenues for abortion and will not fund organizations which advocate it. We support the appointment of judges who respect the sanctity of innocent human life. Our goal is to ensure that women with problem pregnancies have the kind of support, material and otherwise, they need for themselves and for their babies, not to be punitive towards those for whose difficult situation we have only compassion. We oppose abortion, but our pro-life agenda does not include punitive action against women who have an abortion. We salute those who provide alternatives to abortion and offer adoption services.

APPENDIX B *(continued)*
National Political Party Platforms Statements on Abortion

Year	Democrat	Republican
2004	Because we believe in the privacy and equality of women, we stand proudly for a woman's right to choose, consistent with *Roe v. Wade*, and regardless of her ability to pay. We stand firmly against Republican efforts to undermine that right. At the same time, we strongly support family planning and adoption incentives. Abortion should be safe, legal, and rare.	Any effort to address global social problems must be firmly placed within a context of respect for the fundamental social institutions of marriage and family. We reject any treaty or convention that would contradict these values. For that reason, we support protecting the rights of families in international programs and oppose funding organizations involved in abortion.

And while the vast majority of Americans support a ban on partial birth abortion, this brutal and violent practice will likely continue by judicial fiat. We believe that the self-proclaimed supremacy of these judicial activists is antithetical to the democratic ideals on which our nation was founded.

Abstinence from sexual activity is the only protection that is 100 percent effective against out-of-wedlock pregnancies and sexually transmitted diseases, including sexually transmitted HIV/AIDS. Therefore, we support doubling abstinence education funding. We oppose school-based clinics that provide referrals, counseling, and related services for contraception and abortion.

As a country, we must keep our pledge to the first guarantee of the Declaration of Independence. That is why we say the unborn child has a fundamental individual right to life which cannot be infringed. We support a human life amendment to the |

APPENDIX B *(continued)*
National Political Party Platforms Statements on Abortion

Year	Democrat	Republican
		Constitution and we endorse legislation to make it clear that the Fourteenth Amendment's protections apply to unborn children. Our purpose is to have legislative and judicial protection of that right against those who perform abortions. We oppose using public revenues for abortion and will not fund organizations which advocate it. We support the appointment of judges who respect traditional family values and the sanctity of innocent human life. Our goal is to ensure that women with problem pregnancies have the kind of support, material and otherwise, they need for themselves and for their babies, not to be punitive towards those for whose difficult situation we have only compassion. We oppose abortion, but our pro-life agenda does not include punitive action against women who have an abortion. We salute those who provide alternatives to abortion and offer adoption services, and we commend Congressional Republicans for expanding assistance to adopting families and for removing racial barriers to adoption. We join the President in supporting crisis pregnancy programs and parental notification laws. And we applaud President Bush for allowing states to extend health care coverage to unborn children. We praise the President for his bold leadership in defense of life. We praise him for signing the Born Alive Infants Protection Act. This important legislation ensures that every infant born alive—including an infant

APPENDIX B *(continued)*
National Political Party Platforms Statements on Abortion

Year	Democrat	Republican
		who survives an abortion procedure—is considered a person under federal law. In signing the partial birth abortion ban, President Bush reminded us that "the most basic duty of government is to defend the life of the innocent. Every person, however frail or vulnerable, has a place and a purpose in this world."

Source: Party websites

APPENDIX C
Web Resources

Alan Guttmacher Institute
www.agi-usa.org/

American College of Obstetricians and
  Gynecologists
www.acog.org

American Life League
www.all.org/

American Medical Association
www.ama-assn.org

Americans United for Life
www.aul.org

Catholics for Free Choice
www.catholicsforchoice.org/

Center for Reproductive Law and Policy
www.crlp.org/

Christian Coalition of America
www.cc.org/

Concerned Women for America
www.cwfa.org

Democrats for Life of America
www.democratsforlife.org

Eagle Forum
www.eagleforum.org/

Family Research Council
www.frc.org/

Feminists for Life
www.feministsforlife.org/

Feminist Majority Foundation
www.feminist.org

Focus on the Family
www.family.org/

Life Dynamics
www.ldi.org

Life Issues Institute, Inc.
www.lifeissues.org

NARAL Pro-Choice America
www.naral.org/

National Abortion Federation
www.prochoice.org/

National Black Women's Health Project
www.blackwomenshealth.org

National Coalition of Abortion Providers
www.ncap.com

National Network of Abortion Funds
www.nnaf.org/

National Organization for Women
www.now.org/

National Right to Life Committee
www.nrlc.org/

Operation Rescue/Operation Save
  America
www.operationsaveamerica.org

Planned Parenthood Federation of
  America
www.plannedparenthood.org/

Religious Coalition for Reproductive
  Choice
www.rcrc.org/

Republicans for Choice
www.republicansforchoice.com/

The Silent Scream
www.silentscream.org

Traditional Values Coalition
www.traditionalvalues.org/

United States Catholic Conference
www.usccb.org/

Writings of Paul Hill
www.armyofgod.com

Melody Rose is associate professor of political science at the Hatfield School of Government at Portland State University where she teaches courses in American government and politics and is the program director of NEW Leadership Oregon, an affiliate of the NEW Leadership Development Network, which partners with Rutgers University to offer political and leadership training programs to college women in Oregon. Rose has written a number of articles and book chapters on national and Oregon social policy and is writing two books: *She Flies with Her Own Wings*, an analysis of the oral histories of Oregon's first elected political women, and an encyclopedia of primary source documents on abortion history. Rose has served on the board of directors for the Classroom Law Project, a nonprofit organization that seeks to train K–12 teachers in civic education curricula and strategies. She is a regular political analyst on local, state, and national media on matters of elections, voting, and women's political action. Rose lives in Portland with her husband and their four children.